Ana-María Rizzuto and the Psychoanalysis of Religion

Ana-María Rizzuto and the Psychoanalysis of Religion

The Road to the Living God

Edited by
Martha J. Reineke and
David M. Goodman

LEXINGTON BOOKS
Lanham • Boulder • New York • London

Portions of chapter 1 were originally published in McDargh, John. "Creating a New Research Paradigm for the Psychoanalytic Study of Religion: The Pioneering Work of Ana-María Rizzuto." In *Religion, Society and Psychoanalysis*, edited by Janet Jacobs and Donald Capps, 181–199. Boulder: Westview Press, 1997.

Published by Lexington Books
An imprint of The Rowman & Littlefield Publishing Group, Inc.
4501 Forbes Boulevard, Suite 200, Lanham, Maryland 20706
www.rowman.com

Unit A, Whitacre Mews, 26-34 Stannary Street, London SE11 4AB

British Library Cataloguing in Publication Information Available

Library of Congress Cataloging-in-Publication Data Available
Names: Reineke, Martha Jane, editor. | Goodman, David M., editor.
Title: Ana-María Rizzuto and the psychoanalysis of religion : the road to the living God / edited by Martha J. Reineke and David M. Goodman.
Description: Lanham : Lexington Books, [2017] | Includes bibliographical references and index.
Identifiers: LCCN 2017033834 (print) | LCCN 2017027399 (ebook) | ISBN 9781498564250 (Electronic) | ISBN 9781498564243 (cloth : alk. paper) | ISBN 9781498564267 (pbk. : alk. paper)
Subjects: LCSH: Rizzuto, Ana-María. | Rizzuto, Ana-María. Birth of the living God. | Psychoanalysis and religion. | Developmental psychology—Religious aspects.
Classification: LCC BF175 .R593 (print) | LCC BF175 .R593 A53 2017 (ebook) | DDC 200.1/9—dc23
LC record available at https://lccn.loc.gov/2017033834

Printed in the United States of America

Contents

Acknowledgments

We begin by expressing our profound appreciation to Ana-María Rizzuto. From the moment when we approached her with the idea of a symposium reflecting on the achievement of *The Birth of the Living God* through the many stages of manuscript development, Dr. Rizzuto has been a gracious and generous participant. We are especially grateful for the commentaries that Dr. Rizzuto wrote and subsequently revised for publication. Her conversations with the other contributors have made this project a memorable and cherished experience for all.

We also express our thanks to the contributors to this book who spent countless hours on their essays in hopes of offering intellectual and creative sustenance to an interdisciplinary and international readership whose diverse interests and professional pathways cover a broad expanse in psychology and religion. We are especially grateful for the contributors' willingness to count the *Psychology and the Other* community as a place where they can find meaningful engagement with others and contribute their important voices to ongoing conversations.

We also give special thanks to those who have spent considerable energy forging spaces that foster this type of interdisciplinary work. In this instance, the steering and organizing committees for the *Psychology and the Other* conference played a pivotal role in bringing together this group of scholars and embracing their far-reaching work. More specifically, we wish to thank our colleagues Brian Becker, Heather Macdonald, Katie Goodman, Cacky Mellor, David House, Ben Arcangeli, Jacqueline Aug, Abigail Collins, Adeline Dettor, Sam Gable, Jenny Esdale, Kimm Topping, and Danielle Moreno for their hard work and commitment to seeing these types of conversations continue through the conference.

Institutionally, this editorial work and conference planning has received generous and much needed assistance—in terms of time, finances, and space. To Provost Selase Williams, from Lesley University, George Stavros and Lauren Kehoe, from the Danielsen Institute at Boston University, and Fr. James Burns, from the Woods College of Advancing Studies at Boston College, we are grateful for your dedication to this dialog that is increasingly rare in our hyper-specialized and medicalized clinical disciplines. We are enormously grateful, as well, to Brent Slife and his administration of the Richard L. Evans Chair of Religious Understanding at Brigham Young University, which has provided critical material support to actualize this catalytic scholarly and clinical engagement.

We also would like to thank Amy King, Alison Payen, and Molly White at Rowman and Littlefield for their support for this project. We acknowledge also Madhumitha Koduvalli and Kasey Beduhn at Lexington Books for their outstanding efforts on behalf of this project. In particular, Kasey's commitment to the book and her energetic support for the work of its editors are deeply appreciated. Carole Yates offered superb editorial assistance throughout the publication process, for which we are extremely grateful.

I (Martha) want to thank my partner in this enterprise, David, for sharing the vision of the book, offering the *Psychology and the Other* conference as its gestational home, and extending unstinting creative and logistical support as we navigated the complexities of transforming symposium presentations into a published work. Our friendship is a treasured outcome of this book project. I thank my husband, Bill, and daughter, Beth, for their serenity as they have come to accept what they cannot change: my passion for writing which so often takes the form of multi-year projects.

Furthermore, I (David) want to express particular thanks to Martha for shepherding this project from her early and brilliant ideas to this very typesetting. It was her orchestration that brought together these incredible conversations and her persistence that allowed this project to reach print. It is a pleasure to work with her and to watch an individual embody the goodness that she promotes in her scholarship. Thank you for this honor and privilege of partnering. And, as always, I wish to thank my incredible wife, Katie Lynn, who tolerates and supports my incessant over-involvement in these types of ventures. This year, we brought our son—Levi Thomas—into the world and it is my hope that it is a world that continues to hunger for the transcendent. Thank you, Ana-María, for charging us to be curious in this manner.

Introduction

Martha Reineke and David Goodman

In courses on the psychoanalysis of religion, students learn essential vocabulary: for example, the unconscious, the Oedipus complex, transitional objects, sublimation, and illusion. For many students, the terminology is new. As a consequence, we who introduce students to psychoanalysis try to make the unfamiliar more familiar by showing students that they have already experienced features of the world that the special vocabulary of psychoanalysis attempts to capture. We talk with our students about their teddy bears. We discuss films whose main characters are caught in the riptide of the Oedipal complex. We invite students to share their dreams. But even as we introduce students to psychoanalysis, we wonder, how is it possible that students do not know the terms psychoanalysis has assigned to key life experiences? After all, these words, so familiar to us that they seem like common sense, make us feel that we have always known Freud.

This book was born of similar musings. While preparing a course unit on *The Birth of the Living God: A Psychoanalytic Study* I (Martha Reineke) found myself wondering, "Why do I feel that I have always known Ana-María Rizzuto? Surely there was a time when her ideas were new to me." When I opened the book to check its date of publication, one answer to her question was immediately evident. *The Birth of the Living God* was approaching the thirty-fifth anniversary of its publication, long enough for it to have become a fixture in Reineke's library. Yet, as I reflected further, a more substantive answer to the question came into view: the power of Rizzuto's ideas, rather than the long-standing availability of her book, had established the significance of Rizzuto for me. Over three decades, *The Birth of the Living God*, the first empirical and clinical study by a psychoanalyst of the development of God representations in early childhood and their elaboration throughout the life cycle, had become bedrock for the psychoanalysis of religion. Shaping the psychoanalysis of religion in fundamental ways, *The Birth of the Living God* also had established a trajectory for innovative thinking in the field that reaches still into the future. No wonder then, that I could not recall a time when Rizzuto's ideas had not been known. As Mary Lou Randour aptly notes, "If the symbol of Freud as 'father' of psychoanalysis has been used to explain his historical position, certainly Rizzuto is the 'mother' of all attempts to explicate a developmental and clinical psychoanalytic theory of religious experience."[1]

And, quickly switching voices, I (David Goodman) have found *The Birth of the Living God* to have a similar impact in clinical practice. Historically, a combination of ethical codes prohibiting imposition of beliefs, misguided value-neutrality requirements, and inherited enmity toward religion have shaped clinical sensitivities in a way that engendered a profound discomfort with addressing the religious in the context of clinical settings. Even now, it can actually feel as though one is violating basic professional convention to articulate questions about religious belief and God's place in a patient's cognitive and emotional life—these are "taboo" topics in many psychological communities. However, in the last decades, unease about religion in the clinical context has begun to soften following Rizzuto's original contributions to the psychoanalysis of religion and her breach of modern prejudicial assumptions. Those that have taken up her enterprise find themselves with pavement underfoot and a foundation from which to work. That they now stand in possession of strong underpinnings for the exploration of religion is recent to clinical work, and new creative possibilities and approaches are just now beginning to emerge.

As exemplified by the experiences shared here, the editors of this book concur that Rizzuto has made her mark, profoundly enriching the clinical practice of psychoanalysis as well as theoretical scholarship in the psychoanalytic study of religion. Moreover, recognizing that the thirty-fifth anniversary of *The Birth of the Living God* was a fitting occasion to reflect formally on the book that had shaped the psychoanalysis of religion in such fundamental ways, we planned a symposium on *The Birth of the Living God*. It was held at the 2013 Psychology and the Other Conference in Cambridge, Massachusetts. In their presentations, participants in the symposium acknowledged the significance of *The Birth of the Living God* and assessed its ongoing influence in clinical psychoanalysis and psychotherapy as well as in theoretical explorations in the psychology of religion, especially in light of new developments in psychoanalysis, psychotherapy, and the psychoanalytic study of religion.

Following the symposium, we made plans to preserve its achievements in a book that would include presentation authors and additional, solicited essays. Together, these pieces comprise the chapters of this book. Some chapters focus on the clinical context. They demonstrate how Rizzuto's theory, which explores the central role of object relations in the development of religious belief, can inform clinical practice and enhance therapeutic interventions with patients. Other chapters attest to the power of Rizzuto's theory to illuminate and support critical reflection across the breadth of the psychoanalytic study of religion.

Collectively, the chapters that comprise this book are a unique contribution to clinical and scholarly engagement with the psychoanalysis of religion. Rizzuto's work previously has been discussed in multi-contributor anthologies exploring the broad expanse of the psychology of religion[2] or in single-author overviews of key movements, figures, or ideas in the psychology or psychoanalytic study of religion.[3] The chapters in this book focus solely on Rizzuto's work and offer a systematic evaluation of its significance from clinical and theoretical perspectives. Moreover, in explicitly looking to the future in their assessment of Rizzuto's work, the contributors to this book also attest empirically and theoretically to its ongoing significance. As a consequence, this book has unique importance to readers committed to exploring new pathways in clinical practice and engaging in the theoretical study of psychoanalysis and religion.

We are deeply honored that Ana-María Rizzuto attended the symposium on *The Birth of the Living God* and offered commentaries on each presentation. These commentaries, revised for this book, along with commentaries Rizzuto wrote for the additional solicited chapters for this book, add significantly to the usefulness of this work for its readers. Through engaging the authors in discussion, Rizzuto sheds light on her most recent thinking on the psychoanalysis of religion, augmenting her extant scholarship. Rizzuto's insights, sparking critically reflective and creative engagement with her work, promise also to further the ongoing, dynamic reception of her work. We are most grateful to her for furthering important work in the psychoanalysis of religion through generously contributing her keen insights and trenchant observations to this book.

THE SIGNIFICANCE OF *THE BIRTH OF THE LIVING GOD*

In *The Birth of the Living God*, Rizzuto shows that the formation of God representations occurs through a process that is fully integrated with the formation of self-representations. Distinct from God concepts associated with adult religious beliefs, institutional dogma, and the public practice of religion,[4] these God representations are unique to each individual and are born of the dynamic interplay between love and hope, fear and freedom, acceptance and rejection. These all feature in a young child's formative relationships with its parents or other primary caretakers. Building on theories of transitional representations or objects, particularly ideas advanced by D.W. Winnicott, Rizzuto shows that, as a young child develops and separates psychically from its parents, its God presentations become more robust. God is a presence in the child's life capable of great caring, or indifference, or frightening hostility toward the child. Indeed, Rizzuto suggests that, even when humans deny belief in God, as a fact of psychic life, God representations persist: no human power, not even the wishes of the child, can make God disappear.[5]

Rizzuto concurs with Freud in the basic contours of her thinking: God originates in early parental relations. However, her empirical explorations attest to a more complex origin and history of God than Freud imagines. Where Freud emphasizes the role of a child's father at all points in the history of a child's relationship with God, Rizzuto's research shows that God representations derive from mothers, fathers, and even grandparents, if they are the child's primary caretakers. Moreover, these representations are an amalgam not only of real parents, but also of the wished-for and feared parents of a child's own making.[6] Further, and even more significantly, the persistence of God representations in later life is not necessarily a defensive function and anachronistic, as Freud claims. Rather, God representations can be subject to revision: they can play not only a role during the resolution of the Oedipal complex but also in the lives of older children, adolescents, and even adults. Whenever someone experiences challenges in integrating self-representations with life experiences, their God representations may participate in that challenge. Yes, God may be exposed in such instances as an anachronism; however, Rizzuto documents also that, as part of a complex, adaptive process, God may grow, achieving new dimensions as God is integrated within the psychic life of the maturing individual. Neither attacking nor defending the ontological status of God, Rizzuto's attention is focused on how God representations function in important ways in the psychic life of the individual across the life span. For Rizzuto, at the most fundamental level, God is not an idea to which one assents or a belief one professes; rather, God is experienced as an affective act of connection whose roots can be traced to the formative attachments of early childhood.

The Birth of the Living God is most significant for characterizing the complex dynamics that underlie religious belief and practice in ways that do not reductively treat these beliefs and practices as mere psychological categories. As a consequence, rather than assert that psychoanalysis is incompatible with religious beliefs and practices or with spiritual concerns that patients may bring to a therapeutic context, Rizzuto makes room for the coexistence of psychoanalysis and religion in the therapeutic setting. In like manner, her work looms large in theoretical studies of the psychoanalysis of religion. Offering an alternative to positivist readings of religion, she shows psychoanalysis to be a finely tuned instrument, capable of plumbing in compelling and creative ways, the complex depths of human engagement with religion, across history and inclusive of diverse expressions of belief in human culture.

THE IMPORTANCE OF RIZZUTO IN A CLINICAL CONTEXT

Psychoanalysis, like all clinical approaches, teaches a language for suffering and identity that both opens and closes experiential possibilities. That is true for all language traditions. However, one of the primary goals and moral obligations of psychoanalysis is to assist a patient in having access to the fullest range of experience, and never its circumscription. That is part of what Freud critiqued religion for—the maintenance of an illusion that diminished the possibility of experiencing the world and life more fully, as it actually is. But what about psychoanalytic prejudices and ideological frames that become their own form of protection, preventing an individual from encountering the world in its fullest form? Exposing such constraints on human experience is exactly what Rizzuto accomplished for the clinical community: she called on this community to see how its own modern prejudicial forms constrained persons seeking care from gaining access to a full range of life experiences. Rizzuto showed that religion, spirituality, God, and theology are part of the warp and woof of life and cannot be excluded elements. They also cannot be reduced to ready pathologies and weak forms of rationality. Rizzuto's research releases the clinician from the restrictive sets that appeared to be imperatives in "modern" practice. God is not only fair game for the therapeutic context, but profoundly important territory to traverse with patients. Rizzuto makes this case, however, while still respecting and maintaining the tethers and frames that Freud brought to the intellectual and clinical communities. She is not anarchic to the psychoanalytic enterprise. Rather, she enriches it by letting Freud's work breathe more fully without the asphyxiations of modern cultural sets and secularizing "securities." Suspicion, one of the hallmarks of modernity's "masters," is counterbalanced by a curiosity and trust in a patient's experience.

Throughout *The Birth of the Living God*, Rizzuto demonstrates that the developmental history of God she traces is of critical importance within the therapeutic context. Rizzuto's case studies point to ways that therapists may identify a history of God that is closely intertwined with a patient's relational history. The compelling force of Rizzuto's arguments lies with this claim: if a therapist wishes to attend fully to the psychic life of her/his patients—physical, social, interpersonal, and spiritual—the diagnostic value of God representations, especially in relationship to transferential phenomena, must be explored. God functions like any other object relation and is caught up in the "complex choreography" through which an individual abides in, wishes for, or fears relational being. A patient may draw on God representations as a defense in the therapeutic setting or as a productive source for integration of psychic changes over the course of therapy or psychoanalysis. When a therapist invites the complex range of a patient's God representations into the therapeutic space, the affective and lived world of the patient—the assumptions behind repeating cycles, relational needs, prohibitions, and desires—gain more dimensionality and greater opportunity to find voice and inclusion.

THE IMPORTANCE OF RIZZUTO IN A THEORETICAL CONTEXT

Rizzuto's findings also have profound implications for scholarship in the psychology of religion. Insights about the origins of the human capacity for religious belief offered in *The Birth of the Living God* broaden and deepen the frame of inquiry within the psychology of religion. Rizzuto's work suggests that a full examination of the role of religious belief in human psychology and culture must include consideration of the origins of religious belief within a developmental context of very early childhood during which parental and God representations emerge together. Reflections on religion that focus only on the social context of religious dogma, doctrine, belief, and non-belief into which older children are initiated and which they embrace or refuse as they move into adulthood, bypass the deep roots of religious belief within the originating moments of psychic life. Distorted understandings of the role of religion in human life and culture follow.

Rizzuto's theory of God representations not only has important implications for theoretical reflection in the psychology and psychoanalysis of religion but also facilitates the exploration of relationships between culture and religion, individual experience and communal activities, private and socially shared meanings. Rizzuto has named this focus "anthropological medicine" in order to highlight the many dimensions of the human experience.[7] For Rizzuto, cultural meanings with roots in society and culture link with meanings generated by the psyche. Inspired by Rizzuto, individuals who study the power of metaphor from any number of perspectives—psychological, literary, anthropological—can draw on her insights to thematize how, from multidisciplinary perspective, metaphors shape individual and communal experience. Specifically, Rizzuto's focus on God representations can be linked with the scholarly study of religious symbols and ritual expressions. Her theory suggests that symbolizing and ritual are not regressive or anachronistic but point to a telos, a capacity for humans to transfigure their past and productively and creatively shape their futures as individuals and within society.

CHAPTER OVERVIEW

In chapter 1, John McDargh begins this book with a masterful review of Rizzuto's work and assessment of its significance. Situating her project in relationship to Freud, he demonstrates that Rizzuto is indebted to Freud even as she enters into a critical engagement with his work, opening up wholly novel ways of looking at religious beliefs and practices across the life cycle. McDargh traces two formative influences on Rizzuto's groundbreaking work: her upbringing in Argentina in a pre-Vatican II Roman Catholic Church and her training as a physician. He recounts the origins of *The Birth of the Living God* in a research project conducted in a Boston Hospital clinical setting. Most importantly, he offers the definitive accounting of the evolving history of the reception of Rizzuto's work by and impact on various professional communities: psychoanalytic institutes, pastoral and clinical psychologists, and psychologists of religion. Finally, drawing on these insights, McDargh sketches ways in which the future trajectory of Rizzuto's work already is visible in recent applications of her insights.

Chapters 2 and 3 explore the clinical significance of *The Birth of the Living God*, emphasizing, in particular, its reception in Europe. Drawing on his extensive experience in Italy as a psychologist and psychoanalyst, Mario Aletti explores the contribution of Rizzuto to the practice of psychoanalysis, especially for shaping new understandings in psychoanalysis about the religion of the individual. He discusses specific features of Rizzuto's work that attest to her original contributions to clinical practice and to research in the field of the psychology of religion. Aletti considers how Rizzuto writes about God as a transitional object, clarifies her notion of a "God representation," and explores the developmental processes that Rizzuto tracks as "the birth of the living God." Aletti gives special attention to Rizzuto's method, highlighting how she exemplifies an epistemologically valid approach to the psychological experience of religion. Of utmost significance, he points out, is Rizzuto's respect for patients' values, respect that Aletti confirms is essential for the analyst. Aletti concludes his chapter by considering the ongoing significance of Rizzuto's work for elucidating the role of psychoanalysis in a field that increasingly values quantitative research.

In chapter 3, Gry Stålsett, Arne Austad, and Leif Gunnar Engedal offer a case study that exemplifies Rizzuto's profound impact, at the institutional level, on the practice of psychotherapy, pastoral care, and counseling. In 1995, Rizzuto began an ongoing relationship with the Modum Bad Clinic, a psychiatric hospital in Norway. Her research provided the impetus for an integrative treatment model for patents known as the VITA program. In their contribution to this book, Stålsett, Austad, and Engedal report on one patient, Olav, who participated in this program, analyzing his experience in light of Rizzuto's theory. With the case of Olav, they shed light on the meaning and function of God representations in individuals' lives by exploring key metaphors Olav used to describe himself and which he assigned to his God representations. Stålsett, Austad, and Engedal address the existential, narrative, dynamic-relational, and affective sources of these metaphors. They also report on their therapeutic approach to Olav, explaining how they encouraged him to explore and discover multiple layers of meaning in his metaphors. Stålsett, Austad, and Engedal advance Rizzuto's project through a sustained application and analysis of key themes on which she first reported in *The Birth of the Living God*. Their research, building on that groundbreaking book, deepens the readers' understanding of patients' suffering as well as demonstrates how therapies grounded in Rizzuto's research can augment resources for recovery available to psychoanalysts and psychotherapists. By focusing on Olav's metaphors, they bring into focus Rizzuto's key insights: when persons speak in metaphors, they seek listeners, including a listening God they have graphically represented with their metaphors. Only as therapists become attuned to the "conversational" dynamics that swirl around these metaphors will the internal life of the individuals they seek to help be adequately illuminated.

Chapter 4 bridges the clinical and theoretical contributions to this book. Its author, psychiatrist Anthony Stern, explores ways in which Rizzuto's insights extend beyond Western religious traditions about which she has written (Judaism and Christianity) to include Eastern religious traditions. Stern's lyrical reporting on his encounter with a kundalini yoga master named Rudi (Swami Rudrananda) focuses on the flow of energy between two persons, one a spiritual master. In light of his experience, Stern addresses, as have Stålsett, Austad, and Engedal, the power of metaphors. Stern reflects on the role of models of the psyche in relation to that which can only be spoken through the poetry of metaphor. He focuses, in particular, on metaphors of an embodied self and on openings through these metaphors to healing, especially in the context of encounters with spiritual teacher with whom one feels "overwhelmingly in the hands of the living God." Considering the relation between individual psyches and the reality of an other, or Other as well as connections between our selves and others, Stern draws on Rizzuto, Eastern spiritual traditions, Martin Buber's thought, and the contribution of Buber's student, Leslie Farber. Offered from the perspective of someone engaged in the practice of psychotherapy and in spiritually oriented reflection, Stern offers an opening to Eastern spiritual traditions for students of Rizzuto's work at a time when the psychoanalysis of religion is being drawn into increasingly global conversations.

Exploring opportunities for theoretical engagement with the psychoanalysis of religion, in chapters 5 and 6, Martha Reineke and Jacob Waldenmaier address the significance of Rizzuto's work. Reineke begins her chapter recalling that Rizzuto observes that God arrives in children's lives along with a motley crew of monsters, superheroes, witches, gnomes, and fairies. Rizzuto argues that, because parents treat God differently from these other creatures, children learn to discriminate between God, who holds favor with their parents, and these other characters, which do not. Eventually, but for a few bit parts played by the devil, monsters and their kin slip from view in children's lives. Building on Rizzuto's work in hopes of expanding its range of influence, Reineke looks closely at how gods and monsters are deeply embedded in the human psyche and in human culture. Exploring how these metaphors function psychologically and culturally, Reineke revisits Rizzuto's assumption that children leave witches and monsters behind as they mature. Focusing initially on monsters in the sacred scriptures and ritual practices of the world religions, she follows Timothy Beal in arguing that, despite the averred secularism and sophistication of the modern era, monsters remained active forces in art and literature. Reineke draws on the work of Julia Kristeva to locate a maternal rather than paternal referent in the work that monsters do. Rizzuto writes that the mirroring provided by the mother's face in the oral stage of development is the first experience the child uses in the formation of a God representation. However, with Kristeva, Reineke suggests that the maternal matrix, the tain in that mirror, offers more original material: objectless and immediate, a not-yet-a-subject identifies with a not-yet-an-object, the maternal matrix, not yet a "mother." This archaic material contributes not only to the monster representations in early childhood but also to the psychological and cultural function of monsters in world religions, art, and literature. Finally, in dialogue with Rizzuto, Reineke explores Rizzuto's *Why did Freud Reject God?* Exploring maternal referents in metaphors associated with the Philippson bible and Freud's collection of antiquities, Reineke sheds new light on Freud's relationship to religion even as she also highlights the significance of Rizzuto's work in new contexts, thereby extending the legacy of *Birth of the Living God.*

In chapter 6, Jacob Waldenmaier scrutinizes the psychoanalysis of religion from a perspective attuned to key intellectual achievements of the modern and contemporary eras. Viewed through that lens, Waldenmaier shows Rizzuto's work to have enriched across disciplines our understanding of and engagement with the atheism, belief-maintenance, and religious deconversion. Because Rizzuto offers a clinically robust, ontologically neutral, and psychologically sound characterization of God, her insights facilitate our understanding of and engagement with the tensions between faith and reason and between reality and illusion. Reviewing key ways in which continental theology, social theory, and natural philosophy—all three often mingled with atheistic sentiments—contributed to the nascent science of psychology leading up to and during the era in which Freudian psychoanalysis developed, Waldenmaier describes how Rizzuto's interprets the role of religious belief in human life in ways that fully appreciate its importance and relevance even as she makes no discrete ontological claims about theology's referent. Finally, Waldenmaier discusses how Rizzuto maintains the importance and vitality of the God-concept against two incompatible polarities claimed in new atheism—that of reason with faith, and that of reality with illusion—thereby informing in helpful ways the critical reflection on the contemporary resurgence of atheistic sentiment, especially with reference to the psychology of religion.

In diverse ways, the chapters in this book attest to the compelling power of Rizzuto's groundbreaking work thirty-five years after the publication of *The Birth of the Living God*. The contributing authors confirm the originality and indispensable quality of Rizzuto's insights and offer empirical confirmation of claims Rizzuto makes in the case studies she includes in *The Birth of the Living God.* Chapters that focus on clinical practice corroborate Rizzuto's claims that, when her theory is applied within a clinical setting, the theory works. So also do they point to future productive applications of Rizzuto's work within a clinical context. Chapters in this book that focus on theoretical considerations within the psychology of religion demonstrate how Rizzuto aids scholars who want to explore the origins of the human capacity for religious belief, especially in light of modern and contemporary criticism of religious beliefs and practices. These chapters show how Rizzuto's insights can enrich models of religion that want to account for the psychological as well as sociocultural functions of religion. The presence of Rizzuto's own voice in response to these pieces elevates each piece and brings about a "living" conversation with this preeminent scholar. In all these ways, this book attests to and appreciatively celebrates Ana-María Rizzuto's field-defining contributions to the developmental psychoanalytic theory of religious experience and its clinical application.

NOTES

1. Mary Lou Randour, ed. *Exploring Sacred Landscapes: Religious and Spiritual Experiences in Psychotherapy* (New York: Columbia University Press, 1993), 9.

2. *Exploring Sacred Landscapes: Religious and Spiritual Experiences in Psychotherapy*, ed. Mary Lou Randour (Columbia University Press, 1993); *Religion, Society, and Psychoanalysis,* eds. Janet Liebman Jacobs and Donald Capps (Westview Press, 1997); *Religion and Psychology: Mapping the Terrain* eds. Diane Jonte-Pace and William B. Parsons (Routledge, 2002); and *The Image of God and the Psychology of Religion,* eds. Richard L. Dayringer and David Oler (Routledge, 2005).

3. See for example, John McDargh, *Psychoanalytic Object Relations Theory and the Study of Religion: On Faith and the Imaging of God* (University Press of America, 1983); James W. Jones, *Contemporary Psychoanalysis and Religion* (Yale University Press, 1991); Andrew R. Fuller *Psychology and Religion: Eight Points of View* (Rowman and Littlefield, 1994); David W. Wulff, *Psychology of Religion* (Wiley, 1996).

4. Ana-Maria Rizzuto, *The Birth of the Living God: A Psychoanalytic Study* (Chicago: University of Chicago Press, 1981) 48.

5. *The Birth*, 35.

6. ———, 44.

7. Ana-Maria Rizzuto, "An Accidental Psychologist of Religion," in *Psychology of Religion: Autobiographical Accounts*, ed. Jacob Belzen (New York: Springer, 2012), 186.

BIBLIOGRAPHY

Dayringer, Richard L., and David Oler, eds. *The Image of God and the Psychology of Religion*. New York, NY: Routledge, 2005.

Fuller, Andrew R. *Psychology and Religion: Eight Points of View*. Lanham, MD: Rowman and Littlefield, 1994.

Jacobs, Janet Liebman, and Donald Capps eds. *Religion, Society, and Psychoanalysis*. Boulder, CO: Westview Press, 1997.

Jones, James W. *Contemporary Psychoanalysis and Religion*. New Haven, CT: Yale University Press, 1991.

Jonte-Pace, Diane, and William B. Parsons eds. *Mapping the Terrain*. New York, NY: Routledge, 2002.

McDargh, John. *Psychoanalytic Object Relations Theory and the Study of Religion: On Faith and the Imaging of God*. Lanham, MD: University Press of America, 1983.

Randour, Mary Lou ed. *Exploring Sacred Landscapes: Religious and Spiritual Experiences in Psychotherapy*. New York, NY: Columbia University Press, 1993.

Rizzuto, Ana-Maria. *The Birth of the Living God: A Psychoanalytic Study*. Chicago: University of Chicago Press, 1981.

Rizzuto, Ana-Maria. "An Accidental Psychologist of Religion," in *Psychology of Religion: Autobiographical Accounts*, edited by Jacob Belzen. New York, NY: Springer, 2012.

Wulff, David H. *Psychology of Religion: Classic and Contemporary*. Hoboken, NJ: Wiley, 1996.

Chapter 1

The Paradigm-Shifting Research of Ana-María Rizzuto

Origins, Strategy, Reception, and Horizon

John McDargh

Ana-María Rizzuto's work, most notably her landmark publication *The Birth of the Living God*, had an early and positive reception among counseling psychologists, psychologists of religion, and pastoral psychologists. However, it was largely ignored in psychoanalytic institutes or was responded to with hostility in the single published review in a psychoanalytic journal.[1] Now, thirty-five years later, we see a distinctive shift in receptiveness toward a serious engagement with spiritual and religious issues in therapy. This shift is seen in the mental health community and even among many of Rizzuto's fellow psychoanalysts.[2] To support this engagement in this chapter, I situate Rizzuto's project in relationship to Freud's work. I demonstrate that while Rizzuto is uncompromisingly indebted to Freud, she is also thoughtfully critical of Freud in ways that open up new possibilities for a more intricate understanding of the place of religious believing across the life cycle. Within this broad context, I set forth a threefold agenda: First, I locate the origins of Rizzuto's inspiration and motivation for her research in her own unique background as a medical doctor and, eventually, a psychoanalyst who was raised Roman Catholic in Argentina. Second, I describe the evolution and vicissitudes of Rizzuto's distinctive clinical research project. Finally, I account for the evolving reception of her work by, and impact on, various professional communities: psychoanalytic institutes, pastoral and clinical psychologists, and psychologists of religion.[3]

The increasingly positive reception of Rizzuto's work has already been noted by clinical psychologist Mary Lou Randour. Writing fourteen years after *The Birth of the Living God,* in her introduction to an edited collection of essays on "religious and spiritual experiences in psychotherapy," Randour expressed her sense of Rizzuto's contribution: "If the symbol of Freud as 'father' of psychoanalysis has been used to explain his historical position, certainly Rizzuto is the 'mother' of all attempts to explicate a developmental and clinical psychoanalytic theory of religious experience."[4] With the benefit of eighteen more years, we can identify some of that "mother's" flourishing off-spring. Indeed, we can argue that Rizzuto's research has contributed significantly to a fresh appreciation by psychotherapists and counselors for the salience and relevance of careful, skillful, and respectful inquiry into their patients' religious and spiritual lives.

It is not hard to understand why Rizzuto's work is now viewed positively. For the first time, a fully credentialed and well-regarded psychoanalyst has demonstrated, in a careful, rigorous fashion, the *clinical* utility of taking an individual's uniquely personal religious beliefs with great seriousness *both* as another "royal road to the unconscious" for the clinician *and* as a potential resource for the psychic well-being of the patient. Religious beliefs are not *a priori* an index of arrested psychological development nor do they point to a patient's failure to face the reality of human helplessness and aloneness in the universe. One cannot over-emphasize the significance of this shift at the level both of theory and of therapeutic practice.

Foundational to Rizzuto's entire research project is Freud's genius insight that an individual's "religion"—a word derived from *re-ligio*, "to be connected or linked"—is a way of "re-linking with a very significant emotional object."[5] In Freud's case that object was posited to be the father and exclusively the father. Rizzuto's exhaustively detailed investigation of her subjects' conscious and unconscious religious imagination expands considerably beyond Freud's restricted focus to include the mother and other key figures in the child's relational world (grandparents, etc.). For Rizzuto, "The originality of his (Freud's) conception rests on the fact that, for the first time in the history of the psychology of religion, he offered clinical evidence about the *internal psychical processes* that contribute to the formation and maintenance of a relationship with an internally conceived and socially sanctioned divine being."[6] Rizzuto's own originality, however, lies not only in her discovery of the great range of the early childhood relationships that provide the "raw material" for the adult's conscious and unconscious representations of God but also in her challenge to Freud's unrelentingly critical assessment of the value of religious beliefs in the lives of individuals and societies.

Rizzuto finds Freud's corollary conclusion theoretically problematic. Freud stated that uncovering the developmental processes, which link an individual's conscious and unconscious representation of "God" to their primary familial relationships, necessarily entails a negative psychological and moral valuation. He held that these beliefs in God must be outgrown as a person matures intellectually and emotionally. Rizzuto challenges this philosophical position in part by recruiting to her analysis the insights of D.W. Winnicott and other object relations theorists. These psychologists viewed the capacity for imaginative engagement with symbolic objects across the life cycle not as a marker of psychological immaturity but rather as a uniquely adaptive human competency that functionally serves health as much as pathology.[7]

To appreciate how Rizzuto's principled defection from a certain kind of psychoanalytic orthodoxy on the psycho-social status of religious believing has opened a freer space for clinical research and inquiry, it is helpful to remember the long-running influence of Freud's *The Future of an Illusion* on psychotherapy within and beyond the psychoanalytic institutes. In *The Future of an Illusion,* Freud issued an emphatic moral call for what Rizzuto termed "a new psycho-analytic man free from neurotic infantile longings for divine parental protection and from the necessary submission to the will of the divinity found in the religious individual."[8] Freud prophesized the withering away of religion by slowly bringing about an "education to reality" that would encourage persons to renounce these infantile wishes, stand bravely without supernatural support, and rely only on *logos*—reason tutored by the unmasking interrogation of analysis. Practicing psychoanalysts were to be the vanguard of this new moral order.

As Rizzuto sees it, this moral injunction in Freud "evoked a spontaneous self-censorship that prompted analysts to leave aside whatever religion they had at the moment they decided to become Freud's followers. Who would dare to show Freud or his colleagues that he was still clinging to the infantile imago of his father/God?"[9] What happened, predictably, was that religious experiences and any lingering loyalties to religious beliefs were rendered inadmissible in analytic discourse. Rizzuto describes a fairly common occurrence when she began lecturing at analytic institutes about her research. Invariably, two or three psychoanalysts in attendance would seek her out privately after the talk to share a past personal religious experience that had been meaningful to them. She observes, "They regularly ended our conversation with a variation of this sentence, 'I did not tell this experience to my analyst.' They had censored themselves during their analysis because they honestly had felt that religious experience was not acceptable 'analytic material.'"[10] The consistency of these off-the-record confessions is perhaps evidence of how professional loyalty to the authority of Freud, as the author of *The Future of an Illusion,* created a culture of silence around this salient dimension of human experience among psychoanalysts and between analysts and patients.

The consequences of this tacit prohibition were certainly very evident twenty-five years ago when Dr. Gil Levin, director of Einstein Medical School's Summer Cape Cod Institute, took the risk of inviting a team organized by psychiatrist Tomas Agosin to offer a course on "Psychotherapy and Spirituality."[11] The psychologists, psychiatrists, and mental health professionals who subsequently flocked for eleven consecutive summers to this continuing education program frequently spoke of themselves metaphorically as "coming out of the closet." Many attendees showed palpable relief at being able to identify themselves as religiously or spiritually interested therapists who were eager to reflect seriously with fellow professionals about topics that were ignored or actively discouraged in their training and supervision.

What kind of personal formation would give someone the courage, integrity, and determination to swim against the currents of her own professional community and become deeply invested in a strenuous, critical psychoanalytic investigation of the dynamics of religious experience? Moreover, what accounts for Rizzuto's capacity to remain generously open to the Transcendent toward which such experience may point without becoming an apologist for any particular religious world view? Our search for the answers leads us to examine Rizzuto's distinctive personal and professional background.

PERSONAL, THEOLOGICAL, AND CLINICAL BACKGROUND TO RIZZUTO'S RESEARCH

For many years, one consequence of the internalization of Freud's position about the responsibility of psychoanalysts to model the rejection of "infantile" religious longings has been a lack of analysts' professional curiosity about the possible role their own particular religious formation (or lack thereof) may have played in their distinctive practice of psychoanalysis. George Atwood and Robert Stolorow's book, *Faces in A Cloud: Intersubjectivity in Personality Theory,* began to break down this barrier between the personal and professional by looking at how Freud, Jung, and Reich's, metapsychologies duplicated the structures of their subjective worlds.[12] Still, it was easier for these theorists to excavate personal history secondhand than to explore firsthand the role their early childhood and young adult experiences had in shaping their professional trajectory, particularly when an important part of that experience involved their relationships to formative religious and spiritual experiences. Rizzuto stepped across that prohibition as creatively and completely as any theorist writing today. Three importance sources highlight the personal history and cultural "back story" that informs Rizzuto's research, illuminating her achievement.

The first resource is Rizzuto's autobiographical essay, "Roman Catholic Background and Psychoanalysis," published in the journal *Psychoanalytic Quarterly* as a companion piece to an essay by relational psychoanalyst Lewis Aron.[13] With transparency and insight comparable to Rizzuto's, Aron explores the role that his early and ongoing engagement with Jewish thought and the practice of Judaism played in shaping his vocation as a psychoanalyst and psychoanalytic theorist.[14] Both Aron and Rizzuto examine in some detail the enduring influence that the distinctive life-ways and habits of the heart of

Catholicism and Judaism had on the way they engaged the practice of psychoanalysis. As Rizzuto affirms toward the end of her contribution, "I believe that my Catholicism gave me both experiences and conceptual tools to find psychoanalysis a most appealing instrument for understanding people and helping them transform themselves."[15] Her account of the enduring influence of her Argentine Catholic childhood and young adulthood is richly detailed and evocative.

Rizzuto describes growing up in the town of Cordoba embedded in a loving, observant household whose daily, weekly, and seasonal rhythm of life was ordered by the ritual practices of a Catholicism that offered the imagination of a growing child a rich representational world. Not just "God" but also a host of benevolent female and male saints and unseen benefactors mirrored the benign presence of her maternal grandmother and other significant women relatives, all of whom modeled both kindness and strength. In the conclusion of this article, Rizzuto identifies five elements of her Catholic upbringing that were mapped onto the "listening perspective" of psychoanalysis that she would later embrace:[16]

1. "An object-related universe in which people are never alone.
2. A symbolic understanding of all reality, both physical and psychical, that facilitated my comprehension of the defensive and creative symbolic working of the mind.
3. Habits of self-examination that alerted me to the existence of hidden sources of my motivations and hidden regions of my mind.
4. The experience of the transformational power of confessing my sins to an understanding and respectful adult who was intent on helping me.
5. The need to confront reality and oneself in all honesty when it is obvious that one cannot escape or mislead the searching eye of God. Freud within his frame of reference called this the reality principle."[17]

Remarkable in Rizzuto's interrogation of her own childhood experience is her recognition of the deep continuities between elements of those formative years and the habits of the mind and heart she cultivated in her adult life as a working psychoanalytic psychotherapist and a researcher exploring the intricacies of the human process of "believing" in a realm of the unseen.

The second resource that explores how Rizzuto's own life experiences undergird and inspire her theoretical reflections and clinical practice is her 2007 article, "God in the Mind: The Psychodynamics of an Unusual Relationship."[18] This article covers formative early experiences that led Rizzuto into psychoanalytic training and were the originating inspiration for her research on the origin and development of the individual's conscious and unconscious representations of God. This article also surveys the range of responses to her research from therapists, pastoral psychologists, and from her own psychoanalytic community. Finally, "God in the Mind" is the only article to date in which Rizzuto not only discusses the long and winding road to the writing of *The Birth of the Living God* but also traces the arc of her subsequent psychoanalytic investigations that directly build upon that foundational research project. Specifically, Rizzuto provides a detailed narrative of the process of researching and writing *Why Did Freud Reject God?,* the work that nineteen years after the publication of *The Birth of the Living God* resulted in Rizzuto receiving long overdue critical acclaim from the psychoanalytic community.[19] In the final section of this chapter, when we consider new questions that might build upon the path opened by *The Birth of the Living God*, we will discuss the significance of Rizzuto's second major book on the psychology of religious development.

The third and most recent resource that fills in the personal history of Rizzuto's pioneering work in the psychoanalysis of religion is her contribution to *Psychology of Religion: Autobiographical Accounts* edited by a distinguished University of Amsterdam psychologist of religion Jacob Belzen.[20] Between the covers of this book are fascinating first-person narratives written by prominent psychological researchers into religious phenomena from the Netherlands, Belgium, Great Britain, Sweden, Finland, Germany, Italy, the Czech Republic, and the United States. Rizzuto is one of only five Americans featured in the book (the others are David Wulff, Bernard Spilka, H. Newton Malony, and Donald Capps). Moreover, she is distinctive as the only contributor whose lifelong professional identity is that of a practicing psychoanalyst. Perhaps for that reason she has titled her autobiographical chapter with some self-consciousness of her outlier position: "An Accidental Psychologist of Religion." Perhaps also because of her unique status, Rizzuto's chapter is the only chapter in the book that includes the text of an amplifying interview conducted by editor Belzen with Rizzuto.

The title, "An Accidental Psychologist of Religion," is deliberate because, in many ways, Rizzuto's narration of her vocational life story may be told as a series of "accidents"—unpredictable and yet fortuitous encounters, invitations, and circumstance—that in unforeseen ways shaped her journey to the research program in the psychology of religion which is the inspiration for the chapters in this book. Drawing upon these three sources and my own interviews with Dr. Rizzuto, I will note several of these "accidents" before turning to a more detailed description of the research that eventually was published as *The Birth of the Living God.*

The first of these unexpected, life-shaping events was of such defining existential and intellectual significance for Rizzuto that she mentions it in in all three of the autobiographical narratives I cite here. The story is a personal experience that is both poignant and illuminating. It shows how Rizzuto came up against the limitations of the familiar religious listening perspectives of her Catholic culture. She was forced by this experience to recognize that she needed to find a more psychologically, and even theologically, adequate way to empathically hear how human beings make their own personal meaning out of religious messages. This is the story:

During her young adult years, Rizzuto was engaged in volunteer pastoral work in a multiclass Roman Catholic parish where she was involved in social work, organizing, and catechetical work with poorer children and their families. With the support and encouragement of the parish priest, Rizzuto delivered social and pastoral services in a role that gave her the rare opportunity to listen to the personal stories and spiritual struggles of parishioners of all ages and classes. Rizzuto's account deserves to be told in her own words:

> I was in my late teens and was studying to become a teacher in Cordoba, Argentina. On Sundays we went with a group of classmates to a neighboring Catholic Church to teach the catechism to children preparing to receive the first communion. That particular Sunday the conversation was about heaven and going to heaven. A young girl gave clear indications that she did not care to go to heaven. There was pain in her voice, sadness in her face, and conviction in her stance. I decided to let the matter drop and after class to take the time to talk to her in private. Our conversation led to the disclosure that she knew her mother was a prostitute, and she also knew prostitutes did not go to heaven. Her choice had been made: she would go in the afterlife to wherever her mother would go. I reflected about that painful moment with the young child: it was clear that she was choosing her mother over God. I was not only deeply moved, but intellectually challenged by a choice that neither theologians nor catechism writers or my teachers had prepared me. The moments of our painful conversation remain engraved in my mind as a religious and a theoretical question.[21]

One might well see Rizzuto's whole program encapsulated in the seed of this one small, but unforgettable, exchange between a child yearning for a lost mother and a well-intentioned, but puzzled, young woman. The experience challenged Rizzuto to understand each individual's religious beliefs as uniquely personal dynamic creations that may employ the symbolic resources of a religious culture, but in a highly idiosyncratic fashion, and always in the service of constructing an internal world in which one remains vitally connected to, or in relationship with, an "other" whose love and regard is life itself for the human person.

Rizzuto completed her teacher training with a strong emphasis on child and adolescent developmental theory and the work of Maria Montessori. Instead of entering teaching, however, she decided to enter medical school. To that study, she brought her passion for understanding that was initially evoked in those memorable parish encounters. She was determined to find a way of practicing, as she called it, "anthropological medicine" in order to view patients "not as individuals caught by unsuspected diseases, but as persons immersed in the complex web of their internal and external realities."[22] Twenty-five years before Harvard professor of medicine Arthur Kleinman published *The Illness Narratives: Suffering, Healing and the Human Condition*, Rizzuto and a small coterie of like-minded fellow medical students happily found the work of Viktor von Weizsacker (1886–1957) who conducted incisive clinical interviews at patients' bedsides. His work convinced Rizzuto and her colleagues that "physical and psychical illnesses always appear embedded in a life that is made up of networks of personal and cultural meanings. In brief: illness is part of that meaning."[23] As a consequence, though Rizzuto could not have known it at the time, from the very beginning of her days as a medical student, she was on a trajectory that would take her away from an early interest in hematology and toward psychiatry, more particularly toward psychoanalysis.

By the end of her medical education with a specialization in internal medicine and hematology, Rizzuto was maintaining what she called a "triple life": working with the head of hematology at Cordoba Hospital, leading a private practice, and teaching child and adolescent development at the newly established Catholic University of Cordoba. She also had decided that she needed to emigrate from Argentina to the United States to enter psychiatry and to study to be a psychoanalyst. At this juncture, another series of defining invitations to understanding emerged, which began to shape the trajectory for the research program Rizzuto would take to the United States.

The first influence occurred as Rizzuto was completing her medical education at an unprecedented historical moment within the Roman Catholic Church in general and the Argentine church in particular. The years of the Second Vatican Council (1962–1965) virtually coincided with Rizzuto's "triple life" as a medical researcher, a physician, and a professor of developmental psychology. Her path to the psychoanalytic investigation of personal religion tracks along some of the influential intellectual currents in modern Catholic thought that led up to the "*aggiornamento*" (opening of the doors) represented by the Second Vatican Council. For centuries the Roman Catholic Church maintained its dominant position of an unchanging, immutable character to its sacred doctrines and practices—all historical evidence to the contrary notwithstanding. The church, in general, held a suspicion of "modernity" and of modern psychology in particular. This stance translated into seminary education programs that consisted largely of learning from authorized theological manuals how to present church teachings in an orthodox fashion and make judgments about the moral behavior of human beings, particularly in the context of sacramental confession.

From high school on, however, Rizzuto had continued her serious involvement as a layperson in the life of a vibrant, intellectual Catholic community, where certain Continental European and Latin American theologians and philosophers were beginning to be read. Their work would be foundational for the Second Vatican Council. As Rizzuto recounts it, when she accepted an invitation to participate in a select, year-long study group that focused on the problem of the *evolution of dogma* in the Catholic Church, she embarked on a transformative intellectual experience. Working through the writings of such figures as Yves Congar, Gustav Thils, Jacques Leclerq, Henri deLubac, Hans Kung, and Karl Rahner, she encountered, for the first time, a compelling case for seeing the church as a living and growing social organism, rather than as a static and unchanging institution whose divine constitution inoculated it against the necessity of change or renewal. The organic image of the church that emerged from these thinkers is of a dynamic and constantly developing body. This body is composed of all the faithful, priests, and laypersons alike, who respond to the inspiration of the indwelling Spirit to new historical demands and occasions. But if this is true of the church as a collective, then analogically, it must also be the case for individual persons. From this new vantage point, one can appreciate that *the theological door is thrown open to consider human believing as itself a dynamic, continually evolving process.* All this provided Rizzuto with both the theological warrant and the moral imperative to investigate the psychological processes of religious development. But how should she proceed?

Rizzuto found support for putting this theological perspective to practical pastoral use from an unexpected direction. In the years before and during the Second Vatican Council, interest grew in some sectors of the Argentine church in preparing priests and pastoral workers to work with greater psychological awareness of the human foundations of religious belief. The next wholly unexpected and surprising "accident" for Rizzuto came through an invitation from the dean of the Pontifical Seminary of Our Lady of Loretto in Cordoba to accept a position as professor of pastoral anthropology. Rizzuto was invited to design and teach a first-of-its-kind course for clergy and seminarians in Cordoba on "the psychology of belief." Like any good researcher, she immediately sought out available scholarship that would help clergy in training listen with empathy and understanding to the lives of their parishioners. What she discovered was disappointing. Relevant material on the psychology of religion available in French or Spanish featured a limited set of psychologically sophisticated Catholic authors: Roland Dalbeiz, Ignatius Lepp, and H. C. Rumke. The work of Sigmund Freud was available to her, even though it had been condemned in 1934 by Pope Pius XI and was still regarded warily by many Catholics. Given the paucity of research in the psychology of religious development accessible to a Spanish readership, Rizzuto confronted a challenge and an opportunity: she would make the seminarians themselves investigators of the psycho-spiritual lives of their parishioners.

After securing the bishop's assurance that no topics or resources would be considered beyond investigation, Rizzuto responded affirmatively to the invitation and developed an educational strategy that made each course participant an independent investigator. Quite simply, all participating seminarians were asked to pay close attention to what they were hearing and seeing during their ordinary pastoral work and to make that material the substance of their common weekly study. Emphasis was placed on capturing the immediacy of the sharing that had taken place and on taking seriously the "data of the details" of each conversation. The approach was inductive, empirical without being positivistic, and certainly radically different from that of the manuals of penitential counsel and question/answer catechisms that had been the stock-in-trade of Roman Catholic seminary education prior to the Second Vatican Council. Again, we see Rizzuto's conviction growing that the key to understanding religious faith is to enter a mode of careful, systematic observation of the very particular imagery that persons employ to tell their own life stories and to talk about the God of their understanding.

In a certain sense, Rizzuto's research, from its very beginning in Argentina to the project in the United States that became *The Birth of the Living God,* may be said to represent a return to the mode of radical empiricism that characterized William James's original approach to the psychology of religion. She shares with James a fascination with the unlimited plurality and variety of religious experience and a commitment to investigate how "real work is done" by means of the particular beliefs that an individual may choose to embrace. Moreover, like James, Rizzuto felt that one could investigate the pragmatic consequences of believing without needing either to attack or to defend the ontological status of the object of that belief.

In 1965 Rizzuto left Argentina to pursue psychiatric training and arrived in the United States with a potential research design already in mind. The design was grounded in her own considerable experience listening to countless conversations with medical professionals, priests, parishioners, and patients. She would find the key to interpreting these "living human documents" in the psychoanalytic training that she began in Boston in 1968. However, she was developing the basic motivation and vision for her research prior to her formal analytic training. Perhaps as much as any other factor, what accounts for the fresh and original feel of Rizzuto's approach to psychological research is this: she began with an immersion in the *questions* raised by individual religious experiences rather than with a set of interpretations defined by psychoanalysis that were then "applied."

THE RESEARCH PROJECT: DESIGN AND EXECUTION

After an initial year in New York City in 1964–1965 where she worked in rotating internships to revalidate her medical license and board certification, Rizzuto moved to Boston. She hoped that in Boston, the city of William James and a community with a strong academic tradition, she would find a psychiatric community open to the research project she was proposing. What she found was decidedly more mixed. On the one hand, at Boston State Hospital, a large mental institution no longer in existence, she received the superintendent's support to conduct research on her own time in the ward. On the other hand, two successive research supervisors declined to serve as advisers on the project, apparently unable to understand why she might be interested in investigating the psychodynamic processes through which individuals formulate representations of "God." In some ways, this early venture anticipates the profile of Rizzuto's whole professional career as a working analyst and as a psychoanalytic scholar/theorist. From the beginning, she pursued her research almost entirely on her own time without the support of outside grants or funding and without a research team. Nevertheless, while she was at Boston State Hospital, another fortunate "accident" occurred in Rizzuto's life. She gained the support of the much beloved and respected Dr. Elvin Semrad, professor of psychiatry at Harvard Medical School. Regarded by some as the dean of psychiatry in Boston, Dr. Semrad encouraged Rizzuto's research interests even when many, if not most, of her peers and senior colleagues regarded it with little interest or comprehension.[24]

Pulling a heavy Grundig tape recorder through the halls of the hospital day after day on her own time, Rizzuto developed a protocol that enabled her to capture large amounts of data in recorded interviews, as well as questionnaires and projective tests. Her objective was to assemble information on patients' family constellations, their relevant childhood experiences including whatever they might identify as their religious experiences, and their past and present images of "God" or other religious figures. In a sense, her project was a large-scale, one-person application of the methodology she had piloted with the seminarians in Cordoba: *listen first; interpret later*. As she writes, "Finally I decided that I would not bias my learning by imposing preformulated theories of any type upon the material: I would gather the data and let them be until the moment I was ready to look at them and then let them speak for themselves when common patterns, repeated events, similar ways of functioning, and so on appeared in the comparison of cases."[25]

Rizzuto's initial challenge was to verify her own intuition that the psychological dynamics of religious believing are the same across normal and clinical populations, or, to use Harry Stack Sullivan's fortunate phrasing, that we are "all more simply human than not" when it comes to how we function in this vital arena of mental life. Confirming this observation became Rizzuto's goal during a year-long pilot study at Boston State Hospital (1966–1967). Comparing fifteen hospitalized patients with five professional employees at the hospital, Rizzuto satisfied herself on this point: although the specific *contents* of religious believing may vary, the *process* of believing differs in degree but not in kind between mental patients and persons considered "normal."[26]

The next fortunate circumstance in Rizzuto's life was an invitation to work with Dr. Paul Myerson, a psychoanalyst who headed the psychiatry department at Tufts-New England Medical Center. In Rizzuto's fourth year of residency, Dr. Myerson invited her to serve as chief resident and teaching fellow in psychiatry. Myerson gave her permission to use the entire inpatient population as the subjects of her research. As a result, the next critical stage of her research was conducted at Tufts-New England Medical Center. This three-year project (1967–1970) was the empirical basis for *The Birth of the Living God.* She devised the following three-part protocol administered in stages to one hundred and twenty-three inpatients over the period of the study.

Stage 1: During the first week of a standard, two-week hospitalization, the patient was asked to draw a picture of his or her family and was given a family questionnaire, later reproduced in the appendix of Rizzuto's book.[27] The twenty-three-item questionnaire elicited from the patient his or her identifications and associations with various family members (e.g., "Emotionally I resemble my ____ because ____;" "The member of the family I admire the most is my____because____"). The questionnaire also inquired about the patient's sense of the lines of loyalty, subgroupings, and patterns of authority in the family (e.g., "The boss in my family was____because____"). Finally, the patient was asked to identify how old he or she was in the family picture that he or she drew and where the family depicted in the drawing was living.

Stage 2: In the second week of hospitalization, the patient was given a "God Questionnaire" of some forty-five questions.[28] The questionnaire allowed the patient to state if he or she believed or did not believe in a personal God and why. The questionnaire inquired about how the patient perceived God, regardless of whether or not the patient had said they "believed in God" (e.g., "What I like the most about God is____because____" or "What I resent most about God is____ because____"). As will be discussed later in more detail, Rizzuto found it significant that even patients who claimed disbelief in God nevertheless possessed fairly definite notions about the God whose existence they denied. For instance, they were clear about what that God would or would not want of them. The emphasis in the questionnaire was on the patients' affective relationship to the God they imagined and the history of that relationship (e.g., "The day I changed my way of thinking about God was____because____"). A few questions tapped into the patient's relationship to other figures associated with traditional religious imagery, for example, favorite saints or biblical characters, and the devil. However, the primary focus of the questionnaire was on eliciting from the patient how the patient imagined the actions, desires, intentions, and attitudes of the figure they associated with the word symbol "God."

Stage 3: In the final discharge interview, Rizzuto asked the patient to draw a picture of God and discuss that picture with her.

From the 123 completed research protocols, Rizzuto selected twenty patients whose questionnaires were particularly articulate and well developed and whose cases spanned all diagnostic categories. She wrote a painstakingly detailed thirty-page formulation of each of these twenty patients. She also drew upon process notes from over eighteen hours of inpatient therapy as well as from social work and nursing notes in the patients' medical records while on the unit. From this extensive array of data on each individual, Rizzuto organized her twenty patients according to a typology of the conscious way in which individuals described themselves as "believing" or "not believing" in God. The four cases presented in the second part of her book were selected as particularly rich representations of persons from each of these four categories:

1. those who have a God whose existence they do not doubt;
2. those wondering whether or not to believe in a God they are not sure exists;
3. those amazed, angered, or quietly surprised to see others deeply invested in a God that does not interest them;
4. those who struggle with a demanding, harsh God they would like to get rid of if they were not convinced of his existence and power.[29]

With these four cases, Rizzuto offers a nuanced and psychologically differentiated mapping of the terrain of "belief and unbelief." David Wulff, historian of the psychology of religion, lifts up the significance of this mapping, citing Winnicott. Wulff writes, "Whereas the contemporary understanding of belief suggests that only two attitudes are possible—affirmation of the object's existence or denial of it—a third possibility closer to the belief's original meaning is suggested by Winnicott: an intermediate position of complex cognitive and emotional attitudes that include imaginative participation in, solemn appreciation for, or deep engagement with the religious object." Acknowledging the tenacity with which dichotomous thinking about belief-disbelief is maintained, Wulff continues, "Clarifying the possible alternative attitudes that can be taken towards religious content would be one of the greatest services that psychologists of religion could render today." This is the service that Rizzuto, the "accidental psychologist of religion," offers.[30]

Wulff's insights bring to mind Oliver Wendell Holmes, who was famously quoted as saying "For the simplicity on this side of complexity, I wouldn't give you a fig. But for the simplicity on the other side of complexity, for that I would give you anything I have."[31] In the subject before us, "the simplicity on this side of complexity" would be the common view that belief and unbelief are uncomplicated binaries. When someone says, "I believe in God" (or the obverse), we know exactly what they mean—and presume they do as well. Classic theological apologetics or its mirror position—the equally doctrinaire counter claims of the new atheists which Jacob Waldenmaier discusses later in this book—often presume that persons come to this position (belief or unbelief) in some kind of straightforward process of conscious reasoning, or perhaps by means of an equally deliberate suspension of incredulity.

For over ten years, Rizzuto swam in the immense complexity of the dense human data she compiled over countless hours talking with patients and soliciting their reflections on the questions she gave them. One might say, referencing Holmes, that she gave "everything she had" to break through that binary "on the near side of complexity" and arrive at last at four categories which are "the simplicity on the far side." I think they brilliantly organize a comprehensive range of stories underneath which is one story: the lifelong need of all humans to experience themselves as selves in-relation, no matter the conditions under which they have encountered the distinctive vicissitudes of their own life circumstances.

THE RESEARCH PROJECT: FINDINGS

Rizzuto's three observations in *The Birth of the Living God* comprise its most salient findings and account for its influence over three decades on the psychoanalytic study of religion. Let's look at each of these in turn.

1. *No one coming to awareness in a society where the symbol "God" has any cultural currency is without a conscious or unconscious object representation of God.*

In several places in her book, Rizzuto is unequivocal on this point: "In Freud's understanding of the subject, and in my own, *there is no such thing as a person without a God representation*" (emphasis added).[32] This assertion has the capacity to make some other psychoanalysts a bit uncomfortable, or so I personally have observed. At a presentation by Rizzuto to a psychoanalytic gathering some years prior to the publication of *The Birth of the Living God* several analysts in attendance objected defensively. They argued that since they had been "fully analyzed," they could not possibly still harbor an object representation of God. But they misunderstood Rizzuto. She is *not* claiming that individuals such as her psychoanalytic colleagues who profess a disbelief in the existence of God somehow secretly or unconsciously "believe" in God. Rather, she is asserting that an analytic inquiry into the representations of the God these individuals profess *not* to believe in will itself yield evidence of this God's intricate origins in the vicissitudes of their particular family romance and cultural circumstances. Recall here Rizzuto's own discovery in her research for *The Birth of the Living God* that even persons who strongly assert that they did *not* believe in God nevertheless were able to produce detailed associations to "God" and could draw a picture of the God they had rejected as an object of personal belief. None of her subjects, regardless of religious upbringing or current conscious philosophical convictions, failed to produce evidence of associations with a "God" that was available to them at multiple representational levels.[33]

In taking this position, Rizzuto is consistent with Freud, as she reads him; moreover, she also is building upon the theoretical development of Freud's thought associated with British object relations theorists such as pediatrician and psychoanalyst David Winnicott. He proposed that, in the lifelong task of becoming a self, the capacity for "illusory" thinking is an indispensable psychic resource. The child, from a very early age, manages to maintain some basic sense of being a self-in-relationship by means of a process of proto-symbolization, or what Winnicott called the use of "transitional objects." The child invests a toy, a blanket corner, or a particular physical practice (e.g., sucking a thumb or pulling on an ear lobe) with the capacity to evoke certain solacing or soothing self-states that are associated with the care taking of primary adults in the infant's life.[34] This psychic capacity for "illusion" produces the imaginary companions and fantasy figures that populate the child's inner world. This capacity is not "outgrown." Rather, this innate human capability for experience "unchallenged in respect of its belonging to inner or external (shared) reality" evolves into adulthood. There, it "is retained in the intense experiencing that belongs to the arts and to religion and to imaginative living, and to creative scientific work."[35] We shall observe in Rizzuto's third major finding how this recognition of the lifelong value for human flourishing of "illusion" is the ground from which will emerge a more positive assessment of religious believing.

Rizzuto maintains that in most Western societies the term "God," or its functional equivalent (*Allah, Adonai, Ha-Shem*, etc.), is a generally available cultural symbolic resource. Even children raised in irreligious or unobservant households hear persons regularly evoke "God" to bless or curse. They notice "In God We Trust" written on currency. They cannot fail to observe that, although they and their peers are systematically disillusioned about Santa Claus or the tooth fairy at a certain age, generally no such intervention is made regarding this supra-personal figure that seems somehow to hover mysteriously in the background or foreground of other people's lives. In her research, Rizzuto aspired to explain how that pervasively referenced, but invisible, "God" is imagined by a growing child embedded in his or her own network of familial and social relationships and, thus, to understand how this "God" may or may not be available for the lifelong tasks of sustaining a sense of being a self-in-relationship.

Rizzuto's conclusions may vex persons who, like some of her analytic colleagues, fall into the third category of "those amazed, angered or quietly surprised to see others deeply invested in a God that does not interest them." However, her research findings have proved useful to persons who work clinically or pastorally with individuals who fall into her fourth category of "those who struggle with a demanding, harsh God they would like to get rid of if they were not convinced of his existence and power." If one has lived or worked professionally with such persons, then one knows the poignancy of their determined attachment to a God who is punitive and persecutory. Such a God appears to offer neither the kind of compensations and consolations nor the superego control over impulses and desires that Freud had held were some of the psychological motivations for the human creation of a deity. Moreover such an internal relationship often seems impervious either to rational dissuasion or to theological interventions that would propose a less malignant concept of God. Rizzuto offers a more compassionate and clinically useful insight into the function those representations may play in the internal world of such a person. One might, for example, empathically understand these individuals' condition *vis-a-vis* their God representations as analogous to the psychological situation of persons who, having been abused as children, attach themselves as adults to abusive partners. They look to a punishing or harshly judgmental God as others look to an abusive romantic partner for the only reliable version of "love" and attention that they hitherto have known and believe they deserve.

2. *The object representations of God are not simply derived from the child's experience of the historical father; moreover, once fashioned, they do not remain static and unchanging. Rather, they are available for further elaboration, revision, refashioning, or rejection in ways related to the function they are called upon to serve at any given moment.*

Three significant developments beyond Freud are condensed in Rizzuto's second finding from her research project. The first development beyond Freud concerns what sort of psychic "raw material" goes into the individual's mental representation of "God." Freud held that the familial referent for the Biblical God was the male child's father in the flesh: "a personal God is, psychologically, nothing other than an exalted father."[36] By contrast, in the four case studies discussed in *The Birth of the Living God*, Rizzuto presents persuasive evidence that a representation of God is more like a composite photograph that displays together features of a child's patterns of interaction with either or both parents, grandparents, and, in theory, other significant caregivers from the child's earliest life experience.[37]

Rizzuto's second corrective to Freud focuses on the fate of these early representations of God. For Freud, they were psychological anachronisms frozen in the state of their own primitive developmental origins. These necessarily had to be surrendered as the rationally reflective person matured and made his or her own peace with the cosmic aloneness that is the human fate. For Rizzuto, however, that we are wed to the primitive character of our original God representations is no more the case than that we are sentenced to live forever tethered to the earliest representations we formed of our parents. Rizzuto writes, "If one is willing to accept that a mature relationship with one's parents is possible, then a mature relationship with the God representation should also be possible."[38] Our real-time relationship with our parents "in the flesh" is not the only relationship that has the potential to develop and change. Over time, and sometimes with the support of therapy, one may mourn and release attachment to idealized or demonized internalized parental representations. Expressions of appreciation, compassion, and gratitude toward ourselves, and toward our parents, may follow—whether or not they are still living or deceased. What happens to our relationships with our internalized parental object representations may occur analogously in our relationship to our conscious and unconscious representations of "God."

Rizzuto reiterates both her first and second findings in these words:

> It is a central thesis of this book that no child in the Western world brought up in ordinary circumstances completes the oedipal cycle without forming at least a rudimentary God representation, which he may use for belief or not. The rest of developmental life may leave that representation untouched as the individual continues to revise parent and self-representations during the life cycle. If the God representation is not revised to keep pace with changes in self-representation, it soon becomes asynchronous and is experienced as ridiculous or irrelevant.[39]

Although a given person may continue to grow and develop intellectually and emotionally in their relationships to significant others, past and present, there may be no parallel maturation with respect to their "at least rudimentary God representation." If the circumstances of an individual's life wall off their God representations from critical psychological, philosophical, and existential exploration and elaboration, then these representations will remain in a state of arrested development.

An example of a revision of a God representation that keeps pace with changes in self-representation illustrates Rizzuto's point. This example was offered to me by a female colleague. Growing up in a fairly traditional, patriarchal Christian family, her earliest representations of God were strongly organized by her relationship to her idealized, but authoritarian, father as well as by her relationships with male spiritual leaders in her community who were important emotional and moral referents. The sense of a valued-self that she developed was founded on submission and docility toward male authority and brought to expression in cheerful, self-abnegating service to others. Over the course of her college education and in the context of therapy with a secular woman counselor, my colleague's self-representation began to change. Newly incorporated into this representation were elements of self-agency, assertiveness, and a capacity for independent thought that had always been there but had remained un-integrated because it had been devalued by the significant men in her family and by her mother. Only a relationship with a maiden aunt who the family had judged as eccentric and heterodox had countered this devaluation: my colleague felt that the aunt had related to her respectfully as an intellectual peer.

Several years into the process of naming and claiming this more expansive self-representation, my colleague realized that her representations of God had not kept pace with these evolving developments. Forms of worship and prayer that once had been meaningful now felt, to use Rizzuto's words, "ridiculous and irrelevant." Nevertheless, the Christian story was a connection to her family of origin and one she felt could offer her undiscovered resources for meaningful living. She began to study feminist biblical theology under the direction of a respected female minister. More importantly, she cultivated a regular practice of imaginative personal prayer in which she affectively related to images of Jesus as a man who loved and empowered women, including herself. Over time, she observed that her God representations became more synchronous with her changing self-representations. She supported, rather than resisted, those changes.

Rizzuto's second finding differs from Freud in a third way. She follows Winnicott and other object relations theorists who ascribe to the psychological processes that generate our representations of God with *an adaptive potential* that is not outgrown or superseded in the course of maturation. In his various writings on Western religion, Freud saw the psychological formation of "God" as serving only a defensive function. With the resolution of the Oedipal conflict, "God" is installed as an aspect of the superego that projects onto the cosmic screen the authority and protective function of the formerly idealized father. God serves to compensate the individual for the narcissistic injuries inflicted by fate, contingency, and misfortune and for the instinctual renunciation required to live in society. For Freud, the psychologically adult individual, of which he was willing to grant there might be few specimens, is one who recognizes the illusory (i.e., wish-fulfillment-motivated) character of religious belief and surrenders these beliefs to pursue a life informed only by the god *logos,* the still small voice of critical reason.[40]Rizzuto does not deny that, for some individuals, their God representations may serve these compensatory needs at a certain stage of development or even across the life cycle; however, she is persuaded by her study that Freud's description was an impoverished, incomplete, and clinically inadequate account of how religious "illusion" serves human life.[41] Her four case studies might be considered "thick descriptions" of the multiple adaptive and defensive functions of the religious imagination.

In *The Birth of the Living God,* Rizzuto describes theoretically and abstractly these multiple functions of religious believing. They fall into two groups. There are functions that have to do with *mastery,* and these she describes using a language of "integration," "balance," and "equilibrium." Other functions have to do with "meaning making." Here, her language moves beyond the usual terms of psychoanalytic discourse to sound more existential and even theological. The study of the lifelong metamorphosis of the God representations, she wrote, "provides us with a beautiful illustration of the ingenuity and creative symbolic mastery of the human mind in the effort made by the individual to master his present reality, his past, and his contemporary context, *as well as of his need for transcendence and meaning* in the context of the universe at large."[42] Some of the most creative subsequent work that has been stimulated by Rizzuto's project has used the work of analysts such as Stephen Mitchell, Jessica Benjamin, and Christopher Bollas to show how "mastery" and "meaning making" come together around the problem of maintaining a sense of being a self-in-relation.[43]

3. *It is important to distinguish the more preconscious, imaginal, primary process dimensions of an individual's "God" from the more public, secondary process, conceptual elaborations of "God."*

Rizzuto's insight that primary process is more important than secondary process is illustrated in a story from my colleague, a theologically sophisticated scholar. He felt he had subjected his religious formation to intense scrutiny and, he thought, to a thorough demythologizing. "God," insofar as he spoke of a divinity, was something closer to Paul Tillich's "Existential Ground of Being." Yet, he was astonished when he found himself on one very frightening plane ride spontaneously and earnestly addressing God in the words of a long-forgotten bedtime prayer that went back to his evangelical childhood. My colleague was surprised. Rizzuto would not have been. After all, the working distinction between the "God of the philosophers and theologians" and the "living God" whose character and presence is shaped by the individual's whole affective, relational experience is crucial for Rizzuto:

> When dealing with the concrete fact of belief, it is important to clarify the conceptual and emotional differences between the concept of God and the images of God which, combined in multiple forms, produce the prevailing God representation

> in a given individual at a given time. The concept of God is fabricated mostly at the level of secondary-process thinking. This is the God of the theologians, the God whose existence or nonexistence is debated by metaphysical reasoning. But this God leaves us cold. This God is only the result of rigorous thinking about causality and philosophical premises. Even someone who believes intellectually that there must be a God may feel no inclination to accept him unless images of previous interpersonal experience have fleshed out a concept with multiple images that can now coalesce in a representation that he can accept emotionally.[44]

Parsing with care the distinction between a "God concept" and a "God representation" is absolutely crucial to correctly understanding Rizzuto's most basic insights into the phenomenon of religious experience. A God concept is simply a statement or an abstract idea that intends reference to some divine reality. One might think here of Anselm's definition of God as "that than which nothing greater can be conceived," Aquinas's "Unmoved Mover," and Paul Tillich's "Ground of Being." The God Concept may also include myriad metaphors of the Jewish, Christian, and Muslim traditions: "Heavenly Father," "Lord of Hosts," "King of Kings," "Ruler of the Universe," and "The All Merciful and Compassionate One." The names of God are virtually endless. In contrast to the God concept, a God representation comprises the conscious and unconscious feelings, self-states, memories, smells, sounds, physical sensations, tastes, mental images, and associations that cluster at any given moment around the word symbol "God" that may be evoked by any of the metaphors or concepts such as I have just described.

Believing, Rizzuto wants us to understand, is not simply a matter of the head, that is, intellectual submission to doctrines or ideas. More fundamentally, believing is an affair of the heart.[45] "Believing" that matters for vital living depends on how a particular idea or concept about "God" is emotionally resonant with an individual's highly personal, conscious, and unconscious "representations" of God, which may be evoked at the time the concept is encountered. In a talk delivered at the Menninger Clinic, Rizzuto eloquently articulated her conviction that "believing" must be understood psychologically, if not theologically, as a matter of the heart and not simply of the head. Rizzuto affirmed that "Belief is never only something to be believed *in,* a fact of knowledge or dogma alone. It is an interpersonal disposition that affirms the existence of a *mode of relatedness* between the believer and others, be it people, the universe conceived as a living reality or a divine being. Thus belief as a human act of attribution is always, by its very nature, an affective act of connection."[46] With this observation, the overarching significance of Rizzuto's three research findings comes clearly into view.

The process of "believing" with respect to God is grounded in the fundamental need of our species for some reliable internal and external relationship to a reality that responds to our essential psychological need for nurturance, emotional recognition, and mirroring. So profound is this need for connection, in the first instance from the primary caretakers of infancy, that even when the parent "in the flesh" is absent, our imaginative capacity for illusory thought sustains the hope that this connection somehow endures. Rizzuto memorably attested to this need in her poignant conversation with the orphaned young girl in Cordoba who stubbornly insisted that she would rather be in hell with her mother than in heaven without her. But our thinking heart's questioning of how we relate to life does not end with our earliest interpersonal world. Because we are meaning-making beings who are self-conscious of our mortality, finitude, and inter-connectedness, we are drawn to questions that not only encompass particular persons into whose care and company we are born but also include the widest dimension of reality we can imagine: *Who or what is going to be there for me? Am I ultimately safe and somehow upheld in existence, or am I finally alone and abandoned? Is Reality constructed to support or defeat me?*

As Rizzuto demonstrates, for some persons their "mode of relatedness" to an ultimate environment may be mediated either positively or problematically by their representations of God. Even if that is not the case, the way at any given moment that anyone answers those questions of the heart will be shaped in significant ways by their unique relational histories. William James grasped this insight when he wrote, "The universe is no longer a mere It to us, but a Thou, if we are religious; and any relation that may be possible from person to person is possible here."[47] Rizzuto invites us to go further than James. "Religious" is a capacious descriptor not limited to formal institutional affiliation or self-definition; rather, by virtue of being human, all persons are, as the Russian philosopher Nikolai Berdyaev put it, "incurably religious."

EARLY RECEPTION AND CURRENT INFLUENCE OF RIZZUTO'S WORK ON AND THEORY AND PRACTICE

At the conclusion of *The Birth of the Living God*, Rizzuto wrote, "If my own research stimulates more scientific investigation in the fields of psychology, sociology, anthropology, comparative religions, mythology and others, I will consider my efforts well rewarded."[48] Some thirty-six years after that statement, Rizzuto's investigative efforts have indeed begun to be rewarded by a range of research and reflection, mostly in the area of clinical and pastoral theology. Initially, however, the book did not receive the reception from Rizzuto's peers that might have been expected, given Rizzuto's professional standing as a working, well-published psychoanalyst deeply committed to her professional practice and guild and held in high regard among psychoanalysts internationally. *The Birth of the Living God* was appreciatively reviewed in over half a dozen national journals in theology, the study of religion and pastoral care and counseling, such as *Theological Studies, The Journal of Pastoral Care, and The Journal of Religion and Health.* By contrast, it was reviewed at length in only one psychoanalytic journal, *Psychoanalytic Quarterly.*[49] The tone and the content of that review merit analysis for they attest to entrenched resistance on the part of some psychoanalytically committed persons to the implications of Rizzuto's research findings.

The author of that single review, Howard F. Stein, now professor emeritus in the Department of Family and Preventive Medicine of the University of Oklahoma Health Sciences Center, is not a practicing psychoanalyst. Nevertheless, Stein strongly supports Freud's position in *The Future of an Illusion.* Stein begins his essay praising Rizzuto's "masterful review" of the psychoanalytic literature on religion. He then charges Rizzuto with having written a "brief for religion" and of having used object relations theory "as a crypto-Jungian basis for a psychoanalytic theology."[50] The nub of his critique is that Rizzuto fails to embrace Freud's ideal of maturity as the relinquishment of all illusions "in favor of mature, post oedipal love and work." To suggest, as Rizzuto does, that, even in maturity, we never outgrow our need for some form of transitional experiencing is, for Stein, to commit "the error of confusing a persistent group fetish with a true transitional object, that is, an object that is phase-specifically intermediate between lesser and greater self-differentiation and individuation." Stein goes so far as to intimate that Rizzuto's failure to uphold a thoroughly orthodox hermeneutic of suspicion with respect to religion is possible evidence of inadequate psychoanalytic treatment: "There can be no compromise between the pre oedipal and oedipal authoritarian character and the post oedipal human chary of all belief. Any psychoanalysis which admits such a compromise reveals a lacunar resistance, an incompleteness of analysis in the analyst."[51] The curiously *ad hominem* character of Stein's displays the kind of neuralgic response that Rizzuto understood she might invite in writing *The Birth of the Living God.* Overlooked in Stein's review is Rizzuto's straightforward assertion that she is *not* making an argument for the existence of God, about which psychoanalysis on its own terms has nothing to say. To the contrary, she is amassing the clinical data that will allow her to "confirm, complement or correct Freud's statements about the formation of the God representation."[52]

If Stein criticizes Rizzuto for deviating from a certain psychoanalytic orthodoxy regarding religion, other individuals come from the opposite direction to mount a critique. They wonder whether Rizzuto's search for the psychological origins of the representation of God is inherently reductionistic. They object that her theory does not explicitly allow for the possibility that God in God's Self might have real agency to effectively shape, correct, and transform an individual's personal representations of a divine other. From this vantage, some reviewers hold that the consequence of Rizzuto's research makes God "nothing but" the sum of the individual's history of human object relationships as these have been psychologically memorialized, without leaving room for the activity of God as a contributor to the representational process. A senior psychoanalyst Stanley Leavy, himself a convert from Judaism to Catholic Christianity, argues this position.[53] This same argument also appears in criticisms of Rizzuto's work written from an evangelical Christian perspective.[54] The most developed book-length statement of this position is from Moshe Halevi Spero, an Orthodox Jewish psychologist. Spero offers a comprehensive theoretical and clinical model of the representational process that also incorporates the possibility of a "veridically real" God as a player in mental life.[55]

Between these two critiques—the "orthodox" psychoanalytic and the "orthodox" religious—are philosophically and theologically intricate responses to Rizzuto that find in her appropriation of Winnicott the beginning of a profound "postmodern" epistemological shift. This shift judges as inadequate both the scientific positivism of Freud and the theological positivism of those who must regard God as wholly other, outside and beyond the structures of the human psyche. James Jones, who brings to his study of religious belief an interdisciplinary background in psychology, religious studies, and the philosophy of science, has argued that Rizzuto's work exemplifies this "middle way." Her work challenges Cartesian dualisms of subject-object and knower-known in ways that parallel developments in the physical sciences, feminist psychology, and postmodern theology.[56]

This very positive response to Rizzuto's work comes from scholars working within the disciplines of pastoral care and counseling. Their perceptions indicate that Rizzuto's appropriation of psychoanalytic thinking is a valuable resource with which to engage two issues central to their discipline, one clinical and the other theological. The clinical issue is this: in its essential praxis Christian and Jewish pastoral care and counseling may be understood as processes that help persons unmask the false gods or idolatries that limit human freedom and compromise the capacity for love.[57] Rizzuto's developmental model provides the pastoral counselor with a means to sensitively understand this psycho-spiritual process of deconstructing damaging and inadequate images of God.[58]

The theological issue involves negotiating a fundamental paradox: How can we recognize that all human speech about "God" is necessarily an imaginative creation of the human mind and also claim that such speech intends as its referent a transcendent Reality which both exceeds us utterly and yet in which we "live and move and have our being" (Acts 17:28)? Rizzuto's book alerts those in the pastoral disciplines, whose acquaintance with psychoanalysis largely has been limited to Freud and ego psychology, to the possibility that contemporary psychoanalytic object relations theory may well be a uniquely helpful conversational partner for working out this theological *via media.* Writing on the contribution of Winnicott and Rizzuto, pastoral theologian Leroy Howe argues that their articulation of transitional object processes provides an invaluable analogue for thinking about representations of God. By thinking with Rizzuto, pastoral psychology and fundamental theology are delivered from the trap of an either/or binary that would posit God *either* as an invention of our minds *or* as a reality independent of our minds. Howe writes:

> Transitional objects to not "live" simply on one side or the other of Freud's narrowly defined dichotomies of pleasure principle/ reality principle, illusion/ realistic possibility, appearance/reality, or wish fulfillment/ truth. They have their own being, value and power both between and beyond all such dichotomies. They are neither fact nor fancy; they are both and more. What is true of transitional objects is quintessentially true of our God representations and of the world coherence we experience by means of them. What we affirm about God is neither an 'objectively' valid representation of a real but transcendent entity, nor is it a complex of wish-driven abstractions formed in our minds out of other internal object representations and encounters with "real" objects in an empirical, interpersonal world. It is both, inseparably.[59]

With these comments, Professor Howe acknowledges that Rizzuto's formulation of an object relational account of the origins and function of God representations provides pastoral theologians with a creative and theologically liberating "tool to think with" (Erikson) about human religious experience.

Beginning with *The Birth of the Living God*, Rizzuto's work also has stimulated a line of creative empirical research in the field of the psychology of religion. For this reason, Division 36, the Division of the Psychology of Religion of the American Psychological Association (APA), honored Rizzuto in 1996 with its annual William C. Bier award for "outstanding contributions to the field of the psychology of religion." Her paper delivered on the occasion of that award to the annual APA meeting in Toronto was titled "Belief as a Psychic Function."[60] The following year, the Spirituality, Religion and Psychiatry Caucus of the American Psychiatric Association recognized Rizzuto's "outstanding contributions to the dialogue concerning religion, spirituality and psychiatry" with its annual Oskar Pfister Award. This award is named after the Swiss pastor who was welcomed into Freud's inner circle as the first lay analyst and maintained a thirty-year dialogue with Freud that remained warm and open despite serious disagreements over both religion and political issues. Finally, the Italian Society of the Psychology of Religion in 2000 voted to make Rizzuto an honorary member in recognition of her profound impact on Italian scholars of the psychology of religion. Chapter 2 in this book by Mario Aletti, founder and past president of the Italian Society of the Psychology of Religion, discusses in detail this impact of Rizzuto's work.

The multiple honors that Rizzuto has received attest to her groundbreaking contributions to the field of the psychology of religion. Let us consider some of the most significant here and reflect on the difference they have made to the field. The first of these contributions is based on the important distinction that Rizzuto has drawn between "God representations" and "God concepts." As noted above, this distinction is, fundamentally, a differentiation between "secondary process" public ideas about a divinity and the "primary process" ensemble of conscious and unconscious feeling, memories, and mental images that a person may associate to the word-symbol "God." European and North American psychologists interested in religion have been researching the psychological dimensions of the individual's concept of God for over thirty years. Many of these studies, influenced by psychoanalysis, have aimed at understanding how the concept of God may relate to an individual's associations to parental figures or to idealized notions of father and mother. In the main, these research methods have employed adjective checklists or semantic differential scales in order to identify attributional factors of God (loving, controlling, wrathful, etc.), which might then be correlated with other personality variables (e.g., self-esteem, level of ego function, etc.) or with certain religious behaviors.[61]

Into this vigorous research tradition, Rizzuto introduced another order of complexity. For example, by proposing that our representations of God are conscious, preconscious, and sometimes unconscious, Rizzuto's study challenged researchers to devise new ways of accessing this material.[62] Taking up this challenge, psychologists have worked from Rizzuto's clinical findings in developing testing instruments that are subject to greater statistical validation and control than is Rizzuto's God questionnaire and, hence, potentially more useful clinically. One early effort was the Spiritual Themes and Religious Responses Test (STARR), a projective test inviting responses to a series of photographs of persons at prayer.[63] Perhaps the most ambitious and psychometrically sophisticated instrument directly inspired by Rizzuto's distinction between God concept and God image/representation is the God Image Inventory (GII) developed by the Rev. Richard T. Lawrence as part of his doctoral work at Catholic University.[64] The GII develops scales to measure the individual's intuitive felt sense of who God is for him or her that might correlate with various measures of the individual's sense of belonging, goodness, and control.[65] Clinical psychologist Jay Gattis at Rosemead School of Professional Psychology developed for his doctoral dissertation a computer program and an accompanying website that familiarizes therapists and counselors with the foundational distinction in Rizzuto's work between God Concept and God Image/Representation, makes the GII available to qualified therapists and counselors, and provides resources on the site to administer and score the instrument.[66]

Further promising lines of investigation can be traced to questions raised in Rizzuto's study. For example, consideration can be given to ways in which a therapist's own countertransference around religion influences how he or she understands and relates to the religious material of the patient. One suggestive study by the late Dr. Randall Sorenson explored how the God representation of the *therapist* and the therapist's own prior experience of the way in which *his/her own therapist addressed or avoided religious issues* impacts the therapist's present ability to respond to religious issues that arise during treatment. Sorenson's work helps to explain how a certain tone-deafness on the part of some therapists to salient religious themes in treatment is in some ways unconsciously inherited. One after another, therapeutic lineages can get caught in the teeth of a religion-hostile cogwheel.[67]

Other research initiatives have asked how particular traumatic experiences may affect a person's representations of God. Here, Carrie Doehring's (1993) careful empirical investigation of the object representational world of women recovering from sexual abuse is exemplary.[68]

Two edited collections of scholarly articles, Mary Lou Randour's *Exploring Sacred Landscapes* and Mark Finn and John Gartner's *Object Relations Theory and Religion*, offer additional examples of the diverse ways in which psychoanalytic object relations theory, in general, and the work of Rizzuto, in particular, have informed the discourse of contemporary psychology of religion.[69] Finn and Gartner's collection is noteworthy for extending attention to the psychology of religion beyond the Jewish-Christian axis to consider Eastern and, in particular, Buddhist religious traditions as these increasingly have become part of the religious landscape in the United States. Building on these insights, Anthony Stern, in chapter 4 in this volume, engages Rizzuto in conversation from the perspective of Asian meditative traditions.

When looking for the influence of Rizzuto's work on the treatment of patients in inpatient psychiatric hospitals or outpatient counseling centers, it is fair to say that nowhere has Rizzuto's work had a deeper *institutional* impact on the actual practice of psychotherapy and pastoral care and counseling than in Scandinavia.[70] Rizzuto was invited to Norway in September 1995 to deliver a keynote address at that country's most respected center for mental health care affiliated with the Church of Norway, the Institute for Pastoral Care and Counseling (IPCC) at the mental hospital and clinic, Modum Bad Psychiatric Center, established in 1957 in Oslo. Numbers of clinicians and pastoral counselors had been studying *The Birth of the Living God* and wanted the opportunity to engage Rizzuto in conversation at the annual

Modem Bad Seminar in Psychiatry. That first visit had a significant impact: it inspired the formation of a new professional network, the *Norsk Religionspsykologisk Fagforum* (Norwegian Forum for the Psychology of Religion). *The Journal of Pastoral Care and Counseling*, a publication of the IPCC, has spread the influence of Rizzuto's research across Scandinavia. A special issue of the *Journal of the Norwegian Psychological Association* also was devoted to the clinical psychology of religion.

Rizzuto's research provided the theoretical impetus for an integrative treatment model for patients known as the VITA program housed at Modem Bad. Chapter 3 in this book, authored by Gry Stålsett, Leif Gunnar Engedal, and Arne Austad, presents a case study from this program, demonstrating how the program aims to engage the whole patient—emotionally, physically, psychologically, and spiritually. That there is usable "truth" in Rizzuto's work is demonstrated precisely through case studies such as this one. The ever-wise William James, from the standpoint of his philosophical pragmatism, would have agreed. The value or "truth" of an idea ultimately is tested by whether and how it informs effective action in the world. Thus, well-founded assessments over time of Rizzuto's contributions to the psychology of religion will focus on how her ideas inform a therapeutic praxis that contributes to the healing and transformation of suffering persons—and a suffering world.

GROWING EDGES AND HORIZON

When I imagine theoretical and clinical questions that loom on the horizon, which Rizzuto's work may help us engage, I find myself contemplating the dramatic way that the landscape of religion has shifted away from the dense and defining religious culture that would have characterized Argentina during Rizzuto's youth and young adulthood and also the United States at that time, even with its greater religious diversity. In a landmark study from 2007 to 2014, The Pew Research Center for Religion and Public Life documents the unprecedented, rapid increase in the numbers of Americans who do not identify with any single religious community or tradition. In 2007, 16.1% of Americans surveyed self-identified as religiously unaffiliated. Seven years later, in 2014, 22.8% of Americans had joined that demographic cohort, making the religiously unaffiliated the fastest growing "religious" group in America. When the survey breaks out its findings by age among 18–22 year olds, fully one-third (34%) are unaffiliated, compared with 9% of the so-called "Silent Generation" (those born between 1925 and 1945). Numbering fifty-six million persons, the religiously dis-identified are now more numerous that either mainline Protestants or Roman Catholics.[71]

A study of these "nones" in 2012, conducted jointly by the Pew Research Forum on Religion and Public Life and the PBS television program Religion & Ethics Newsweekly, offers a fascinatingly complex picture of this population of the religiously unaffiliated. While 32% of this growing group describe themselves as atheist and agnostic, about 68% claim to "believe in God" and more than a third identify themselves as "spiritual but not religious." Scholars of the sociology and psychology of religion show an increasing interest in the meaning of this self-designation of "spiritual but not religious." On the one hand, "spiritual but not religious" suggests distrust of or disillusionment with what is commonly described as "institutional religion"; on the other hand, this descriptor seems to speak of a deeper, persistent yearning to connect with "Something More."[72] At the same time, professional chaplains and others who offer both spiritual and psychological care share an emerging recognition that this growing, religiously unaffiliated sector of our society deserves pastoral support that can meet the "nones" where they are, offering respect and understanding.

Two senior hospital chaplains in Boston—the Rev. Mary Martha Thiel, director of Clinical Pastoral Education at Hebrew Senior Life, and Rev. Mary Radner Robinson, director of the Chaplaincy at Boston Children's Hospital—have developed a three-part training module, "Spiritual Care of the Nonreligious," for the national readership of the HealthCare Chaplaincy Network. They write in the introduction to the module:

> Professional chaplains need education and humility to provide skillful and sensitive spiritual support to the growing numbers of nonreligious persons—the so-called "spiritual but not religious," unaffiliated, agnostics, and atheists—in their institutions. Training should encourage increased awareness of why persons are nonreligious, a clear understanding of the chaplain's role as a caregiver of all, inclusive assessment tools, and an enlarged toolkit of spiritual care interventions. Because professional chaplains are often socialized and trained in religious settings, the spiritual care of nonreligious persons requires intentional cultural humility.[73]

I would suggest adding Rizzuto's work to this "enlarged toolkit" as a valuable, psychoanalytically informed resource which also models "intentional cultural humility."

Rizzuto's offerings for the mental health or pastoral professional engaged with the nonreligious or "unbeliever" are best exemplified by her book, *Why Did Freud Reject God?*[74] This second major work on the psychology of religion, published nineteen years after *The Birth of the Living God,* was recognized in 2001 with the Gradiva Award for Best Book (Religious Subject) by the National Association for the Advancement of Psychoanalysis.[75] I want to describe the process Rizzuto used to come to the subject of this second major book on psychoanalysis and religion—an investigation of Freud's own conscious and unconscious relationship to the religion of his childhood—because that process shows how her work is as relevant to the endeavor to understand religious doubt and unbelief as it was previously pertinent to the effort to comprehend religious belief.

Rizzuto locates the origins of the book *Why Did Freud Reject God?* in the exhibition "The Sigmund Freud Antiquities: Fragments from a Buried Past," which had a profound impact on her when she viewed it in Boston in 1992. Originally created by the Freud Museum in 1989, the exhibit commemorated the 50th anniversary of the death of Freud.[76] Rizzuto describes her book as a fascinating detective story and writes of needing to become something of a "psychoanalytic Sherlock Holmes" as she conducted research for the book. What was the mystery to be unraveled? The title of the book points to what she wanted to resolve: How might one understand psycho-dynamically the "God" that Freud needs to reject? In her role as a detective, Rizzuto engaged in a painstaking recovery of the dynamic meaning of the images from the Philippson Bible that belonged to Freud's father, the same Bible that the young Sigmund Freud encountered in his home and which Rizzuto viewed in the Boston exhibition. These meanings in hand, Rizzuto could connect them to Freud's lifelong passion to collect ancient statuary.

Significantly, *Why Did Freud Reject God?* offers an empathic and respectful application to the life of Freud of the very hermeneutics of personal religious representation worked out in *The Birth of the Living God.* This text demonstrates the potential relevance of Rizzuto's hermeneutic for understanding both belief *and* unbelief and for mapping the complex ways in which humans hunger for meaning. Humans' need for an enduring symbolic connection to primary familial relationships of affirmation can be identified even in persons growing up in what putatively is a "post-religious" culture.

The reader interested in the specifics of how Rizzuto believes that she resolves the case of Freud's a-theism will find a close reading of *Why did Freud Reject God?* in chapter 5 by Martha Reineke later in this book. Here, I want to lift up the tone of deep respect for the way in which Freud, working within the unique cultural and familial circumstances of his life, came to the positions he held. Rizzuto's *Why did Freud Reject God?* is not, as some might imagine, an apologia for the value of traditional, biblical religion, a "gotcha" unmasking of the conflictual origins of Freud's atheism. To the contrary, Rizzuto's analysis opened for her and for her readers a new set of questions about what she calls "the believing function," a process inseparable from the constitution and maintenance of the person's sense of vital selfhood.[77] She writes,[78]

> Freud's belief in the capacity of psychoanalysis to "increase the love of man and the decrease of suffering" was profound and sincere. It was his belief, to which he committed his life and his indefatigable intellect. The writing of *Why did Freud Reject God?* convinced me that, whether we are ordinary religious believers or psychoanalysts who believe in psychoanalysis, we organize our lives around profoundly significant beliefs. We do not choose them. They are so dynamically oriented into the fabric of our psychic being that we have to believe. At the end of my research on Freud I had become very fond of him as a person who struggled with very difficult life circumstances. I felt affectionate compassion for the child he had been and profound respect for the great man he made himself in his search for meaning and a cause to commit himself to. He had unveiled to me the genesis of his need to believe in psychoanalysis. He also prompted me to ask a wider question, a general question and not a religious one: What is the psychic function of believing, the action of believing, not just the function of the belief content?

With this question, Rizzuto brings us back and points us forward, in a fresh and more expansive way, to the value of a functional approach not only to the study of our images of God but also to the examination of the myriad ways in which human persons "believe themselves into being." In our time of "nones" and the "spiritual but not religious," Rizzuto's insights enable us to read with deeper understanding the conclusion of the *Varieties of Religious Experience*. Here, William James quotes with approval his colleague James Henry Leuba:

> The truth of the matter can be put . . . in this way: *God is not known, he is not understood; he is used*—sometimes as a meat-purveyor, sometimes as moral support, sometimes as a friend, sometimes as an object of love. If he proves himself useful, the religious consciousness asks for no more than that. Does God really exist? How does he exist? What is he? are so many irrelevant questions. Not God, but life, more life, a larger, richer, more satisfying life, is, in the last analysis, the end of religion.[79]

Ana-María Rizzuto's scientific work and her clinical practice, first and last, may be understood as one in service to this "larger, richer, more satisfying life."

DISCUSSION

Ana-María Rizzuto

John McDargh's detailed and accurate presentation of my itinerary as the writer of *The Birth of the Living God* is a delight to read. He shows himself as a fellow scholar and friend and a faithful chronicler of my early awakening to the mysteries of a living God, when I so carefully listened to a distraught girl who chose her mother over God as her companion for eternity. McDargh's description of my work from that moment on is precise and well documented. It gathers in a short piece what actually happened and continues to happen to a research project I carried out under the intellectual and psychological sense of obligation to understand the human need to create divine beings in the mind, and, most specifically, the type of relationship we form with our divinities that is experienced as either an existing reality or as a being whose existence must be rejected or avoided.

McDargh documents how strange and esoteric my subject matter appeared to seasoned researchers and senior psychoanalysts. A few believed that I was out of my mind. Others gave me a compassionate look and suggested that the best I could do was to write a short paper. There were three exceptions. Milton Greenblatt, the superintendent of Boston State Hospital, without challenging my subject matter, gave me freedom to work on it on my own time. Elvin Semrad, professor of psychiatry at Harvard, gave me his free time to discuss the project and approved of it. Finally, when I moved to the Department of Psychiatry at Tufts-New England Medical Center, Paul Myerson trusted the seriousness of my enterprise and made it possible for me to carry out the most significant part on my research. I owe them my deepest gratitude.

Once I had done my work, I had to find a publisher. Those interested in the field of religion saw in the word 'psychoanalysis' something not far from a message from a destroyer of faith. Those in the field of psychoanalysis saw in religion an atavistic remnant of infantile dependency not worth considering as a serious matter. Caught between these two polarities, I came to realize that my publishing salvation was to be found with the university presses. I called the big ones, Harvard, Princeton, Columbia, and Chicago. I found their chief editors respectful, interested, and most gracious in wanting to help me. The editor of The University of Chicago Press, David T. Brent, said the magic words: "Send me the manuscript." In a couple of months, I received the letter accepting the book for publication. I also owe David T. Brent my deepest gratitude: his vision of the significance of the book and its value as a contribution to the literature were beyond my capacity to recognize. I knew I had done good and thoroughly documented research; nevertheless, as an outsider to the main stream of the psychology of religion, as McDargh documents in this chapter, I had no idea where my contribution would fit. To use McDargh's words: that was the final "accident" that gave long-lasting life to *The Birth of the Living God.* The indisputable prestige of The University of Chicago Press provided my book with the strong support that it had failed to obtain up to that point. Much to my slightly vengeful satisfaction, one of the analysts who had doubted my common sense exclaimed: "Dr. Rizzuto has just published a book with The University of Chicago Press!"

McDargh documents very well the reception of the book by different groups of professionals and scholars. Psychoanalysts remained tepid for a very long time; and, when they began to warm up to some of the ideas, they promptly replaced "God" and "religion" with "spirituality." Freud's rejected God remains taboo for many. "Spirituality" as a human disposition is more manageable and does not risk the founder's condemnation that individuals who are drawn to religion have remained attached to an infantile clinging for protection.

Those who welcomed my book have called it a major contribution, a turning point in the psychology of religion, a watershed, a new paradigm, and other wonderful and enhancing terms. Mary Lou Randour bestowed motherhood on me when she said, as McDargh cites, "If the symbol of Freud as 'father' of psychoanalysis has been used to explain his historical position, certainly Rizzuto is the 'mother' of all attempts to explicate a developmental and clinical psychoanalytic theory of religious experience."[80]

I am most grateful for all these enhancing words, and I joyfully accept their significance for me and for my work. However, nothing pleases me more than McDargh's assertion that "there has been a blossoming of creative empirical work following the publication of *The Birth of the Living God.*" He concludes,

> *We see the conviction growing in Rizzuto that the key to understanding religious faith is to enter a mode of careful, systematic observation of the very particular imagery that persons employ to tell their own life stories and to talk about the God of their understanding.*[81]

This conclusion opens the door for our unprejudiced and respectful exploration of all types of religious experiences, regardless of how sublime or bizarre they may appear to the external observer. To reach this conclusion, I am, as a psychoanalyst, indebted to Freud who insisted that to know the private life of a person we must invite him/her to speak without censoring what comes to mind. We are called to listen with absolute seriousness to the vagaries of the human mind. This method of Freud opened for good the-up-to-that-moment closed realm of human unconscious life. His change of paradigm facilitated my own change of paradigm.

It is my hope that the commitment to the many diverse empirical studies of religious experience in all their variety continues to evolve and that all of us researchers remember that the heart and mind of the believer, or of the unbeliever, harbor the special key to access the private reality of his/her religious experience.

I have been grateful to many in this discussion. John McDargh, my friend, colleague, and fellow researcher, deserves my last "thank you" for his very articulate narration of my life journey as the author of *The Birth of the Living God.*

NOTES

1. Howard Stein, Review of "The Birth of the Living God. A Psychoanalytic Study by Ana-María Rizzuto," *Psychoanalytic Quarterly* 50 (1981): 125–130.

2. One indication of this emergent interest has been the publication by the American Psychological Association over the last sixteen years of two major collections of articles that variously explore ways to address the dimension of spirituality and religion in clinical practice. The first was William R. Miller, *Integrating Spirituality into Treatment: Resources for Practitioners* (Washington, DC, American Psychological Association, 1999). This book is organized thematically with such chapters as "Assessing Spirituality," "Spirituality and the 12 Step Programs," "Meditation and Mindfulness," and "Diversity Training in Spiritual and Religious Issues." A more recent volume was Len Sperry and Edward Shafranske, eds., *Spirituality Oriented Psychotherapy* (Washington, DC: American Psychological Association, 2005). That collection is organized by therapists' theoretical orientation: psychoanalytic, cognitive-behavioral, Jungian, humanistic, etc. It is an index of Rizzuto's standing in this widening professional conversation that she was asked to contribute a contextual chapter on the entire project with the specific chapter demonstrating a psychoanalytic approach written by Edward Shafranske.

3. This chapter is a reworking and substantive updating of an earlier essay: John McDargh, "Creating a New Research Paradigm for the Psychoanalytic Study of Religion: The Pioneering Work of Ana-María Rizzuto" in *Religion, Society and Psychoanalysis: Readings in Contemporary Theory,* ed. Janet Liebman Jacobs and Donald Capps. (Boulder, CO: Westview Press, 1997),181–193.

4. Mary Lou Randour, ed., *Exploring Sacred Landscapes: Religious and Spiritual Experiences in Psychotherapy* (New York: Columbia University Press, 1993), 9.

5. Ana-María Rizzuto, "One Hundred Years After Freud Declared That Religion Was a Universal Obsessional Neurosis," in *Changing the Scientific Study of Religion: Beyond Freud? Theoretical, Empirical and Clinical Studies from a Psychoanalytic Perspective,* ed. Jacob A. Belzen (New York: Springer, 2009), 37.

6. Rizzuto, "One Hundred Years After," 37.

7. For an extended and insightful analysis of how the emergence of a "new psychoanalysis" has the potential to shift the traditional negative assessment of the processes of religious "believing," see James W. Jones, *Contemporary Psychoanalysis and Religion: Transference and Transcendence*" (New Haven: Yale University Press, 1991).

8. Rizzuto, "One Hundred Years After," 37.

9. Rizzuto, "One Hundred Years After," 38.

10. Rizzuto, "One Hundred Years After," 38.

11. The convener of the "Agosin Group" was Chilean psychiatrist Tomas Agosin, M.D. (1948–1991) who, before his untimely death, was assistant professor of clinical

psychiatry at Albert Einstein College of Medicine. Even after his passing, the Cape Cod Institute summer course "Psychotherapy and Spirituality" continued each summer for ten years, a remarkable testimony to the serious interest among counseling psychologists, psychiatric social workers, clinical psychologists, and psychiatrists to explore the nexus of therapy and spirituality/religion. At various times, the "Agosin Group" included myself, and clinical psychologists Mark Finn, Peter Cohen, Nancy Kehoe, and Fredrika Halligan. For a more journalistic effort to situate the story of Dr. Agosin and this teaching team within the history of a contemporary psychological *rapprochement* with spirituality and religion see Russell Shorto, *Saints and Madmen: How Science Got Religion* (New York: Henry Holt, 1999), 61–87.

12. Robert D. Stolorow, and George Attwood, *Faces in a Cloud: Intersubjectivity and Personality Theory* (Northvale, NJ: Jason Aronson, 1993).

13. Ana-María Rizzuto, "Roman Catholic Background and Psychoanalysis," *Psychoanalytic Psychology* 21 (2004): 436–441.

14. Lewis Aron, "God's Influence on My Psychoanalytic Vision and Values," *Psychoanalytic Psychology* 21(2004): 442–451.

15. Rizzuto, "Roman Catholic Background," 441.

16. Regarding the formative influence of Rizzuto's Catholic upbringing on her psychoanalytic research, I would add that there is another way in which the distinctiveness of a Catholic vision of reality and mode of theologizing informs her project. I argued in a paper delivered at the seventy-fifth anniversary meeting of the American Academy of Religion that a characteristically "Catholic" concern in the study of psychology has been to find the *continuity* between the divine and the human. The fundamental Catholic assumption is that the activity or grace of God necessarily must build upon human nature *(gratia perficit naturam).* I would contrast this integrated vision of divine/human reality with a more typically "Protestant" concern to assert the *discontinuity,* or the radical "otherness," of God and material creation as a way of defending against the danger of idolatry. This "Catholic" loyalty to a unified vision of the human person looks for evidence of a "*fit*" between God and the human person in the unfolding structure of human psychic life. It is, I believe, implicit throughout Rizzuto's work and may account for why she is unafraid to rigorously examine human developmental patterns. The Catholic "analogical imagination" derives in part from a confidence that whatever can be known truly about the human person will also provide metaphorical clues to a transcendent reality that ultimately, however, can never be fully grasped (*Deus semper major,* "God is always greater"). See John McDargh, "Theological Uses of Psychology: A Retrospective and Prospective," *Horizons: Journal of the College Theology* Society 12 (1985): 247–264.

17. Rizzuto, "Roman Catholic Background," 441.

18. Ana-María Rizzuto, "God in the Mind: The Psychodynamics of an Unusual Relationship," *The Annual of Psychoanalysis* 35 (2007): 25–46.

19. Ana-María Rizzuto, *Why Did Freud Reject God? A Psychodynamic Interpretation* (New Haven: Yale University Press, 1998).

20. Ana-María Rizzuto, "An Accidental Psychologist of Religion," in *Psychology of Religion: Autobiographical Accounts,* ed. Jacob Belzen (New York: Springer, 2012), 185–200.

21. Rizzuto, "An Accidental Psychologist," 185–186.

22. Ibid., 186.

23. Ibid., 186. See also Arthur Kleinman, *The Illness Narratives: Suffering, Healing and the Human Condition* (New York, NY: Basic Books, 1988).

24. For nearly half a century, Elvin Semrad (1909–1976), psychiatrist and psychoanalyst, influenced generations of young sychiatrists not by his scholarly writing or contributions to theory but by the embodied quality of his empathy and capacity for sustained, skillful presence with even the most challenging of psychotic patients. Dr. Semrad's most enduring legacies were the clinicians like Rizzuto who he encouraged to believe in their own good judgment, common sense, and innate compassionate wisdom. The record of his own wisdom is found in an edited collection of student notes and recordings of his supervisory talks to psychiatric residents in training at Harvard's Massachusetts Medical Center in the 1960s compiled by his junior colleagues after his death. Susan Rako and Harvey Mazer, eds., *Semrad: The Heart of a Therapist* (New York: Aronson, 1980).

25. Rizzuto, "An Accidental Psychologist," 189.

26. Rizzuto, *Birth of the Living God*, 181.

27. Ibid., 217–219.

28. Ibid., 91.

29. Ibid., 91.

30. David M. Wulff, "Beyond Belief and Unbelief," *Research in the Social Scientific Study of Religion* 10 (1999).

31. *Holmes-Pollock Letters: The Correspondence of Mr. Justice Holmes and Sir Frederick Pollock, 1874–1932* (Cambridge, MA: Belknap Press, 2nd ed., 1961) 109.

32. Rizzuto, *Birth of the Living God*, 47.

33. In Rizzuto's contribution to Belzen's collection of the autobiographies of psychologists of religion, she argues succinctly that in her insistence on this conclusion she is only asking the followers of Freud to be consistent with the implications of Freud's own position—even if he himself was not. To put it another way, in so far as our psychic representations of "God" are formed in the crucible of our primary relationships, they have an enduring presence. However, over time, *how* any given individual may consciously or unconsciously choose to relate to, or use, that representation may fall into any of the four disparate possibilities Rizzuto sets out. She writes: "Freud, in *Future of an Illusion,* enjoined all human beings to give up their God and to follow him, the mature psychoanalyst, in accepting the tribulations of life without having to cling to a fictional fatherly divinity. I had to confront Freud with his own contradictions: a God that has been shaped from the affection connection with primary objects can neither be erased nor neglected. It can only be dealt with, as Freud himself had said, by using the ordinary defenses we use in relation to any of our internal objects. The particular personal use of the divinity as an internal object and the defenses against its psychic presence need to be understood as part of the motivational and conflicted stance of the individual in relation to his personal God and the objects that contributed to the God representation. In this respect the divine being shares its dynamic fortunes and misfortunes with the other internal objects in the person's psychic life. From the technical point of view of a practicing analyst, to

neglect the psychic functions of the divinity ends up as equivalent to ignoring some of the critical transformations of internal primary objects at the service of psychic life." Rizzuto, "An Accidental Psychologist," 193.

34. For a particularly accessible summary of Winnicott's thought and its contribution to the study of religious phenomena, see James W. Jones, *Contemporary Psychoanalysis and Religion: Transference and Transcendence* (New Haven, Yale University Press, 1991).

35. David W. Winnicott, "Transitional Objects and Transitional Phenomena," in *International Journal of Psychoanalysis* 34 (1953): 14.

36. Freud, *Leonardo DeVinci and a Memory of His Childhood* (London: Hogarth Press, 1910), 123.

37. "The type of God each individual produces as a first representation is the compounded image resulting from all these contributing factors–the pre-oedipal psychic situation, the beginning stage of the oedipal complex, the characteristics of the parents, the predicaments of the child with each of his parents and siblings, the general religious, social and intellectual background of the household." Rizzuto, *The Birth of the Living God*, 45.

38. Ibid., 52.

39. Ibid., 200.

40. Sigmund Freud, *The Future of an Illusion* (New York, W.W. Norton, 1927).

41. For a discussion of the lifelong adaptive function of "illusion," see the work of Paul Pruyser, *Beyond Belief and Unbelief* (New York, NY: Harper & Row, 1974).

42. Emphasis added. Rizzuto, *Birth of the Living God*, 90.

43. Edward Shafranske, "God Representation as the Transformational Object" in *Object Relations Theory and Religion: Clinical Applications*, eds. Mark Finn and John Gartner.(Westport, CT: Praeger Press, 1992) 57–72. And James W. Jones, "The Relational Self: Contemporary Psychoanalysis Considers Religion," *Journal of the American Academy of Religion* 59 (1991): 119–135.

44. Rizzuto, *The Birth of the Living God*, 47–48.

45. The most exacting philological analysis of the origins of the words *faith* and *belief* was done by Wilfred Cantwell Smith, founder of Harvard University's Center for the Study of World Religions. Smith demonstrated that the Latin word *Credo,* which is most often translated as "I believe" in English, is the combination of two Latin words *Do/dere* (to put or to place) and *Cor/cordis* (heart). Thus, "to believe" originally meant "to put or place the heart upon." Smith argues that originally faith and belief were relational and affective terms with a connotation of trusting or relying upon another and that it was understood that way up until the early modern era. Wilfred Cantwell Smith, *Belief and History* (Charlottesville: University Press of Virginia, 1977), 41–45. See also Marcus Borg, *The Heart of Christianity: Rediscovering a Life of Faith* (New York: Harper Collins, 2004), 25–41. Rizzuto, from a psychoanalytic perspective, has in many ways retrieved that more ancient and more psychological understanding of what is entailed in "believing."

46. Rizzuto, "Psychodynamic Aspect of Religious Beliefs," (unpublished paper delivered at the Menninger Clinic, March 10, 1995).

47. William James, *The Will to Believe and Other Essays in Popular Philosophy* (New York: Dover, 1956), 27–28.
48. Rizzuto, *The Birth of the Living God*, 211.
49. Howard Stein, "Review of *The Birth of the Living God* by Ana-María Rizzuto," *Psychoanalytic Quarterly* 50 (1981): 125–130.
50. Ibid., 127.
51. Ibid., 127.
52. Rizzuto, *The Birth of the Living God*, 10.
53. Stanley Leavy, *In the Image of God: A Psychoanalyst's View* (New Haven, CT: Yale University Press, 1988). See also Stanley Leavy, "Reality in Religion and Psychoanalysis," in *Psychoanalysis and Religion*, eds. H. Smith and S.A. Handelman. (Baltimore, MD: Johns Hopkins University Press, 1990), 43–55.
54. Nancy S, Duvall, "Religious Representations," Review of "Object Relations Theory and Religion: Clinical Applications," by Mark Finn and John Gartner, eds, Journal for Theology and Psychology 22 (1994): 429–432.
55. Moshe Halevi Spero, "Parallel Dimensions of Experience in Psychoanalytical Psychotherapy of the Religious Patient," American Journal of Psychotherapy, 35 (1900): 565–575. And Religious Objects as Psychological Structures. A Critical Integration of Object Relations Theory, Psychotherapy and Judaism (Chicago: University of Chicago Press, 1992). Two other less tendentious efforts to make a place in the psychotherapeutic process for the theological perspective of a religiously committed therapist while working within Rizzuto's paradigm are Owe Wikström, "God as an 'Acting Agent' in Psychotherapy?" in Clinical Psychology of Religion. Emerging Cultural and Multicultural Questions from European and North American Voices, eds. Valerie DeMarinis and Owe Wikström (Stockholm: Forskningsrådsnämnden, 1996): 96:4. And John McDargh, "Concluding Clinical Postscript: On Developing a Psychotheological Perspective," in *Exploring Sacred Landscapes: Religious and Spiritual Experiences in Psychotherapy*, ed. Mary Lou Randour (New York: Columbia University Press, 1993): 172–193.
56. James Jones. *Contemporary Psychoanalysis and Religion: Transference and Transcendence* (New Haven: Yale University Press, 1991) and "The Relational Self: Contemporary Psychoanalysis Reconsiders Religion," *Journal of the American Academy of Religion* 59 (1991): 119–135.
57. Merle Jordan, *Taking on the Gods: The Task of the Pastoral Counselor* (Nashville: TN: Abingdon Press, 1995).
58. Daniel J. Heinrichs, "Our Father which Art in Heaven: Parataxic Distortions in the Image of God," *Journal of Psychology and Theology* 10 (1982): 120–129.
59. Leroy Howe, *The Image of God: A Theology for Pastoral Care and Counseling* (Nashville, TN: Abingdon Press, 1995), 110. Howe eloquently summarized this "middle position" between two "orthodoxies" that Rizzuto's work opens up for the psychologically serious and theologically committed thinker. "Object relations theory in psychology and 'existential' forms of contemporary theology converge in repudiating modes of thinking held captive by a narrow 'subject-object' framework. Classical psychoanalysis betrays its bondage to such a framework when it takes its own differentiations between actuality and illusion as absolute and then consigns

God to the realm of the latter. Religious believers holding out for a God who is all actuality and no illusion are no better off for their orthodoxy. Their God is an object of belief, 'out there' and we are left with no helpful way of accounting for beliefs about 'him' that appear *not* to correspond with 'his' objective reality. By contrast, if beliefs about God are viewed as another kind of transitional object, it becomes readily understandable how and why some beliefs go awry. As all contractors know, weak materials make for weak structures. And when we attempt to construct a representation of a 'good' deity out of 'bad' internal objects, the result will be an object that can make life transitions more difficult rather than easier. The God whom we represent to ourselves and to others 'is' *both* a contrivance of our imagination *and* that supreme architect, artificer, imaginer, and Creator whose love towards us truly is an 'all excelling' love. Beliefs about God will be consistently misunderstood if we do not respect this all-important 'both-and.'" Howe, *The Image of God*, 182.

60. Ana-María Rizzuto, "Belief as a Psychic Function," *Psychology of Religion Newsletter of Division 36 of the American Psychological Association* 22 (1997): 1–5.

61. Antoine Vergote et al., "The Concept of God and Parental Images," *Journal of the Scientific Study of Religion* 8 (1969): 79–87. It is a commentary on the consequences of the way in which Rizzuto was forced to conduct her research largely without the benefit of a network of supportive colleagues in religious studies and without formal academic affiliation that she did have the opportunity to encounter Professor Vergote and the research tradition of the Center for Religious Psychology at the Catholic Universities of Leuven and Louvain until fairly late in her ten year research program. Belgian religious educator Christiane Brusselmans had been a visiting lecturer at Harvard Divinity School in 1974 where Rizzuto met James Fowler and the Harvard moral developmental psychologists (Lawrence Kohlberg, Carol Gilligan, Robert Kegan). In 1979 Dr. Brusselmans found sponsorship for the First International Conference on Moral and Religious Development at the French Abbey of Senanque that brought together twenty scholars of moral and religious development from European, American, and Canadian universities. James Fowler (Candler School of Theology) and William Rogers (Harvard Divinity School) had been my professors and I had introduced them to the work of Rizzuto who they invited to participate in that remarkable gathering. The papers for the conference were published as James Fowler and Antoine Vergote, eds., *Toward Moral and Religious Maturity* (Morristown, NJ: Silver Burdett, 1980). Rizzuto's contribution to the volume was "The Psychological Foundations of Belief in God," *Toward Moral and Religious Maturity,* 115–135.

62. Individuals and representative examples of scholarship by those who have taken up the challenge include: Beth F. Brokow, "The Relationship of God Image to Level of Object Relations Development" (PhD diss., Rosemead School of Professional Psychology, Biola University, 1992), and Katherine Spear, "Conscious and Unconscious God Concepts" (PhD diss., Fuller Theological Seminary, Pasadena, CA, 1994); Owe Wikström, "God as an 'Acting Agent' in Psychotherapy?" Clinical Psychology of Religion. Emerging Cultural and Multicultural Questions from European and North American Voices, eds. Valerie DeMarinis and Owe Wikström. (Stockholm: Forskningsrådsnämnden, 1996), 96:4; Carlos Dominguez Morano, S.J., professor of the psychology of religion on the faculty of Theology of Granada and past president

of the A.I.E.M.P (International Association of Medical-Psychological and Religious Studies), author of *Creer despues de Freud (Belief After Freud)* (Cordoba, Argentina: San Pablo Press, 2010); John McDargh, "Concluding Clinical Postscript: On Developing a Psycho-theological Perspective," in *Exploring Sacred Landscapes: Religious and Spiritual Experiences in Psychotherapy,* ed. Mary Lou Randour (New York: Columbia University Press, 1993), 172–193; and Ryan Hays, "Fashioning Our Own Freuds: Psychoanalysis and Religion" (PhD diss., Emory University, The Graduate Institute of the Liberal Arts, 2008).

63. Marilyn Saur and William Saur, "Transitional Phenomenon As Evidenced in Prayer," *Journal of Religion and Health* 32 (1993): 55–66.

64. Richard T Lawrence, "The God Image Inventory: The Development, Validation and Standardization of a Psychometric Instrument for Research, Pastoral and Clinical Use in Measuring the Image of God," (PhD diss., Catholic University of America, Washington, DC, 1991).

65. Richard T. Lawrence, "Measuring the Image of God: The God Image Inventory and the God Image Scales," *Journal of Psychology and Theology* 25 (1997): 214–226. The abstract of this article reads in part: "The God Image Inventory (GII) is an 8-scale, 156-item, psychometric instrument to measure the image of God, developed for clinical and pastoral use in N = 1 cases. For research use with a large N, the God Image Scales (GIS), in a 6-scale, 72-item format, or a 3-scale, 36-item format, are preferred subsets of the GII. The GII and GIS are designed on the basis of Ana-María Rizzuto's distinction between the God concept and the God image. They explore issues of belonging (Presence and Challenge scales), goodness (Acceptance and Benevolence scales), and control (Influence and Providence scales). The scales of the GII have demonstrated internal reliability and preliminary validity work has been done. Standards have been developed on an N = 1580 sample of U.S. adults, but are applicable, at least to date, only for Christian subjects." The GII was reviewed by Todd W. Hall and Randall Lehmann Sorenson in *Measures of Religiosity*, edited by Peter C. Hill and Ralph W. Hood, Jr. (Birmingham, AL: Religious Education Press, 1999): 326. See also Jacqueline L. Noffke and Todd W. Hall, "Attachment Psychotherapy and God Image," in *God Image Handbook for Spiritual Counseling and Psychotherapy: Research, Theory, and Practice, eds.* Glendon Moriarty and Louis Hoffman. (New York: Haworth Pastoral Press, 2008).

66. See Jay Gattis' website www.godimage.org (2015). The site contains useful background material including Lawrence's 1997 article and Rizzuto's unpublished address, "Critique of the Contemporary Literature in the Scientific Study of Religion" delivered to the 1970 Annual Meeting of the Society for the Scientific Study of Religion, a particularly concise formulation of the God Concept/ God Image distinction. Access to the inventory itself on the site is appropriately monitored by the requirement that clinicians who would like to use it professionally take an on-line test on their grasp of the theoretical foundations of the inventory and certify that they are qualified to administer it.

67. Randall Sorenson, "Therapists' (and Their Therapists') God Representations in Clinical Practice," *Journal of Psychology and Theology* 22 (1994): 325–344. And "Transcendence and Inter-subjectivity: The Patient's Experience of the Analyst's

Spirituality," in *The Soul on the Couch: Spirituality, Religion and Morality in Contemporary Psychoanalysis* (Hillsdale, NJ: Analytic Press, 2003).

68. Carrie Doehring, *Internal Desecration: Traumatization and God Representations* (Lanham, MD: University Press of America, 1993).

69. Mary Lou Randour, ed., *Exploring Sacred Landscapes: Religious Experiences in Psychotherapy* (New York: Columbia University Press, 1993); Mark Finn and John Gartner, eds., *Object Relations Theory and Religion: Clinical Applications* (New York: Praeger Press, 1993).

70. Several Scandinavian books present Ana-María Rizzuto's research and writing so that she has become a standard reference in the clinical psychology of religion in these countries. Theologian and psychotherapist Goran Bergstand in 2004 published an important book that located Rizzuto's contributions within the history of the development of a psychoanalytic understanding of religion *En Illusion och dess Utveckling: Om Synen på Religion i Psykoanalytisk Teori* ("An Illusion and Its Development: Understanding Religion in Psychoanalytic Theory.") Students of the psychology of religion in Scandinavian universities have since 1999 been introduced to the work of Rizzuto by way of a widely used Swedish text written by Uppsala professors A. Geels and O. Wikstrom, *Den Religiosa Manniskan* ("The Religious Man: An Introduction to the Psychology of Religion," 2012). Two new books have both given an important place to Rizzuto's work: *Religionspsykologi* ("Psychology of Religion") eds. L. J. Danbolt and Lief G. Engedal et.al., (Oslo: Gyldendal Akademisk, 2014); and a book that includes both a psychological and philosophical/theological assessment of her work by a professor at the MF Norwegian School of Theology, J. O. Henrikson, *God and the Self: Dynamic Interplay* (2013).

71. See "Nones on the Rise" Pew Research Center for Religion in Public Life, accessed October 9, 2012, http://www.pewforum.org/2012/10/09/nones-on-the-rise/ and "America's Changing Religious Landscape," accessed May 12, 2015, http://www.pewforum.org/2015/05/12/americas-changing-religious-landscape/

72. See Linda Mercadante, *Beliefs without Borders: Inside the Minds of the Spiritual but Not Religious* (New York: Oxford University Press, 2014).

73. Rev. Mary Martha Thiel and Rev. Mary Radner Robinson, *Spiritual Care of the Nonreligious Part Two,* 13, 4 (New York: Plain View, Healthcare Chaplaincy Network, 2016).

74. Ana-María Rizzuto, *Why Did Freud Reject God? A Psychodynamic Interpretation* (New Haven: Yale University Press, 1998).

75. I refer to this deliberately as her second major book "on the psychology of religious development" to make the point that, parallel to her research and writing on religion and psychoanalysis, Rizzuto has published extensively on a wide range of topics relevant to psychoanalysis and psychotherapy, most of which, like *The Birth of the Living God,* are grounded in fresh creative readings of the original work of Sigmund Freud. Her most recent book represents her long standing interest in the complex role of the speech act in the "talking cure" that is psychoanalysis. This is based on a careful reconsideration of Freud's rarely discussed 1891 monograph "Aphasia." See Ana-María Rizzuto, *Freud and the Spoken Word: Speech as a Key to the Unconscious* (New York: Routledge, 2015).

76. Rizzuto, "God in the Mind," 34–41.

77. The interest in studying "believing" as both a social and a personal phenomenon is one that Rizzuto shares with a rich tradition of investigation prominent among European psychologists of religion going back to the seminal work of Dutch psychologist H.C. Rumke (1939). See Corveleyn and Hursebaut (1994). The essay she wrote that pursues her interest in exploring the centrality of "the believing function" is "Believing and Personal Religious Beliefs" (Rizzuto, 2002).

78. Rizzuto, *Why Did Freud,* 40–41.

79. William James, *Varieties of Religious Experience*, 1902. Cambridge, MA: Harvard University Press, 1985, 399. Emphasis in original.

80. Mary Lou Randour, ed., *Exploring Sacred Landscapes: Religious and Spiritual Experiences in Psychotherapy* (New York: Columbia University Press, 1993), 9.

81. John McDargh, "The Paradigm Shifting Research of Ana-María Rizzuto."

BIBLIOGRAPHY

Aron, Lewis. "God's Influence on My Psychoanalytic Vision and Values." *Psychoanalytic Psychology* 21(3), 2004: 442–451.

Benson, Peter, and Bernard Spilka God Image as a Function of Self Esteem and Locus of Control. *Journal for the Scientific Study of Religion* 12(3), 1973: 297–310.

Borg, Marcus J. *The Heart of Christianity: Rediscovering a Life of Faith.* New York, NY: Harper Collins, 2004.

Brokaw, Beth F. "The Relationship of God Image to Level of Object Relations Development." PhD diss., Rosemead School of Psychology, Biola University, 1992, *Dissertations Abstracts International,* 52, 6077B.

Corveleyn, Josef, and Dirk Hutsebaut, eds. *Belief and Unbelief: Psychological Perspectives.* Amsterdam: Rodopi, 1994.

Danbolt, L. J., and Leif G. Engedal. *Religionspsykologi.* Oslo: Gyldendal Akademisk, 2014.

Doehring, Carrie. *Internal Desecration: Traumatization and God Representations.* Lanham, MD: University Press of America, 1993.

Duvall, Nancy. Review of *Object Relations Theory and Religion,* by Mark Finn and John Gartner. *The Journal of Psychology and Theology* 22, 1994: 429–432.

Finn, Mark, and John Gartner, eds. *Object Relations Theory and Religion: Clinical Applications.* New York, NY: Praeger Press, 1993.

Freud, S. *Leonardo Da Vinci and a Memory of His Childhood.* In *Standard Edition* 11(1910/1958), translated by James Strachey. London: Hogarth Press and the Institute of Psychoanalysis.

——— 1913. *Totem and Taboo.* New York, NY: W. W. Norton, 1952.

——— 1927. *The Future of an Illusion.* New York, NY: W. W. Norton, 1961.

Geels, A., and Owe Wikstrom. *The Religious Man: An Introduction to the Psychology of Religion.* Stockholm: Natur och Kultur, 2012.

Gorsuch, Richard. "The Conceptualization of God as seen in Adjective Ratings." *Journal for the Scientific Study of Religion* 7(1), Spring, 1968: 56–64.

Hall, Tisdale, and Beth F. Brokaw. "Assessment of Religious Dimensions in Christian Clients: A review of Selected Instruments for Research and Clinical Use." *Journal of Psychology and Theology* 22(4) (1994): 395–421.

Hays, Ryan. "*Fashioning Our Own Freuds: Psychoanalysis and Religion.*" PhD diss., Emory University, 2008.

Heinrichs, Daniel J. "Our Father which Art in Heaven: Parataxic Distortions in the Image of God." *Journal of Psychology and Theology* 10(2), 1982: 120–129.

Henrikson, Jan Olav. Relating God and the Self: Dynamic Interplay. New York: Routledge, 2013.

Homans, Peter. "Review of '*The Birth of the Living God: A Psychoanalytic Study,*" by Ana-María Rizzuto, *Journal of Religion* 62(4), 1982: 445–446.

Howe, Leroy T. *The Image of God: A Theology for Pastoral Care and Counseling.* Nashville, TN: Abingdon Press, 1995.

James, William. *The Will to Believe and Other Essays in Popular Philosophy.* New York, NY: Dover, 1956.

———. (1902). *The Varieties of Religious Experience.* Cambridge, MA: Harvard University Press, 1985.

Jones, James W. (1991a). *Contemporary Psychoanalysis and Religion: Transference and Transcendence.* New Haven, CT: Yale University Press.

———. (1991b) . "The Relational Self: Contemporary Psychoanalysis Reconsiders Religion." *Journal of the American Academy of Religion* 59(1): 119–135.

Jordan, Merle R. *Taking on the Gods: The Task of the Pastoral Counselor.* Nashville, TN: Abington Press, 1985.

Kehoe, Nancy, and Thomas G. Gurhiel. "Ministry or Therapy: The Role of Transference and Counter Transference in a Religious Therapist," In *Exploring Sacred Landscapes: Religious and Spiritual Experiences in Psychotherapy,* edited by Mary Lou Randour, 55–80. New York, NY: Columbia University Press, 1993.

Kochems, Tim. "Countertransference and Transference Aspects of Religious Material in Psychotherapy: The Isolation or Integration of Religious Material," In *Exploring Sacred Landscapes: Religious and Spiritual Experiences in Psychotherapy,* edited by Mary Lou Randour, 34–54. New York, NY: Columbia University Press, 1993.

Lawrence, Richard T. "*The God Image Inventory: The Development, Validation and Standardization of a Psychometric Instrument for Research, Pastoral and Clinical use in Measuring the Image of God*" PhD diss., Catholic University of America, Washington, DC, 1991.

Leavy, Stanley A. *In the Image of God: A Psychoanalyst's View.* New Haven: Yale University Press, 1988.

———. "Reality in Religion and Psychoanalysis." In *Psychoanalysis and Religion,* edited by Joseph H. Smith and Susan A. Handelman, 43–55. Baltimore, MD: Johns Hopkins University Press, 1990.

McDargh, John. *Psychoanalytic Object Relations Theory and the Study of Religion.* Lanham, MD: University Press of America, 1983.

———. "Theological Uses of Psychology: A Retrospective and Prospective." *Horizons* 12(2), 1985: 247–264.

———. "God, Mother and Me: An Object Relational Perspective on Religious Material." *Pastoral Psychology* 34(4), 1986: 251–263.

———. "Concluding Clinical Postscript: On Developing a Psycho-theological Perspective." In *Exploring Sacred Landscape: Religious and Spiritual Experiences in Psychotherapy,* edited by M. Randour. New York: Columbia University Press, 1992.

———. "Creating a New Research Paradigm for the Psychoanalytic Study of Religion: The Pioneering Work of Ana-María Rizzuto." In *Religion, Society and Psychoanalysis: Readings in Contemporary Theory,* edited by Janet Liebman Jacobs and Donald Capps. Boulder, CO: Westview Press, 1997.

Mercadante, Linda. *Beliefs without Borders: Inside the Minds of the Spiritual but Not Religious.* New York, NY: Oxford University Press, 2014.

Meissner, William W. *Psychoanalysis and Religious Experience.* New Haven: Yale University Press, 1984.

———.*Life and Faith: Psychological Perspectives on Religious Experience.* Washington, DC: Georgetown University Press, 1987.

———. "The Role of Transitional Conceptualization in Religious Thought." In *Psychoanalysis and Religion,* edited by Joseph H. Smith and Susan A. Handelman. Baltimore, MD: Johns Hopkins University Press, 1990.

Miller, William R. *Integrating Spirituality Into Treatment: Resources for Practitioners.* Washington, DC: American Psychological Association, 1999.

Morano, Carlos Dominguez. *Belief After Freud (Creer despues de Freud).* Cordoba, Argentina: San Pablo Press, 2010.

Noffke, Jacqueline, L. Noffke, and Todd W. Hall. "Attachment Psychotherapy and God Image," in *God Image Handbook for Spiritual Counseling and Psychotherapy: Research, Theory, and Practice*, edited by Glendon Moriarty and Louis Hoffman. (New York, NY: Haworth Pastoral Press, 2008.)

Pruyser, Paul W. *Beyond Belief and Unbelief.* New York: Harper &. Row, 1974.

Rako, Susan, and Harvey Mazer, eds. *Semrad: The Heart of a Therapist.* New York, NY: Aronson, 1980.

Randour, Mary Lou ed. *Exploring Sacred Landscapes: Religious and Spiritual Experiences in Psychotherapy.* New York: Columbia University Press, 1993.

Rizzuto, Ana-María. "Object Relations and the Formation of the Image of God." *British Journal of Medical Psychology* 47 (1974): 83–94.

———. "Freud, God and the Devil and the Theory of Object Representation." *International Review of Psychoanalysis* 3 (1976): 165–180.

———.*The Birth of the Living God: A Psychoanalytic Study.* Chicago: University of Chicago Press, 1979.

———. "The Psychological Foundations of Belief in God." In *Toward Moral and Religious Maturity,* edited by James Fowler and Antoine Vergote, 115–135. Morristown, NJ: Silver Burdett, 1980: 115 –135.

———. "The Father and the Child's Representation of God: A Developmental Approach." In *Father and Child: Developmental and Clinical Perspectives,* edited by Stanley H. Cath, Alan R. Gurwitt, and John M. Ross, 357–381. Boston, MA: Little, Brown and Co, 1982.

———. "Exploring Sacred Landscape." In *Exploring Sacred Landscapes: Religious and Spiritual Experiences in Psychotherapy,* edited by Mary Lou Randour. New York, NY: Columbia University Press, 1993.

———. "Psychodynamic Aspect of Religious Beliefs." Paper delivered at the Menninger
Clinic, March 10, 1995.

———. "Belief as a Psychic Function." *Psychology of Religion Newsletter of Division 36 of the American Psychological Association* 22 (1997): 1.

———.*Why Did Freud Reject God? A Psychodynamic Interpretation.* New Haven, CT: Yale University Press, 1998.

———. "Roman Catholic Background and Psychoanalysis." *Psychoanalytic Psychology* 21, 3 , 2004: 436–441.

———. "God in the Mind: The Psychodynamics of an Unusual Relationship." *The Annual of Psychoanalysis* 35, 2007: 25–46.

———. "One Hundred Years After Freud Declared That Religion Was a Universal Obsessional Neurosis." In *Changing the Scientific Study of Religion: Beyond Freud?: Theoretical, Empirical and Clinical Studies from Psychoanalytic Perspectives,* edited by Jacob A. Belzen. New York, NY: Springer, 2009.

———. "Accidental Psychologist of Religion." In *Psychology of Religion: Autobiographical Accounts,* edited by Jacob A. Belzen. New York, NY: Springer, 2012.

Rumke, Henricus C. *Karakter en aanleg in verband met het ongeloof.* Amsterdam: Ten Have, 1939. Published in English as *The Psychology of Unbelief.* London: Rackliff, 1952.

Saur, Marilyn, and William Saur. "Transitional Phenomenon as Evidenced in Prayer." *Journal of Religion and Health* 32 (1993): 55–66.

Schaefer, Charles A., and Richard L. Gorsuch. "Dimensionality of Religion: Belief and Motivation as Predictors of Behavior." *Journal of Psychology and Christianity* 11 (1992): 244–254.

Shafranske, Edward. "God-representation as the Transformational Object." In *Object Relations Theory and Religion: Clinical Application,* edited by Mark Finn and John Gartner. Westport, CT: Praeger, 1992.

Shorto, Russell. *Saints and Madmen: How Science Got Religion.* New York, NY: Henry Holt, 1999.

Smith, William Cantwell. *Belief and History.* Charlottesville, VA: University Press of Virginia, 1977.

Sorenson, Randall. "Therapists' (and their Therapists') God Representations in Clinical Practice." *Journal of Psychology and Theology* 22 (1994): 325–344.

———. "Transcendence and Intersubjectivity: The Patient's Experience of the Analyst's Spirituality." In *The Soul on the Couch: Spirituality, Religion, and Morality in Contemporary Psychoanalysis* (Relational Perspectives Book Series), edited by Charles Spezzano and Gerald J. Gargiulo. Hillsdale, NJ: Analytic Press, 2003.

Spear, Katherine. "Conscious and Pre-conscious God-concepts: An Object Relations Perspective." PhD diss., Fuller Theological Seminary, Pasadena, CA, 1994.

Spero, Moshe H. "Countertransference in Religious Therapists of Religious Patients." *American Journal of Psychoanalysis* 35 (1981): 565–576.

———. "The Reality of the Image of God in Psychotherapy." *American Journal of Psychotherapy* 39 (1985): 75–85.

———.*Religious Objects as Psychological Structures: A Critical Integration of Object Relations Theory, Psychotherapy and Judaism.* Chicago, IL: University of Chicago Press, 1992.

Sperry, Len, and Edward Shafranske. *Spiritually Oriented Psychotherapy.* Washington, DC: American Psychological Association, 2005.

St. Clair, Michael. *Human Relationships and the Experience of God: Object Relations and Religion.* Mahwah, NJ: Paulist Press, 1994.

Stein, Howard. Review of "The Birth of the Living God. A Psychoanalytic Study by Ana-María Rizzuto." *Psychoanalytic Quarterly* 50 (1981): 125–130.

Stolorow, Robert, and George Attwood. *Faces in a Cloud: Intersubjectivity and Personality Theory.* Northvale, NJ: Aronson, 1993.

Thiel, Rev. Mary Martha, and Rev. Mary Radner Robinson. "Spiritual Care of the Non-Religious, Part 2" *Plain Views* (Healthcare Chaplaincy Network) 13, 4 (April 20, 2016).

Vergote, Antoine, Alvaro Tamayo, Luiz Pasquali, Michael Bonami, Marie-Rose Panyn, and nne Clusters. "Concept of God and Parental Images." *Journal of the Scientific Study of Religion* 8, 1969: 79–87.

Winnicott, David W. "Transitional Objects and Transitional Phenomena." *International Journal of Psychoanalysis* 34, 1953: 14.

Wulff, David M. "Beyond Belief and Unbelief." *Research in the Social Scientific Study of Religion* 10, 1999.

Chapter 2

Becoming a Believer, Becoming an Unbeliever

The Contribution of Ana-María Rizzuto to the Psychology of Religion in the Light of Clinical Practice

Mario Aletti

Jacob A. Belzen, editor of the book *Changing the Scientific Study of Religion: Beyond Freud?,* wonders at its outset "whether and to what extent progress has taken place during one century of the psychoanalytic psychology of religion," as he calls it.[1] In my opinion, quite remarkable progress has occurred in this past century, as new attention has been given to a focus on the individual's religion. Further, that focus now enables us to assess the value of the work of Ana-María Rizzuto to the psychology of religion: her research has played a crucial role both for psychoanalytic practice[2] and for understanding the attitude of psychoanalysis toward the religion of the individual.[3] Rizzuto's contributions can be traced to her capacity to combine in a masterful way theory and clinical practice. Her book, *The Birth of the Living God*, is only the most important and influential publication stemming from a larger body of work that Rizzuto has authored over a period of fifty years. Such work materialized not only in *The Birth of the Living God*, but also in other books and papers, which can be considered as the preparation for that book, an in-depth analysis of its achievements after the fact, and extensions of its method and findings into new areas of research. Above all, Rizzuto has profoundly impacted our understanding of the individual's attitude toward religion in the light of psychoanalysis.[4]

In this chapter, I want to discuss specific features of Rizzuto's work that attest to her original contributions to clinical practice and to research in the field of the psychology of religion. But first, I want to clarify what I mean by the phrase "in light of psychoanalysis."

IN THE LIGHT OF PSYCHOANALYSIS

That I use the phrase "in the light of psychoanalysis" in this chapter is no accident. I believe that the more concise expression "psychoanalysis of religion" is inappropriate. As a matter of fact, it is mainly used by non-psychoanalytic practitioners: philosophers, theologians, sociologists, and also psychologists interested in the so-called "applied psychoanalysis." The term "psychoanalysis of religion" can be misleading for at least two reasons. On the one hand, psychoanalysis is not interested in religion as such or in its philosophical or theological truth. Psychoanalysis doesn't focus on religion as a cultural phenomenon, on its origin and history, or on its social or evolutionary role. Psychoanalysis limits its focus to the experience of the individual, that is, to dynamic processes involved in the internal representation of God. On the other hand, psychoanalysis does not attend exclusively to one isolated attitude of a patient, for instance, a patient's attitude toward religion. Every psychoanalysis is an analysis of a person in his or her complex, individual wholeness. Therefore when I talk about reflecting on the patient "in the light of psychoanalysis," this phrase delimits the boundaries of the field so described: *I focus on the individual's experience in all of its complex wholeness.*

Moreover, I want to emphasize that psychoanalysis aims not at the truth of religion but at the truth of the subject: it aims not at the truth of belief but at the truth of the believer.[5] The currently rekindled debate about psychoanalysis and the truth of religion is no real issue. The fact that psychoanalysis doesn't verify the actual truth of religion is part of a wider analytical perspective. Psychoanalysis is not interested in the "material truth" but in the "historical truth";[6] ultimately, that truth emerges from attention given by psychoanalysis to processes attributable to the subjective experience of the individual. As a consequence, the focal point for the psychology of religion is the discourse of individuals, their representations of God, and their relationships with the religion they encounter in the culture to which they belong.

Keeping our attention on the individual in all its complexity in the light of psychoanalysis, including the individual who would describe him or herself as "a believer" as well as the individual who would claim to be "an unbeliever," let's consider five aspects of Rizzuto's work that contribute most significantly to the value of her work for the psychology of religion.

GOD, AN ILLUSORY TRANSITIONAL OBJECT

As is widely known, according to Rizzuto, "God, psychologically speaking, is an illusory transitional object."[7] Rizzuto studies the formation, the transformation, and the use of this representation throughout the human life-cycle.[8]

She traces the God representation back to its origins in the dialectic between representations of the self and those of primary objects.[9] From a logical and methodological point of view, Rizzuto's work prioritizes the revision of the idea of "psychical representation of objects" in the psychoanalytical literature. In her work, she strongly underscores that object representations and self-representations are composite memory processes, mainly unconscious and pre-conscious, ongoing and interacting, which are derived from the adaptation of the organism to its environment. These representations recall memories of the psycho-physical organism, leaving to the "I" the job of their organization at any level: visceral, sensorimotor, eidetic, iconic, and, later, also conceptual.[10]

A particularly stimulating area of Rizzuto's work is the attention that she gives to the relationship between the God representation, mainly unconscious or pre-conscious and rooted in the dimensions of the primary process, and depictions of God and ideas about God that evolve at the level of a secondary process. Rizzuto is perfectly aware that "belief and unbelief are always the result of dynamic processes in which the sense of self and the prevailing God representation are linked in a dialectic of compatibility or incompatibility in the satisfaction of relational needs."[11] Therefore, the same dynamic processes can structure the conscious attitude of belief and non-belief.

Rizzuto's awareness of these processes and the emphasis she places on the idiosyncrasy and dynamicity of the God representation encourages scholars to better explore and define the idea of "*unconscious* God representations." At the same time, when we recognize the significance of these God representations to our understanding of the individual, one of the primary achievements of *The Birth of the Living God* comes into view. Above all, the contribution of this book rests with making visible the possible developmental paths of the birth of the believing person (or of the non-believing person, as in Freud's case).[12] Indeed, Rizzuto states as much when she writes, "Personal religion results from the person's intertwining, in dynamically organized patterns, private dimensions of meaning that combine in diverse proportions the offering of public religion with very private experiences and beliefs."[13] This blending of the private with the public into a personal religion, so clearly described by Rizzuto, constitutes the summative trajectory of the developmental path the individual traverses, whether to belief or non-belief.

THE QUESTION OF THE UNCONSCIOUS GOD REPRESENTATION

One of the most important contributions by Rizzuto to the psychology of religion actually has been a point of considerable misunderstanding. In order that we appreciate her contributions, a brief review and assessment of that misunderstanding is appropriate. Some scholars who cite Rizzuto's works actually are unaware of how she has elaborated psychoanalytically on the concept of representation, and they misunderstand the meaning Rizzuto ascribes to the notion of representation. Some scholars confuse her notion of a God representation with the conscious picture that an individual makes of God, or with the concept of God elaborated by culture, or with the presentations of God offered by various religions and espoused by assorted theologians. In a word, the mental God representation, about which Rizzuto writes, is sometimes identified with the God of a specific cultural tradition.[14] Thus, in spite of a strong and deep rooting of the unconscious and pre-conscious dynamics of a God representation in the individual, as described by Rizzuto, her expression "unconscious God representation" has proved confusing. How can God, some scholars wonder, be "unconscious" when cultures and their institutions attest to God all the time? I assert, as far as a God representation is unconscious, it is not oriented by a name; it can't be defined with any specification; it cannot be captured by an adjective or a noun, or with an "of. . . ." Nevertheless, and notwithstanding our inability to capture a God representation in so many words, the God representation does exist. As Rizzuto stated during a debate with Edward Shafranske, "The representation, by definition, cannot be an expression of nothing. Rather, the opposite is true. A religious desire reveals the search for an object whose representation promises transformations that are deemed necessary."[15]

Adding to the confusion that some scholars have experienced when attempting to understand what Rizzuto means by "God representation" is this: Rizzuto uses the term *God representation*, but the term has often been called a *representation of God* in literature. Perhaps because of this, the term "God presentation" sometimes has been misunderstood even to the point that some individuals have mistakenly interpreted Rizzuto to refer with this term to a kind of crypto-Jungian archetype.[16]

Because the "unconscious" God representation is among the most important points to which Rizzuto draws our attention in her work, it is important to address the confusion. On my understanding, a culture and the religions within that culture, in a secondary process, name the object of desire (or need to believe), identifying it with God. Psychologically speaking, God is a cultural product, and what is unconscious cannot be religious. As a consequence, the unconscious object representation more adequately can be thought of as a never saturated matrix, as a way of relating always open to change, as a shapeless magma that is therefore able to shape every actual object. Indeed, we could liken this unconscious representation, at a psychological level, to a stem cell, primary and non-specialized, that is able to transform in many other typologies of body cells through a process of cell differentiation.

In their efforts to eliminate potential sources of confusion from their descriptions of the individual's experience in all of its complex wholeness, some scholars define the experiences of primary object relations, whose imprints can be found in the attitude toward religion, not as non-religious, but as *pre-religious*. Many religious professionals who bring pastoral or apologetic aims to their interest in the psychology of religion agree with this approach. But, in my opinion, such a categorization as "pre-" should require a relationship with the religious experiences to which the "pre-" religious ones lead. Indeed, forging such a relationship justifies employing the prefix "pre" and accounts for its proper use. But that relationship does not exist. We would see this clearly were we, in like manner, to attempt to adhere to a similar explanatory scheme for understanding atheism. No explanation could be given for the atheistic outcomes of an individual's developmental path, since nobody would use the expression "pre-atheistic" to describe processes that would lead to the outcome "atheism."

Further research, rooted in clinical practice, could clarify how interactions between the representation of the Self and the representation of primary objects shape the representation of an abstract object (I mean, not perceivable or concrete), like God. I believe that further research would be able to show more precisely how, as a possible response to specific cultural stimuli, God is not unconscious nor is God in the unconscious. Personal religion is not innate in the *homo religiosus* but results from the interaction and the dialectics of the subject with organized religion.

THE "PERSONAL RELIGION" OF AN INDIVIDUAL

Another important feature of Rizzuto's contribution to the psychology of religion rests with her use of the work of Donald Winnicott to illuminate, as never before, the specific developmental process that Rizzuto tracks as "the birth of the living God." Let's consider key moments in the process, as described by Rizzuto, while giving due consideration not only to the individual who emerges from this process as a believer, but also to the atheist.

The nature of the unconscious psychological process animating the God representation, starting from the Self representation and the representation of the parents, is still debated and investigated. To be sure, religious beliefs aren't satisfactorily explained by the theoretical concept of projection (one of the weakest in the psychoanalytical theory concerning religion). What does constitute a more satisfactory account? "Symbolic transference"[17] is more convincing, as a concept, as shown in the therapies to which Rizzuto sometimes refers and which I also have verified as a practitioner. In the therapeutic context, that the vicissitudes of transfer impact the attitude of the patients toward the parents and God is readily apparent. The attribute "symbolic" underscores that what is transferred is not only an "imago" of the real parents but also the outcome and the expectations included in the symbol "father" in the culture to which a person belongs. I refer to the idea of "fatherhood" that sometimes leads some patients to tell us, while recalling their past, "I never had a *true* father."

In this regard, the "personal religion" of an individual is not a natural and innate feature. To the contrary, it is the outcome of complex and interacting relations among intra-psychical, inter-psychical, and cultural levels. Such relations presume psychological preconditions (which are non-specific, and of course non-religious), such as the capacities to "believe" and to trust, the capacity to have sufficiently structured object relations, the capacity for symbolisation, the capacity to attribute meaning to events, and finally, the ability to distinguish between objects and their use, as these features of development have been eloquently delineated by Winnicott. The religion of the individual also entails the capacity to name specifically the general (and unavoidable for the human being) experience of believing (to "believe in anything at all").[18] Such specificity comes from the interaction of the subject with the symbolic system and the organized forms of religion; for Christians, it also presumes the revealing Word of God, as well as the ability to respond with all their being to God's interlocution.

Furthermore, I would like to add that, as part of the process of religious maturation, one could construct the God representation as something that is deeply connected with primary objects, while at the same time, assuming the capacity to take the necessary distance from personal desires and projections.[19] In Winnicott's words, maturation also includes mastering "the capacity to be alone."[20]

Rizzuto maintains the universality and, therefore, inescapability of the God representation in the minds of contemporary individuals, at least in the Western world.[21] The human is religious within a culture, a language, and a symbolic universe. There is no religion without a culture that enables it to express itself and that affects it. The name of God doesn't resound in the *vacuum* of other words or in the silence of other speakers.[22] Consequently, the atheist too has a God representation and will necessarily do something with it. That accounts for why a psychology of religion is always, at the same time, a psychology of atheism. And, if we use the words of Rizzuto, the notion of the "psychology of the religious subject" highlights how the psychology of religion would have us study the attitude of the subject. The content of the discipline of psychology directs us to focus on the person's attitude "toward" the religion he finds in his own milieu. At the same time, the birth of the believing human transpires as a process closely connected with personality development. As a consequence, the appropriation of the culturally transmitted idea of God, which is a symbolic-linguistic interactional process, presupposes unconscious pre-linguistic representations, which provide an orientation.

We can sum up the complex phenomenon, whereby an individual develops a capacity for belief, if we reflect closely on all the ways that we can answer the question, "When a person says God, what is he actually saying? Who speaks, about what, to whom?" Answering this question can not only be a matter of semantics. Religious words are emotional and relational too. We think, for example of God the "Father." Powerful feelings, positive and negative, are evoked by the word "Father." These feelings cannot help but inform feelings about God as well. Moreover, when a religious person believes that it is God who speaks, such belief already is a relationship with God and linked with an image of God. God speaks to the religious person in the language of a culture. The specificity of that communication is made possible as well by the capacity the person has developed to understand language and to relate to others.

We engage an idea of God that has been passed on to us within and by the culture to which we belong, but which is bound also in idiosyncratic ways to our individual histories. Winnicott's statement about the child creating the mother he finds[23] applies also to the believer. The believer "creates" the God he or she "finds" in culture.[24] Using different words from Winnicott but attesting to the same phenomenon, Rizzuto confirms that "religion as a concept calls for a living subject who does or experiences something that in his understanding is 'religious'".[25]

A MASTERFUL METHODOLOGICAL WORK

Another extremely relevant contribution of Rizzuto to the psychology of religion is her methodological approach to the exploration of religious belief. Rizzuto's research is a prime example of an epistemologically valid approach to the psychological experience toward religion. She investigates the psychic dynamics of belief; however, she doesn't make statements concerning the truth of religion or the ontological existence of God.[26] Specifically, Rizzuto shows respect for the patient's values—a respect that is mandatory for the analyst—even as her research advances from a position of neutrality about those values.

Furthermore, Rizzuto upholds the principle of the methodological exclusion of the transcendent, introduced by Theodore Flournoy,[27] as an essential requirement for the psychology of religion. Rizzuto attests to her methodological convictions in the introduction to her book when she states: "This is not a book on religion. It is a clinical study of the possible origins of the individual's private representation of God and its subsequent elaborations."[28]

Rizzuto emphasizes that the psychoanalyst has no access to God, but she or he does have access—via and only via the narrative of the patient—to the latter's representation of God. God is not an object of psychoanalytical work; however, the psychic process involved in belief (and in non-belief) in God certainly is an object of this work.

Building on these principles, Rizzuto has combined in a masterful manner theory and clinical practice to produce important and influential work. Fundamental to her project has been its empirical basis. Her first steps in developing the project that was to become *The Birth of the Living God* were to collect data using a variety of methods and techniques (clinical interviews, projective techniques, questionnaires, structured interviews).[29] She subsequently interpreted that data in the light of a critical revision of the theories of Freud about the origin of religion.[30] In following such a path, Rizzuto shed substantial light on the dynamics of the development of a "personal religion" and on the "personal God" in childhood.[31] Indeed, as a result, Rizzuto's project became a model for inquiry in the psychology of religion.

Elaborating on this pivotal model of the God representation in a later project, Rizzuto contributed to the literature in the field of the psychology of religion a psycho-dynamic interpretation of Freud titled *Why did Freud reject God?*[32] A fascinating reconstruction of Freud's attitude toward religion, this book also is a captivating "historical novel" (*historischer Roman*) in exactly the same way that Freud used this word in 1934 to describe, in the unpublished preface, the project of *Moses and Monotheism.* [*Der Mann Moses: Ein historischer Roman*].[33] In Rizzuto's project we hear echoes also of Freud's suggestion in *Leonardo da Vinci, A Memory of his Childhood* that his "picture of Leonardo's course of development" could be considered a "*psychoanalytic novel.*" Describing others' reactions to his description of these works as novels, Freud writes: "If in making these statements I have provoked the criticism, even from friends of psychoanalysis and from those who are expert in it, that I have merely written a psychoanalytic novel, I shall reply that I am far from over-estimating the certainty of these results."[34] The creativity of the analyst in offering an interpretation that reconstructs the personality of Leonardo by connecting and integrating both positive and merely probable data is notable and enlightening. We can say as much for Rizzuto and her work on Freud.

In other essays, Rizzuto enables us to perceive how the model she has developed works, enabling the analyst to follow the vicissitudes of Self, object, and God representations during psychoanalysis,[35] especially those that often take place in transference; since, as she says, "the analyst, as a transferential and real object, occupies the *locus parentis*, a position that facilitates the revival of intense emotions bestowed by the analyst and upon the divine representations."[36] Rizzuto's work remains always strongly connected to psychoanalysis, which she applies rigorously. Describing how she approaches her work, she writes: "My stance, therefore, is strictly psychoanalytic. That means that I attempt to understand any conscious phenomenon or event as the organized manifestation of simultaneously present unconscious processes, developmental modalities, and genetic and dynamic expressions of internal responses to circumstantial and relational concrete psychic moments."[37] In spite of the huge task she has undertaken, Rizzuto doesn't call herself a "psychoanalyst of religion"; instead, she says, "My self-definition favors the term 'psychoanalyst of people's experiences with their internalized religious objects and beliefs'."[38] With this description of herself, Rizzuto exemplifies what it means to work "in the light of psychoanalysis," delimiting as the boundaries of her inquiry the individual's experience in all its complex wholeness.

"I AM OFFERING SNAPSHOTS"

A final contribution that Rizzuto makes to the psychology of religion consists of elucidating the role of psychoanalysis in a field that increasingly values quantitative research. Recently, in a debate with a scholar who suggested replacing psychoanalysis with attachment theory—which he saw as more certain, scientifically proven, and predictive—in the psychology of religion,[39] Rizzuto clarified the relationship that exists between quantitative group research and qualitative individual case studies and explained their differences.[40] According to her, psychoanalysis "is first and foremost a method for acquiring unique personal knowledge—a method based on a disciplined relationship, unique in its fundamental rules and emerging events, aimed at discovering the inner workings of the mind. What makes psychoanalysis an unsurpassed instrument for investigating is the possibility it provides to explore the workings of the mind in a living situation in which affective relational engagement is the cornerstone of a transformational process."[41]

From my point of view, I can affirm Rizzuto's statement. The psychoanalytic method is post-dictive, hermeneutical, and constructivist: it is neither homogeneous, nor commensurate with the objective and pre-dictive method of experimental research that seeks to find a generalization and a causal explanation of the observed facts. Rather, with its own clinical method and long and deep observation of psychic processes as they unfold over time, psychoanalysis offers extremely profound and refined insights into the mental processes observed in an individual. Starting from here, empirical researchers could be encouraged to study some of these processes, in a quantitative manner, on a sample of subjects.[42]

Rizzuto accounts for and enhances the value of her approach with a metaphor: "I am offering snapshots."[43] In other words, with her case studies, she simply offers meaningful portraits of her patients. In photography, it is necessary to select a specific image in order to communicate a particular message; however, that doesn't affect the truth of the snapshot nor the ability the photo has to represent a feature of the real world, cut from that world and captured in the photo. The same can be said for the case study in psychoanalysis. As Rizzuto said some years ago, "Psychoanalysis, with its method of free association and reconstruction of early and later psychic acts and experiences, offers a unique access to the subjective, representational, and affective components of all religious experiences."[44]

One can glimpse in this discussion an issue that is intrinsic to psychology as a science. Scientific knowledge aims at general results: generalization is intrinsic to sciences. Even so, one would be remiss not to notice that there is no other thing so individual as the psyche, which is, moreover, constantly evolving. What empirical research, inspired by *hard* scientific principles, gains in the number of cases it investigates and in its experimental repeatability, it must lose when, in the interests of generalizability, it bypasses idiosyncratic information, the information, I mean, that comprises the unique qualities of an individual. We should be afraid that, by renouncing individuality, psychology could lose its soul: in the meaning both of losing the soul (psyche) as its own object and of losing the specific purpose of *psycho*-logy. Hence there is a necessity for the psychologist of religion to always focus on the complexity of the person and on his or her distinctive interactions within a cultural framework in the current universe of religion.

The term "model" can be used when referring to a general schema of psychic functioning. It is only at this stage that the understanding of the person undergoing clinical psychoanalytic therapy can become useful to psychologists of religion. It is worth keeping in mind that these are reference schemas, that is, a synthesis of many cases, and not an exact and definitive anthropology. Mindful of this point, Donald Winnicott did not like calling his notion of transitional phenomena a "model"; he did not want it to be understood in a too rigid manner. Winnicott wrote, "The thing I am referring to is universal and has infinite variety. It is rather similar to the description of the human face when we describe one in terms of shape and eyes and nose and mouth and ears, but the fact remains that no two faces are exactly alike and very few are similar."[45] Thanks to Rizzuto's work, we are now well equipped to take on this challenging, but ultimately rewarding, task of describing in the light of psychoanalysis the individual's universal, but infinitely varied, religious experience in all of its complex wholeness.

DISCUSSION

Ana-María Rizzuto

Thank you, Professor Aletti, for your presentation of my ideas and for your clarification of some significant points. In my necessarily brief discussion, I will focus on what deserves further elaboration.

A God of Culture

I fully agree with Aletti's assertion that the believer "creates" the God he or she finds in his or her culture. In the same way that Italian children speak Italian and Chinese children speak Chinese, children pick up the god they have to wrestle with from the offerings of culture: God for monotheists and Hindu gods for Hindu children. Even the absence of any god, which is culturally a modern phenomenon, has its impact. A friend of mine, raised during the Mao Revolution in China in a culture that strictly prohibited any religion, soon after his arrival to the United States asked me continuously, "What is God?" I failed to offer him any description that did not prompt his gracious laughter and comment: "But all is matter; there is nothing else." After twenty-five years of exposure to American culture and its "In God we Trust" motif on our currency, he has progressed so far as to say with a smile,"Life is mysterious." I conclude that the coercive Maoist culture in which he grew up not only deprived him of a cultural divinity but also burdened him with the deadly prohibition and fear of even thinking about the "mysterious" realities of existence. On the other hand, we Westerners have God everywhere and feel the opposite of my friend. We have a psychical need to make sense of the word "God" as well as a certain obligation to deal with the divine presence in our culture and with the demands it imposes upon us.

The God Representation

I want to clarify that I speak about a "God representation" and not about a "representation of God." God as understood in our culture is not representable. There is no such thing as the representation *of* God. What I have described in my work is that the child who has grasped in a certain manner the word "God" offered to her for the first time and who finds no tangible referent for it, as she has for other words such as "chair" or "doll," must become creative in her own mind. God is described to her with personal attributes—God is there; God wants, loves, feels, rewards, and punishes. The child thus is given a certain hint of what God might be like and what the divinity's intentions might be. The God "found" in the culture of the parents comes without a photograph. It has to be "created" by the child through internal processes capable of integrating the God offered by the culture with what the child has available to bestow upon this God as a private personally and psychologically significant internal form. In this manner, God representations are idiosyncratically individualized and become *analogically* compatible with the God of culture. The God thus created belongs to the subject as a personal private reality. But what does a child have available in her mind to carry out such a *spontaneously creative* task? As Aletti reminds us, my response has been that we have available to us memorial processes of preexisting human interactions that are now also available to form representational functions during our exchanges with ourselves and others.

What is a Representation?

My first answer to this question points to very complex processes of integration of multiple experiential sources to form our internal conception of an object or a person. From the process point of view, a representation is never a concrete, completely fixed organization of perceived sensory experiences that is established once and for all. To the contrary, and following a strict Freudian conception, a representation always is expandable and constituted from many moments of exchanges with either a physical or a human object. It may include internal contradictions and even incompatible components. Let me illustrate briefly.

A maternal representation must include a multitude of experiential exchanges registered as memorial processes: the maternal voice and its affect and capacity or lack thereof to address the child; her manner of holding the child; her style of feeding her baby; the type of physical contact between them during bodily ministrations; the maternal countenance and her capacity to establish eye contact with her child and see her; and many other aspects of the multisensory/affective mother-child interactions and their non-conscious and explicit intentions. Each one of these components has contrasting alternatives as illustrated by the maternal voice being mostly kind but at times harsh and rejecting. All of these perceptual and memorial processes constitute an extraordinarily complex maternal representation. The same may be said about the paternal representation and other people's representations. The mental processes involved are unconscious in themselves; but some of these processes may be consciously retrieved by recollecting a moment of the past, such as the day the father bought the little girl a pretty dress.

The memorial processes I have just described are potentially available to contribute to the formation of the God representation. Frequently, the interpersonal quality of the moment in which a parent presents God to the child has much to contribute to the selection of the components of maternal and parental representations that would be non-consciously chosen to give representational form to the divine being. Components of different memories and of each parent or close relative may combine to form the private non-conscious God representation. Some of these components may become conscious when the child attempts to objectify God in her mind.

My description suggests that it is erroneous to speak of *a* singular maternal, paternal, or God representation. The richness of the creative process brings about a multifaceted and compounded representation that exceeds the possibility of accessing it in a single conscious moment. As happens with all representations of human beings, we must unveil different aspects *successively* if we want to know in what way we conceive of them. God is no exception.

The preceding description prompts me to reject *a* singular God representation as exhausting our private conception of the divine being or of any person. The expression "image of God" is seriously misleading if it refers to internal processes and not to the technical tools—such as a drawing—that permit one to objectify in a test a given aspect of the divine being at a particular moment.

THE BIRTH OF A BELIEVING PERSON

The preceding considerations permit me to fully agree with Aletti when he calls our attention to the "birth of the believing person." I consider that the birth of the living God and of the believing person are dialectically coterminous in their potential to create a credible divinity and a believing individual or to create its opposite—a God undeserving of a person's belief.

In my 2002 paper, "Believing and Personal and Religious Beliefs: Psychoanalytic Considerations,"[46] I proposed that believing is related to an attribution of *intentionality* between partners involved in dealings with each other. This component is essential for the non-conscious selection of memories to form a believable God representation or one that does not deserve our belief. The memorial processes accessed to create or re-elaborate the God representation *always* involve an interactional moment with the person that provides a particular characteristic of the divinity. The maternal soothing words in a moment of hurt in past experiences may reappear in the feeling of a consoling God. The paternal guidance in the innumerable moments involved in teaching a child to play a sport may sustain the conviction that "God is my shepherd." On the other hand, the humiliating and harsh punishments of rejecting parents may convince the potential believer that God does not care for him or her and is not interested in looking on that person with kindness. Such beliefs in the type of intentional interactions between parents and child and God and the potential believer create the conditions for belief and non-belief. When the *intentionality* is complementary, belief ensues and the believing person is born.

I thank Professor Aletti for the opportunity to clarify some of these issues.

NOTES

1. Jacob A. Belzen, "Past Freud - Beyond Freud. On Progress in the Psychoanalytic Psychology of Religion," in *Changing the Scientific Study of Religion: Beyond Freud? Theoretical, Empirical and Clinical Studies from Psychoanalytic Perspectives*, ed. Jacob A. Belzen (London-New York: Springer, 2009), 5. The phrase "psychoanalytic psychology of religion" is Belzen's terminology. I use "psychology of religion" in this essay.

2. Ana-María Rizzuto, "Psychoanalysis: The Transformation of the Subject by the Spoken Word," *Psychoanalytic Quarterly* 72 (2003).

3. Ibid, "Belief as a Psychic Function," *Newsletter of Division 36 (Psychology of Religion) of the American Psychological Association* 22, no. 1 (1996–1997); Rizzuto, "Believing and Personal and Religious Beliefs: Psychoanalytic Considerations," *Psychoanalysis and Contemporary Thought* 25 (2002).

4. Ibid.

5. Mario Aletti, "The Question of Religious Truth in the Light of Psychoanalysis" (paper presented at the biannual Congress of the International Association for the Psychology of Religion, Lausanne, Switzerland, August 27–30, 2013).

6. Sigmund Freud, "Moses and Monotheism. Three Essays," in *Standard Edition* (London: Hogarth Press, 1964). (Original German Edition 1939).

7. Ana-María Rizzuto, *The Birth of the Living God. A Psychoanalytic Study* (Chicago-London: The University of Chicago Press, 1979), 177.

8. Ibid, "Freud, God, and the Devil and the Theory of Object Representation," *International Review of Psycho-Analysis* 31 (1976).

9. Ibid, "The Father and Child's Representations of God," in *Father and Child*, ed. Stanley H. Cath et al. (Boston: Little, Brown, 1982), 357–82.

10. Rizzuto, *The Birth*, 54–59.

11. Ana-María Rizzuto, *Why Did Freud Reject God? A Psychodynamic Interpretation* (New Haven, CT-London: Yale University Press, 1998), 264.

12. Mario Aletti and Paolo Ciotti, "The Birth of the Believing Man. Prospects for and Problems with the Object Relations Theory Applied to Religion," in *L'illusione Religiosa: Rive e Derive*, ed. Mario Aletti and Germano Rossi (Torino: Centro Scientifico Editore, 2001).

13. Rizzuto, "Believing and Personal": 461.

14. Mario Aletti, "Religion as an Illusion: Prospects for and Problems with a Psychoanalytical Model," *Archiv für Religionspsychologie/Archive for the Psychology of Religion* 27 (2005).

15. Ana-María Rizzuto, "Afterword," in *Object Relations Theory and Religion. Clinical Applications*, ed. Mark G. Finn and John Gartner (Westport, CT-London: Praeger, 1992), 162.

16. Howard F. Stein, Review of *The Birth of the Living God. A Psychoanalytic Study*, by Ana-María Rizzuto. *The Psychoanalytic Quarterly* 50 (1981): 125–30; See also James W. Jones, *Contemporary Psychoanalysis and Religion. Transference and Transcendence* (New Haven, CT: Yale University Press, 1991).

17. Giancarlo Milanesi and Mario Aletti, *Psicologia della Religione* (Torino: Elledici, 1973), 108–20.

18. Donald W. Winnicott, "Children Learning," in *Home is Where We Start From* (London: Penguin Books, 1968), 143.

19. Mario Aletti, *Percorsi di Psicologia della Religione alla Luce della Psicoanalisi,* 2nd ed. (Roma: Aracne, 2010), 94–97.

20. Ibid.

21. Ana-María Rizzuto, "One Hundred Years after Freud Declared That Religion Was a Universal Obsessional Neurosis," in *Changing the Scientific Study of Religion: Beyond Freud? Theoretical, Empirical and Clinical Studies from Psychoanalytic Perspectives*, ed. Jacob A. Belzen(London – New York: Springer, 2009), 35–55.

22. Mario Aletti, "Religious Experience, Gender Differences and Religious Language," in *Religione o Psicoterapia? Nuovi Fenomeni e Movimenti Religiosi alla Luce della Psicologia* [Religion or Psychotherapy? New Phenomenai and Religious Movements in the Light of Psychology], ed. Mario Aletti (Roma: LAS, 1994).

23. Donald W. Winnicott, "The Use of an Object and Relating through Identifications," in *Playing and Reality* (New York: Basic Books, 1971, orig. 1969).

24. Aletti, *Percorsi di Psicologia della Religione*, 87–94.

25. Ana-María Rizzuto, "An Accidental Psychologist of Religion," in *Psychology of Religion: Autobiographical Accounts*, ed. Jacob A. Belzen (New York: Springer, 2012), 195–196.

26. Ibid, "Psychoanalytic Psychotherapy and Pastoral Guidance," *Journal of Pastoral Care* 52, no. 1 (1998).

27. Théodore Flournoy, "Les Principes de la Psychologie Religieuse," *Archives de Psychologie* 2 (1902).

28. Rizzuto, *The Birth*, 3.

29. Rizzuto, *The Birth*.

30. Ana-María Rizzuto, "Object Relations and the Formation of the Image of God," *British Journal of Medical Psychology* 47 (1974); Rizzuto, *Why Did Freud?*

31. Ibid, "Religious Development. A Psychoanalytic Point of View," *New Directions for Child Development* 52 (1991).

32. Rizzuto, *Why Did Freud*?

33. See Pier Cesare Bori, "Oskar Pfister, "Pfarrer in Zurich" e Analista Laico," *Psicoterapia e Scienze Umane* 24, no. 3 (1990).

34. Sigmund Freud, "Leonardo Da Vinci and a Memory of His Childhood," in *Standard Edition* (London: Hogarth Press, 1957), 134. (First German Edition 1910).

35. Ana-María Rizzuto, "Psychoanalytic Treatment and the Religious Persons," in *Religion and the Clinical Practice of Psychology*, ed. Edward P. Shafranske (Washington, D.C.: American Psychological Association, 1996), 409–31; Ana-María Rizzuto, "Vicissitudes of Self, Object, and God Representations During Psychoanalysis / Trasformazioni delle Rappresentazioni del Sé, dell'oggetto e di Dio in Psicoanalisi,"

in *L'illusione Religiosa: Rive e Derive* [The Religious Illusion: Shores and Adrifts] ed. Mario Aletti and Germano Rossi (Torino: Centro Scientifico Editore, 2001), 25-55; Ana-María Rizzuto, "Does God Help? What God? Helping Whom? The Convolutions of Divine Help," in *Does God Help? Developmental and Clinical Aspects of Religious Belief*, ed. Salman Akhtar and Henri Parens (Frankfurt: Northvale, NJ – London, 2001), 19–51.

36. Rizzuto, "Vicissitudes of Self," 26.

37. Ana-María Rizzuto, "Religious Development Beyond the Modern Paradigm Discussion: The Psychoanalytic Point of View," *The International Journal for the Psychology of Religion* 11 (2001), 201.

38. Rizzuto, "An Accidental Psychologist of Religion," 194.

39. Pehr Granqvist, "On the Relation between Secular and Divine Relationships: An Emerging Attachment Perspective and a Critique of the 'Depth' Approaches," *The International Journal for the Psychology of Religion* 16 (2006).

40. Ana-María Rizzuto, "Discussion of Granqvist's Article 'On the Relation between Secular and Divine Relationships: An Emerging Attachment Perspective and a Critique of the 'Depth' Approaches," *International Journal for the Psychology of Religion* 16 (2006).

41. Rizzuto, "Believing and Personal," 26.

42. Mario Aletti, "My Concern with Psychology of Religion: Defending Psychology, Respecting Religion," in *Psychology of Religion: Autobiographical Accounts*, ed. Jacob A. Belzen (New York: Springer, 2012), 35–39.

43. Rizzuto, "An Accidental Psychologist of Religion," 148.

44. Ibid, "Religious Development: A Psychoanalytic Point of View," 50.

45. Donald W. Winnicott, *Playing and Reality* (New York: Basic Books, 1982). (First publication 1971), xii.

46. "Believing and Personal and Religious Beliefs: Psychoanalytic Considerations." *Psychoanalysis and Contemporary Thought* 25 (2002).

BIBLIOGRAPHY

Aletti, Mario. "My Concern with Psychology of Religion: Defending Psychology, Respecting Religion." In *Psychology of Religion: Autobiographical Accounts*, edited by Jacob A. Belzen, 19–41. New York, NY: Springer, 2012.

———. *Percorsi di Psicologia della Religione alla Luce della Psicoanalisi* [Pathways to the Psychology of Religion in the Light of Psychoanalysis]. 2nd ed. Roma: Aracne, 2010.

———. "Religion as an Illusion: Prospects for and Problems with a Psychoanalytical Model." *Archiv für Religionspsychologie/Archive for the Psychology of Religion* 27 (2005): 1–18.

———. "Religious Experience, Gender Differences and Religious Language." In *Religione o Psicoterapia? Nuovi Fenomeni e Movimenti Religiosi alla Luce della Psicologia* [Religion or Psychotherapy? New Phenomenai and Religious

Movements in the Light of Psychology], edited by Mario Aletti, 381–91. Roma: LAS, 1994.

———. "The question of religious truth in the light of psychoanalysis." Paper presented at the biannual Congress of the International Association for the Psychology of Religion, Lausanne, Switzerland, August 27–30, 2013.

Aletti, Mario, and Paolo Ciotti. "The Birth of the Believing Man. Prospects for and Problems with the Object Relations Theory Applied to Religion." In *L'illusione Religiosa: Rive e Derive* [The Religious Illusion: Shores and Adrifts], edited by Mario Aletti and Germano Rossi, 297–302. Torino: Centro Scientifico Editore, 2001.

Belzen, Jacob A. "Past Freud - Beyond Freud. On Progress in the Psychoanalytic Psychology of Religion." In *Changing the Scientific Study of Religion: Beyond Freud? Theoretical, Empirical and Clinical Studies from Psychoanalytic Perspectives*, edited by Jacob A. Belzen, 3–31. London-New York: Springer, 2009.

Bori, Pier Cesare. "Oskar Pfister, "Pfarrer in Zurich" e Analista Laico." *Psicoterapia e Scienze Umane* 24, no. 3 (1990): 3–36.

Flournoy, Théodore. "Les Principes de la Psychologie Religieuse." *Archives de Psychologie* 2 (1902): 33–57.

Freud, Sigmund. "Leonardo Da Vinci and a Memory of His Childhood." In *Standard Edition*, Vol. 11, 57–137. London: Hogarth Press, 1957. (First German Edition 1910).

———. "Moses and Monotheism. Three Essays." In *Standard Edition*, Vol. 23, 7–137. London: Hogarth Press, 1964. (Original German Edition 1939).

Granqvist, Pehr. "On the Relation between Secular and Divine Relationships: An Emerging Attachment Perspective and a Critique of the 'Depth' Approaches." *The International Journal for the Psychology of Religion* 16 (2006): 1–18.

Jones, W. James. *Contemporary Psychoanalysis and Religion. Transference and Transcendence*. New Haven, CT: Yale University Press, 1991.

Milanesi, Giancarlo and Mario Aletti. *Psicologia della Religione*. Torino: Elledici, 1973.

Rizzuto, Ana-María. "An Accidental Psychologist of Religion." In *Psychology of Religion: Autobiographical Accounts*, edited by Jacob A. Belzen, 185–200. New York, NY: Springer, 2012.

———. "Afterword." In *Object Relations Theory and Religion. Clinical Applications*, edited by Mark G. Finn and John Gartner, 155–75. Westport, CT-London: Praeger, 1992.

———. "Belief as a Psychic Function." *Newsletter of Division 36 (Psychology of Religion) of the American Psychological Association* 22, no. 1 (1996–1997): 1–7.

———. "Believing and Personal and Religious Beliefs: Psychoanalytic Considerations." *Psychoanalysis and Contemporary Thought* 25 (2002): 433–63.

———. *The Birth of the Living God. A Psychoanalytic Study*. Chicago-London: The University of Chicago Press, 1979.

———. "Discussion of Granqvist's Article 'On the Relation between Secular and Divine Relationships: An Emerging Attachment Perspective and a Critique of the

'Depth' Approaches'." *International Journal for the Psychology of Religion* 16 (2006): 19–28.

———. "Does God Help? What God? Helping Whom? The Convolutions of Divine Help." In *Does God Help? Developmental and Clinical Aspects of Religious Belief* edited by Salman Akhtar, and Henri Parens, 19–51. Frankfurt: Northvale, NJ – London, 2001.

———. "The Father and Child's Representations of God." In *Father and Child,* edited by Stanley H. Cath, Alan R. Gurwitt, and John Munder Ross, 357–82. Boston, MA: Little, Brown, 1982.

———. "Freud, God, and the Devil and the Theory of Object Representation." *International Review of Psycho-Analysis* 31 (1976): 165–70.

———. "Object Relations and the Formation of the Image of God." *British Journal of Medical Psychology* 47 (1974): 83–99.

———. "One Hundred Years after Freud Declared That Religion Was a Universal Obsessional Neurosis." In *Changing the Scientific Study of Religion: Beyond Freud? Theoretical, Empirical and Clinical Studies from Psychoanalytic Perspectives*, edited by Jacob A. Belzen, 35–55. London – New York: Springer, 2009.

———. "Psychoanalysis: The Transformation of the Subject by the Spoken Word." *Psychoanalytic Quarterly* 72 (2003): 287–323.

———. "Psychoanalytic Psychotherapy and Pastoral Guidance." *Journal of Pastoral Care* 52, no. 1 (1998): 69–78.

———. "Psychoanalytic Treatment and the Religious Persons." In *Religion and the Clinical Practice of Psychology*, edited by Edward P. Shafranske, 409–31. Washington, D.C.: American Psychological Association, 1996.

———. "Religious Development Beyond the Modern Paradigm Discussion: The Psychoanalytic Point of View." *The International Journal for the Psychology of Religion* 11 (2001): 201–14.

———. "Religious Development. A Psychoanalytic Point of View." *New Directions for Child Development* 52 (1991): 47–60.

———. "Vicissitudes of Self, Object, and God Representations During Psychoanalysis / Trasformazioni delle Rappresentazioni del Sé, dell'oggetto e di Dio in Psicoanalisi." In *L'illusione Religiosa: Rive e Derive* [The Religious Illusion: Shores and Adrifts] edited by Mario Aletti and Germano Rossi, 25–55. Torino: Centro Scientifico Editore, 2001.

———. *Why Did Freud Reject God? A Psychodynamic Interpretation.* New Haven, CT-London: Yale University Press, 1998.

Stein, Howard F. Review of *The Birth of the Living God. A Psychoanalytic Study*, by Ana-María Rizzuto. *The Psychoanalytic Quarterly* 50 (1981): 125–30.

Winnicott, Donald. W. "Children Learning." In *Home Is Where We Start From*, 142–49. London: Penguin Books, 1968.

———. "The Use of an Object and Relating through Identifications." In *Playing and Reality*, 86–94. New York, NY: Basic Books, 1971. (Original Work, 1969).

———. *Playing and Reality.* New York, NY: Basic Books, 1982. (First publication 1971).

Chapter 3

The Persecuting God and the Crucified Self

The Vital Role of Metaphors in Psychotherapy

Gry Stålsett, Arne Austad, and
Leif Gunnar Engedal

The title of our chapter presents two powerful metaphors: "the persecuting God" and "the crucified Self." The genesis of these metaphors is found in the self-presentation and treatment of a very troubled psychiatric patient. They came to play a significant role as dynamically related and interacting metaphors in his therapeutic process. When examining these metaphors and learning more about their crucial function in the healing process, a door is opened toward insights into the vital role of metaphors in profound personal processes in psychotherapy.

Ana-María Rizzuto highlights the crucial importance of metaphors in two groundbreaking theoretical and clinical publications.[1] Rizzuto develops key therapeutic concepts in what could be named "a philosophy of language for psychotherapists." In this 'philosophy,' special attention is given to the meaning and function of *affect* and *metaphors* in the patient's idiosyncratic ways of talking. Rizzuto[2] sums up a key theoretical perspective concerning the relation between *language and affect* in the following core sentence from Andre Green:[3] "Without affect there is no effective language. Without language there is no effective affect." Reflecting on the meaning and function of metaphors, Rizzuto describes what a metaphor contains as follows: "In the creation of an internally perceived object, the metaphor becomes a source of self-discovery, a way of refinding our feelings, our objects, our forgotten human objects and perceptions. . . . The metaphor's function is to capture an aspect of ourselves that claims attention but has no other way of finding expression."[4] Rizzuto underlines the important dynamic function of the metaphors as mediators of hidden feelings and aspects of ourselves that have no other way of finding expression.

As the following case presentation demonstrates, these basic theoretical perspectives are highly relevant and fruitful in the examination of what is going on in the therapeutic process of our patient, here named "Olav."[5] In another format and with different analytical foci, "the case of Olav" has been presented[6] and commented on by three experts in the field—James Jones, Scott Richards, and M.S Malitzky—in relation to a previous publication.[7] When now revisiting this case study, our purpose is to shed light on the meaning and function of selected key metaphors that the patient used. While looking into the many layers a metaphor may contain, we will address *existential, narrative, dynamic-relational,* and *affective* sources. The therapeutic task is to encourage the patient to explore and discover multiple layers of information enveloped in his/her personal choice of metaphors. This process of inquiry will increase the patient`s ability to *mentalize*. Therapy facilitates the patient's ability to harbor ambivalent and contradictory emotions and to learn to know the difference between feelings and reality. This is the main therapeutic way of overcoming a "psychic equivalent mode."[8]

THE VITA PROJECT

The VITA Project: *Existential and Religious Issues in Psychotherapy* was designed in 1998 by this chapter's three authors at Modum Bad Clinic, a psychiatric hospital in Norway. Previous publications outline how this model addresses existential suffering and/or religious concerns accompanying treatment-resistant depressions. An effectiveness study compared the Vita Model with a "treatment as usual" comparison group of patients with treatment-resistant depression and Cluster C comorbidity.[9] Through Stålsett's doctoral dissertation, the Vita Treatment Model was shown to be an evidence-based treatment model for comorbid depressive disorders.[10]

We designed the project to develop a new treatment model for psychiatric patients with existential and religious issues formulated as a part of their presented problem.[11] The treatment meets a largely neglected issue in psychotherapy by focusing on relational and existential aspects in religious belief.

The main theoretical foundation for this project is drawn from psychoanalytic object relations theory[12] developed by Rizzuto,[13] existential psychology,[14] modern affect theory,[15] and narrative psychology.[16] Strategies from these traditions and newer research on relapse prevention are integrated into the case. Insights on what fosters changes in maladaptive belief systems[17] and affect organization[18] are included. Unlike many other spiritual or religious forms of therapy,[19] VITA emphasizes *psychological* approaches and means. This implies that religious issues and belief systems are considered from a psychological point of view, that is, explored for their psychological function.

THE THERAPEUTIC GROUP: STRUCTURE AND STRATEGIES

The treatment is a 12-week, group-based program organized in groups that focus on different aspects of the patients' suffering and life experiences. Every day starts with a morning meditation group and ends with a short relaxation group reporting on actual affects. There are also groups for psychodynamic therapy, art therapy, narrative therapy, existential reflection, and regular psycho-education group sessions.

The treatment program is structured in three phases, each four weeks long. Each phase contains some repetitive treatment activities, for example, writing a personal faith history three times and drawing self-, father-, mother-, and God-representations three times in the art therapy group. The art therapy facilitates change through projective techniques by providing the possibility of bringing forward unconscious material and making it available for identification, verbalization, differentiation, and reflection. The overall objective is to facilitate transformation of rigid object representations and to address existential and religious issues, such as God image, meaning, freedom, trust, loneliness, shame, and guilt. Since Rizzuto`s research on the inner representation and dynamic components of religious belief came to our knowledge, it has proven to be a very powerful clinical approach,[20] as illustrated by the following case study. This case study demonstrates the powerful dynamic meaning related to the patient's use of metaphors in the therapeutic process.

THE PATIENT OLAV—A SHORT PRESENTATION

Olav was a 35-year-old divorced lawyer who had been hospitalized in closed psychiatric wards for more than seven years. He manifested severe, treatment-resistant depression, transient psychotic episodes, self-destructive behavior, and suicidal attempts. He had a strict religious upbringing with high moral standards. He was born a twin, but his twin brother died at eighteen months of age.

Olav was told that God had taken his twin brother home as an angel because he (the twin) was good, making Olav feel bad, "the not-chosen," both by his father and by God.

Olav was very close to his mother. His father was described as emotionally distant, demanding submission, admiration, and reverence. During Olav's adolescence, his parents were divorced and his mother left the family to live her own life. During the divorce process, Olav felt obliged to side with his father as well as achieve perfection to obtain his father's love. The father said about the mother: "She was crazy, and she was a whore." She was condemned to hell.

Olav's own growing marital problems in his late twenties and a relatively minor professional mistake eventually contributed to a severe psychic breakdown. He regressed, and for a long time he expressed inhibited anger and longing. These feelings were captured in his saying, "*I would rather be in hell with my mother than in heaven with my father.*" Repeated hospitalizations provided only temporary relief from his restricted life. He felt tortured by condemning inner voices belonging to what he called *The Committee*. As long as *The Committee* dominated his life, he lived with a painful self-experience presented through several powerful personalized metaphors: He was *a Crucified Child* and an *Occupied Land*. In *The Committee*'s continuous condemnations, he heard the sacred voices of God, his father, people he had offended, and people who he felt had abandoned him.

Olav's former treatment was in a traditional psychiatric setting, governed by a symptom-oriented and medical culture. Olav often presented his pain and suffering in poetic language and made extensive use of powerful metaphors like those mentioned above. But Olav's way of articulating his inner world was not validated and explored by the psychiatric team. Instead, he was advised to stop giving attention to and to reject the malevolent and toxic God; however, when he tried to do so, he became worse.

When Olav entered VITA, there seemed to be no distance between the metaphorical world he created and the real world. This lack of differentiation between symbol and reality showed Olav's mental function in a regressed, psychic equivalent mode and reflected a severe lack in his ability to mentalize. As we will see in the following case presentation, his lack of capacity to mentalize changed significantly due to intensive work with the affective loading and narrative contexts that gave power and meaning to the metaphors.

The Therapeutic Process–Key Issues

In the preparation phase of therapy, Olav had to learn how to look closely at his inner world to find another language for communicating his experience. When he said, "*The Committee* says" and so forth, he was told by the therapists that his fellow patients might react as if he were crazy. He responded to this suggestion of possible reactions with good humor, suggesting that he understood the implications. He was able to talk about *The Committee* in new ways, inserting phrases into his speech such as "what I call," "what I perceive as," or "what I experience as." Through such effort, a struggle not without anxiety attacks, he was able to mentalize a little more through his language use.

In the initial treatment phase, Olav felt scared about challenging his inner world, and it seemed strange to him to start to look at the function of *The Committee*. Gradually, his experience changed, and he could obtain an attitude of inquiry toward himself without feeling that he risked being attacked by *The Committee*. He felt ashamed by his self-exposure in the group and wrote in his diary that he hated himself for his depressiveness. He told both fellow patients and the therapists about his fear and anger at his father and God. He felt that his right to live had been stolen for most of his life, and he believed he was denied God's blessing. When drawing an image of himself the first time, he could not do it because he felt empty. He struggled intensively with *The Committee,* with its harsh, condemning voices depriving him of freedom and giving him his painful sense of being *a Crucified Child*. While exploring his feelings, he felt loneliness, guilt, despair, and jealousy toward all the other fellow patients who had lives of their own. He also explained his competition with his dead brother and his experience of being ranked by his father as "the second best" or not good enough. Elaborating, he reflected that there was only one solution: to get ill as kind of a paradoxical opposite to competition. He commented, "If you need to be seen, you have to be the sickest. I feel like a loser."

During the first phase of the treatment, Olav began to realize that he had taken on guilt that was not his own. He could see in glimpses that *The Committee* actually might be a self-attack related to his deeply felt shame of being unable to have a life of his own.[21]

In the next phase of treatment and in accordance with the therapeutic aim of integration of affects, his affective capacity was strengthened. He became more able to express and tolerate anger, and he dared to feel moments of happiness as well as vitality. In relation to this process, he created and gave meaning to a new significant metaphor called *Inner Wolf*. He could hear and identify "the howls from his *Inner Wolf*," and he began to represent his *Inner Wolf* as opposed to, and in conflict with, *The Committee*. This new metaphor marked Olav's emergent ability and willingness to experience his angry feelings, rather than to project them onto *The Committee*. By drawing an image of his mother, Olav got in contact with his anger about being abandoned as well as with forbidden affects related to his desperate longing for her. He painted his mother in red color, reflecting his intense love and hurt, a rage of abandonment because of her departure when she left the family. Commenting about the drawing, he wrote: "There are black whirls of pain, rage, and chaos. She is stretching out her hand towards me, and I get absorbed in her. I can feel her love, but also ambivalence. It is scary and attractive to glimpse in her eyes a flirt. I am longing to be close to her, but also afraid. I do not feel safe. I am struggling to keep trust in her love."

With comments such as these, Olav articulated that his feelings for his mother were deeply ambivalent and threatening. He expressed guilt, shame, and anxiety by his forbidden longing for a mother who was sexualized and whom his father had characterized as a whore. Such feelings needed to be persecuted. In general, due to painful feelings of abandonment, he had developed a profound ambivalence—a longing for closeness and an intense anxiety tied to issues of closeness. He started to allow himself to feel his feelings toward his mother, and he experienced that feelings in themselves were not dangerous.

Olav's drawings of God began to change as well. In his first drawing of God in the art therapy session, he painted a picture mainly in black with five dark eyes and a big blue cross with a crucified child set against the darkness. When commenting on this picture, Olav said: "The crucified little child, nailed to the big cross, is me. I cannot get loose. I am watched by God, not the good God, but *The Committee* who reminds me of the last judgment. The eyes of *The Committee* are God's angels sent from heaven to watch that I don't get his blessing."

Here we see how Olav employed his metaphors to describe a psychological position of being trapped. He was both being watched and condemned by *The Committee*; further, he was denied God`s blessing for which he also longed.

This God representation, in many ways modeled through his religious upbringing by his perceived demanding father, eventually started to be transformed as Olav began to entertain the possibility that God might be different. This process of transformation obviously had multiple sources. Significant for Olav were his experiences in the pastoral counseling sessions with the hospital chaplain in the church room. Counseling sessions with the hospital chaplain were offered on a voluntary basis to all the patients. Olav felt the chaplain and two of his therapists were allies against the power of *The Committee*. With them, Olav could express his anger at God. He said that he felt God had turned away from him, abandoned him, and shown contempt for him. The chaplain encouraged him to give words to his feelings. When Olav and the chaplain's staff were gathered together in the church, strong feelings surfaced, and Olav screamed loudly: "Fuck you, God!" When reflecting on this afterwards in his diary, he wrote: "I don't know what I felt most strongly: God's betrayal or my own. I wept and sobbed loudly. I let go of my despair and anger. I felt calm afterwards."

Olav's mixed emotions, partly expressed through feelings about betrayal, nevertheless moved him toward resolution and a sense of calm. He discovered that some of his feelings related to God had sources within himself.

Olav's slowly growing ability to give words to and express his feelings marked a significant change. This change was related also to new "here and now" relational experiences.[22] He gradually dared to experience and express anger at a number of individuals: his parents, the individual therapist, a fellow male patient, and God. Along the way, he struggled to summon the resistance necessary to reduce the power of *The Committee* and to open himself to new ways of understanding. In his relations with therapists and group members, he also hesitated to admit and accept his growing vitality. He reported he feared he would lose the comforting he received from fellow patients and staff if he developed more autonomy and maturity. This resistance illustrated his developmental arrest.[23]

In the last phase of treatment, Olav gradually became more capable of mentalizing his anger and longings without falling apart in shame and guilt. However, in the relaxation group, he had an outburst of rage and anger toward *The Committee* for having damaged his life. The anger was followed by deep weeping. The individual therapist present at the time identified this episode as a turning point in Olav's treatment.

In the existential reflection group, different sources of guilt were addressed. Olav struggled with guilt and shame related to his forbidden longings for his mother. He eventually could take responsibility for turning his back on God, neglecting values for which he wanted to stand, and acting in ways that had offended himself and others. Olav realized that he no longer needed to fall back on *The Committee* to dissociate from his feelings of anger. He said, with great insight: "Now I have the responsibility. The voices of *The Committee* are my own lack of mercy to me."

Olav's comments point to the development of a new capacity for self-reflective discernment by accepting the responsibility for his life and integrating the projected feelings. He attained new insights. He began to resolve his split feeling and express his ambivalence. He became more nuanced toward his parents. He no longer treated his mother as an all-good object, and he expressed his anger over what he experienced as her abandonment of him when she divorced his father and left home. Moreover, he empathized more with his father's own psychological pain without having to let go of his own angry feelings. At the time of discharge, Olav experienced increased anxiety. He expressed his anxiety about *The Committee* coming back when he faced painful experiences of loneliness. His strong resistance to accepting and identifying with his achieved strength and to face his recovery was addressed.

Outcome

During his former hospitalizations, Olav was diagnosed with a long-lasting depressive disorder and psychotic episodes. His condition was assessed as chronic with only short periods of symptom relief when he felt safe in hospital environments. Compared to the very high pre-treatment global scores for symptom distress, after his treatment at Modum Bad Clinic with the VITA model, his symptoms were reduced to moderate levels at post-treatment and to sub-clinical levels at the one-year follow up. This was a remarkable improvement compared to the regular relapses Olav had experienced after former hospitalizations. He also achieved reliable improvement in interpersonal functioning. At the one-year follow up, there was no Axis I diagnosis.

On Axis II, Olav no longer met diagnostic criteria for paranoid and borderline personality disorders, but had some narcissistic traits.[24] Olav reported that *The Committee* had been dismissed to the distant mountains. The fear, guilt, and rage toward God were diminished, more nuanced, and integrated with feelings of closeness and tenderness toward a benevolent God. According to his own goals before treatment, he felt he had achieved his freedom. He also expressed his experience of being received and accepted as Olav. He no longer experienced himself as being imprisoned in *an Occupied Land*. He began to sense what he described as inner peace, and he expressed with increasing confidence that his faith was his own and that his inner peace was received by grace. In Olav's inner struggle and transformation, he felt empowered by rituals he carefully chose for himself and employed in the hospital chapel. He expressed that he had found his way to a merciful God for whom he desperately had longed through years of struggle. During the treatment process he regularly went to the chapel and sang this classical hymn as his prayer:

Lead, Kindly Light, amid the encircling gloom.
Lead Thou me on.
The night is dark, and I am far from home.
Lead Thou me on.
Keep Thou my feet; I do not ask to see
the distant scene—one step enough for me.

This hymn beautifully captures Olav's feelings as he concluded his treatment.

DISCUSSION: THE MEANING AND FUNCTION OF METAPHORS

As the presentation of Olav's case demonstrates, metaphors played a significant role in his self-experience and in his ability to work through emotionally charged issues in the therapeutic process. In the following discussion, we look more closely at a several crucial metaphors this patient created in his struggle to achieve autonomy and to reach his expressed goal: freedom to be Olav.

As mentioned in the introduction, our point of departure is the understanding of the function of metaphors in psychotherapy developed by Rizzuto. For our discussion of the Olav case, two related perspectives are important. The first addresses the *genesis and sources* of personal meaningful metaphors. The second establishes the *interpersonal and communicative significance* of the metaphors. The description of the fourfold sources of the VITA Treatment, related to existential, narrative, developmental-relational and affect layers, gives a plausible understanding of how metaphors can be meaningfully used to explore Olav's inner world. As to the first point, Rizzuto writes: ". . . the metaphors we create to talk about what is ineffable about ourselves refer directly or indirectly to scenes with four elements: ourselves, directly or in disguised forms; significant others; a particular type of psychic event; and the depiction of an interpersonal experience. This conception suggests that personal metaphors are very crowded events, layered with history and stories."[25]

With this observation, Rizzuto reminds us of the multiple and diverse sources of our personal metaphors. She also argues in favor of their deep and complex dynamic roots and interpersonal functions. These issues are clearly demonstrated in the case of Olav.

As to the second point, Rizzuto says, "All metaphors, regardless of their unquestionable function, are created for another person, an intended listener who must hear them. The listener is always a real person, or a person one believes is real, such as God. Be it in internal discourse or in explicit verbal communication, the metaphor is addressed to another, even if to oneself."[26]

Rizzuto's claim is insightful. She observes the interpersonal and communicative function of personal metaphors. As a form of silent language, they are loaded with meaning and, as such, they search for a listener who will try to understand their messages.

Both perspectives are highly relevant in our discussion of the case of Olav. His ability to create sophisticated, multilayered, and expressive metaphors gives ample evidence to the fundamental role of metaphors in psychotherapy as Rizzuto has described. Let us look at some of the key metaphors Olav used.

The Committee

The core metaphor of *The Committee* gave shape to and expressed a partly conscious, partly unconscious, inner dynamic of vital defensive importance to Olav. At the same time, this metaphor functioned as a powerful way of expressing his inner struggle with his therapists, his surroundings in the group, and with himself. Regarding the communicative meaning, Olav's struggle with *The Committee* demonstrated throughout the process how this metaphor asked for "an intended listener who must hear them." *The Committee* communicated a powerful set of symbolic meanings to the responsible therapist and fellow patients, as well as to Olav himself and to God. Let us now explore in some depth the genetic and dynamic experiences that sustained Olav's most powerful metaphor.

A key quote from Olav's own reflections on *The Committee* is found in his comments on his first drawing of God in the art therapy session. The picture is dominated by a big blue cross with a crucified child at the center. The color is mainly black with five huge dark eyes watching in the sky. However, the right side includes a bright yellow area with five persons in it. Olav said,

> I have not painted God the right way. I did paint what he has done to me. In the light area are people, my family, living in the blessing of God. The crucified little child, nailed to the big cross, is me. I cannot get loose. I am watched by God, not the good God, but *The Committee* who remind me of the last judgment. The eyes of *The Committee* are God's angels sent from heaven to watch that I don't get his blessing. I shall not be given a good life because I have turned away from God. The darkness is despair, sorrow, and rage. I have to hang on the cross to carry the pain and cleavage in my family. I feel guilty for having moved away from God, because I will not kneel to ask for forgiveness. To do so would imply being engulfed for the sake of the others.

With these comments on his relation to *The Committee*, Olav gave a vivid and comprehensive illustration of what Rizzuto said when she underlined that "personal metaphors are very crowded events, layered with history and stories." She pointed out that such metaphors "appear . . . to be complex narrative events that must be allowed to unfold if they are to convey the rich experiential processes the patient is trying to articulate."[27]

Thus, as Rizzuto's comments helped us understand, Olav's reflections presented a complex web of metaphors and story lines that gradually unfolded their meaning and functions during the therapeutic process. In a certain sense, it is fair to say that the entire analytic process in the case of Olav circled around the gradual uncovering of the dynamic-relational genesis, the affects, and the personal existential concerns of this crucial metaphor. The gradual uncovering of such dynamic and existential concerns also corresponded with Rizzuto's point of view when she stated that "the entire analytic process is metaphorical and is carried out by the progressive exploration and understanding of the genetic and dynamic experiences that sustain the verbal and enacted metaphors that organize the patient`s psychic life."[28] As such, Rizzuto helped us to see that Olav's use of metaphors in his treatment was of crucial importance to communicate his inner relational dynamics. These metaphors were deeply connected to his life story and to his existential and religious concerns. They organized his psychic life.

The Persecuting God

Relating the overall interpretative perspective above to more specific issues in Olav's experience, we observe the close dynamic relation between *The Committee* and Olav's God image. Olav obviously belongs to a group of individuals Rizzuto described as those who struggle with a demanding, harsh God who they would like to be rid of if they were not convinced of his existence and power.[29] Prevailing characteristics of the God representation viewed in a developmental perspective included Olav's early life conditions and traumas. These contributed to his elaboration of a particular God representation and are powerfully expressed in the metaphor *The Persecuting God*. This God representation was closely intertwined with, and functioned as, a significant and powerful part of *The Committee*. Olav experienced the voices of *The Committee* as sent from God as guardians with cold, watching eyes to insure that Olav did not receive God's blessing. Thus, they condemned him to suffer alone in darkness, excluded from his family. He faced *existential isolation* (loneliness) and *guilt*. *Narrative* sources for the metaphor obviously can be attributed to his religious culture. Even though pathological, the metaphor contributed to significant meaning construction, filling needs for defense against threatening and painful events and feelings.

As consultants to Olav's case, both Rizutto and William Meissner[30] suggested that *The Committee* also might serve as a defense against forbidden incestuous longings, which were awakened at his first breakdown and dynamically contributed to the emergence of *The Committee*.

What can be seen as the developmental and dynamic background for this intertwining of *The Committee* and God? *The Persecuting God* and *The Committee* seemed to have traits from Olav's father and his father's God. The first drawing of his father showed the father as hiding behind a stone wall, locked in a triangle symbolizing God. Olav commented, "A stone wall; father is behind the wall where he hides because of his own helplessness and weakness, making him unable to show care and compassion. His face is divided; the red is warm feeling and humor, the black is heaviness and helplessness. The triangle is his God; it fills the space not giving room for gods other than him alone."

This complex and conflictive relation to his father, together with a strict religious upbringing and traumatic experiences in relation to his parents' divorce and his mother's abandonment of the family, may have contributed to a powerful image of a condemning and persecuting God. At the same time, several elements indicate a split in Olav's God representation. Olav gave strong and repeated expressions of longings for another God, one who was not represented by *The Committee*: a merciful, loving God modeled on his longtime longing for his mother.

We hypothesized that adult life conflicts had led to Olav's breakdown because of his underlying, impaired, and highly vulnerable self-image and self-structure.[31] His defenses regressed to a paranoid and borderline level, including splitting, projective identification, denial, primitive idealization, and devaluation which all contributed to exaggerating negative aspects of self and others. Thus, Olav's defensive operations led to his inner creation of *The Committee, The Persecuting God*, and *The Crucified Self* which he experienced with panic attacks, shame, guilt, and severe depression. These creations seemed to help him avoid aggression toward his parents by projecting the aggressive feelings onto *The Persecuting God*, thereby making it possible for him to turn his anger against himself.

Olav's God image was split into a harsh, punishing God, and a benevolent God: he both longed to be rid of this God and for closeness to this God, who he described as "the light in the gloom of his inner darkness." His harsh God image and his father image seemed to be fused in *The Committee*. Any thought of open revolt against his father fueled his guilt feelings. He was anxious lest he add to the burden of his father's suicidal despair when his wife left him. Both Rizzuto and William Meissner, as consultants to Olav's case, proposed that Olav needed *The Committee* as a defense, until he had developed a milder superego and a more compassionate sense of self. The defense seemed affectively rooted in excessive guilt and shame related to his forbidden longings and arrested rage.

The Crucified Self

Olav's attempts to live up to his father's perfectionist standards led to chronic self-attack, not only by forbidding positive feelings, but also by the constant guilt he felt before *The Committee*, who condemned him for moving away from God. Metaphorically speaking, he felt crucified, nailed, and bleeding as a little child on a big cross, doomed to suffer for the break-up of his family. He also used "sacrificed" as a metaphor about himself with the Biblical roots of this metaphor reflecting his deep painful feelings of being abandoned and left alone.

On the *existential* level, the metaphor carries information of an excessive guilt burden and a need for atonement. The metaphor is a part of a *narrative* context in which Olav identified himself with the main story from the New Testament: Jesus was crucified, carrying all our sins to save us. *Dynamically*, from a self-psychological point of view, we might see that he not only seeks his twinship self-object "Jesus," but also becomes him. He becomes his own chosen personalized metaphor. In an object relational perspective, Olav took on the guilt instead of going through a de-idealization process in relation to his parents to achieve autonomy. The narrative may contain affects like guilt, anxiety, possible inward anger, and shame, just as the cross might be seen as the cross of shame. On the other hand, in his own perception, the metaphor expresses the burden of taking on guilt in order to save his family.

Occupied Land

Olav's use of the self-representing metaphor *Occupied Land* reflects an existential situation in which he was invaded and deprived of his freedom.

An invaded self is a diminished self, which contributed to his experience of a lost and unlived life. The metaphor is narratively rooted in the language of war and constructed as meaningful information about Olav's existential experience of being at war, on the battlefield. The enemies are dynamically aspects of himself. A key question is, "Who is the narrator?" The battlefield is an intrapsychic battle between introjects, where different self states are struggling. The core affects seem to be fear, arrested anger, and blocked positive affects.

The Wolf

Existential issues reflected in the metaphor of *The Wolf* seem to relate to the ultimate concern of freedom. Olav wanted to be himself as Olav and not merely a prolongation of his father`s ambitions. Narrative parts of the wolf metaphor may stem from the culture and stories told and read to Olav when he was growing up. He was reading Hermann Hesse's *Steppenwolf* while he was in treatment. This novel obviously delivered important metaphorical material, which helped him deal with his painful inner conflicts related to forbidden feelings and longings. Psychoanalytically, the wolf metaphor is not new. It is famous through Freud's *The Wolf Man* case study, which helped Freud elaborate on his theory of psychosexual development.[32] Dynamic and relational sources can promote further development in the understanding of the metaphor. As we understand these sources, they can be related to Olav's identification with his mother. Seen from this perspective, the metaphor of *The Wolf* attests to Olav's efforts to break free from his arrested autonomy. As such, *The Wolf* is related to his unresolved psychosexual issues, separation anxiety,[33] and persecutory God representation. Identifying *affects* addresses issues such as wildness, aggression, and sexuality, which in Olav's case were related to his need for expression of repressed and denied disowned affects.

CONCLUSION

In this chapter we have argued that, in the VITA treatment program, patients' ways of expressing themselves and their sufferings through powerful personal metaphors provide a rich source of interpretative material that moves beyond classical psychiatric language. Key metaphors in this case study articulate the inner landscape of dynamic conflicts and affects in a profound way. Our analysis has shed light on an existential struggle of the self and on ongoing transformations of rigid self- and object representations, both striving for and fighting against recovery. When clinicians address metaphors in therapy, they may uncover powerful and liberating means that patients use to interpret their existential suffering. Patients create their own significant and deeply personal metaphors that may serve a crucial role in a recovery process.[34]

Studying the self in the process of expressing suffering and in the process of recovery through analyzing the use of metaphors is an emerging area in psychotherapy.[35] By exploring the psychological roots of this universe of meaning and validating metaphors as a significant way of patients' self-description, clinicians can observe how a transformative process can be set in motion. The patient's use of metaphors may be seen as an agent of change, as the patient digests the layers of information carried by his or her own personalized metaphors. When patients take part in discovering the information the metaphors carry and they learn to differentiate and address the layers of affects attached to the metaphors, the patients will demonstrate an increased ability to mentalize. Impairment in mentalization involves impairment in reflective functioning. As Malitzky stated of Olav, ". . . from the point of view of mentalization, we can hypothesize that an environmental failure led Olav to a defensive retreat from reflective functioning."[36]

When Olav suffered under the weight of being *crucified* and *imprisoned* and experienced himself as an *occupied land*, he was out of control, not in charge, and immobilized. He was not able to act as an agent and to take charge in his own life. When his therapists invited Olav to explore the metaphoric construction of meaning, they enabled Olav to develop a deeper self-understanding, experience self-acceptance, and display increased reflexive functioning. As Rizzuto stated, "All modalities of representations include an affective valuation," and listening carefully to patients' metaphors allows access to the "ineffable experiences of the mind."[37] The different modalities of representations carry their own "affective valuation" and there are connections between them that form a personal narrative. This narrative contributes to individual meanings by which a person may live. These meanings have an affective impact and, through the therapists' inquiry about the patient's metaphors, the patient can transform these images and the rigidly held world view associated with them.

According to psychotherapy research, the main question of research should be, "What specific factors in psychotherapy are responsible for change?"[38] Among professionals who have commented on this case study, Malitzky made the argument that ". . . the promotion of mentalization in the VITA program was *the* essential element in Olav's cure."[39] Olav`s extensive use of metaphors, which were highly charged affective representations of his inner drama, conveyed "the rich experiential processes the patient is trying to articulate."[40] In other words, "the metaphor becomes a source of self-discovery, a way of refinding our feelings."[41]

In the Case of Olav, his growing ability to mentalize around the affectively charged self-and God-related metaphors appears to have been a crucial factor responsible for change. He was able to track his dynamic roots and narrative maladaptive conclusions from his past in a safe therapeutic culture of inquiry. He could increasingly integrate and own his affects, and he became less anxiety driven. He was no longer, metaphorically speaking, *persecuted* and *crucified.* He was able to bring a new, liberating meta-perspective to the metaphors he had been using.

Our discussion demonstrated the vital importance of paying attention to patients' metaphors. The analysis proved the validity of Rizzuto's statement when she suggested that "*personal metaphors are very crowded events, layered with history and stories.*"[42] Having focused our attention on Olav's metaphors, we hope with this single case study to have contributed to future research that will deepen our understanding of our patients' suffering as well as augment their resources for recovery. Thus, we encourage psychotherapists to cultivate the wisdom of listening carefully to patient's metaphors. For, as Rizzuto wisely said, "All metaphors, regardless of their unquestionable function, are created for another person, an intended listener who must hear them. The listener is always a real person, or a person one believes is real, such as God."[43]

DISCUSSION

Ana-María Rizzuto

This rich paper presents: 1) the *unique* therapeutic model of the VITA program at Modum Bad Sanatorium in Vikersund, Norway; 2) a conceptualization of the processes of transformation of representations, affects, and self-appraisal achieved by the program; and 3) Olav's case to illustrate how the model works and its therapeutic effectiveness.

THE VITA MODEL

The VITA Model is an *original* program to treat patients suffering from religious and existential issues interfering with their life. It is a short-term treatment program involving three separate periods of three weeks and a final evaluation a year later.

The treatment focuses on the articulation—mentalization—and transformation of the patient's representations and affects. Its foundation is psychodynamic in the best sense of the term. Patients are selected not based on DSM diagnostic categories but on the careful assessment of conflictual existential and religious struggles that besiege them. Such criteria allow the VITA therapists to treat patients with severe diagnoses after some preparation to get them ready to benefit from the program.

The VITA core idea consists in creating a "culture of inquiry" for its participants. The principle of abstinence guides the entire model: the therapist does not resort to religious involvement, but remains exclusively within the dynamic understanding of the person's experiential reality as the only means to facilitate *his [the person's] own psychic transformation* under the guidance offered by the program. This approach involves an absolute respect for the *psychic reality* of each patient, the patient's pathogenic conflicts, representations, and affective experiences. Such respect is based on the conviction that the psychic reality of each individual not only is the source of pathology, but also is endowed with the potential to be transformed and used in the healing of the self. In other words, the VITA Model implies that pathology results from the thwarting of developmental processes that have never completely surrendered their search for redress, transformation, and healing.

The groups that constitute the essence of the program offer multiple approaches to integrate private dynamic processes and to articulate existential experiences in open exchanges with fellow sufferers and therapists. In this manner, from the start, the patient is invited to share, in actual conversations with others and in art groups, the experiences, memories, and representations the patient has never before articulated for himself. The diverging and converging different groups appear to me as a very efficacious way of assisting the person in articulating his or her experiences in several modalities, thus offering a welcome *redundancy* that facilitates the patient's consideration of the same experience from multiple angles, in private as well as in the presence of others.

CONCEPTUALIZATION OF THE PROCESS OF TRANSFORMATION

For each patient, the process of *actualizing* in a functionally integrated series of groups and exchanges the representational and affective processes that contribute to his psychic suffering facilitates two processes. First, it allows the progressive integration of exposed and now re-experienced and examined representations and feelings into the experience of the self alone and in the presence of others, thus contributing to psychical change. Second, the sharing with the community of patients and staff of previously private thoughts, feelings, convictions, and self-narratives contribute significantly to their integration with the *reality* the person shares with others and the progressive concomitant feeling of being actually known as the person s/he is. The willingness of the participant in the VITA program to submit personal experiences to the scrutiny of others spurs and facilitates the articulation of previously inchoate beliefs and fantasies transforming them into conscious and mentalized processes endowed with perspective, comparison, and verbal expressions of the experiential self and its biographical underpinnings. The most critical element of the VITA program rests with the patient assuming *responsibility* for his/her own transformation. No one in particular heals the patient's suffering. The patient willingly and actively participates in the processes of inquiry, self-exposure, and private and public articulation of thoughts and feelings shared with others. The combination of biographically repeated narratives, drawings of significant objects including the divinity, and exploration of intensely felt personal metaphors allow for a rich and multifaceted exploration of representations and feelings. The inclusion of religious representations and experiences as required by the treatment model indicates to the patient that his/her faith and existential predicaments are a critical component of who the patient is as an individual in his/her immediate and transcendent context. The benefit of these multiple explorations of every aspect of the VITA resident's life contributes to a new *personal knowledge* different from anything the person experienced before. Such knowledge is mediated by repeated processes of accessing the patient's representations and feelings and submitting them to a new articulation under the patient's own responsibility.

HOW THE MODEL WORKS AND ITS THERAPEUTIC EFFECTIVENESS

Olav's case presents the processes involved in Olav's psychic improvement and documents the *objective* changes in his psychological tests and his representational world. Olav had become a hospitalized chronic patient for seven years with a DSM diagnosis of major depression with psychotic features and borderline, paranoid, and narcissistic traits. He had made suicidal attempts. After the completion of the VITA treatment, his psychological testing at the one-year follow up documented no DSM's Axis I and II diagnoses, but did show some persistent narcissistic traits. I learned from another publication[44] that five years after his treatment Olav had maintained his gains, had remarried, and was working. What processes account for such remarkable change? In "Dissolution of 'The Committee': Mentalization and Psychic Transformation in the Case of Olav," Max Malitzky comments that "the promotion of mentalization in the VITA program was *the* essential element in Olav's cure" in a patient who had retreated defensively from reflective functioning. Malitzky concludes that "issues of faith provided the *medium* for transformation of self and object representations and the growth of mentalization."[45]

I want to reflect on the connections between the mentalizing function and representation as I have understood it and as it is so clearly illustrated in Olav's case. Mentalization is defined as the "*genetically* prepared, experience-expectant capacity to spontaneously, implicitly, *and* explicitly ascribe, interpret, and represent intentionality, meaning, and mental states"[46] (my italics) perceived in oneself and others. It is a biological and psychical capacity present, in my appraisal, from the beginning of life and mediated by *perceptual* processes and indispensable *biological and relational needs*. The refinement of this mental function evolves during development; however, it is clear to me that the intentionality of the other is registered *from the start* by the mediation of our senses so delicately attuned to the affective involvement of the other with us. Mentalization proper, defined as a developmental achievement and therapeutic tool, involves the *conscious* participation of the individuals involved.

The limitations of *conscious* mentalization in a person such as Olav stem from the pathological developmental and defensive inhibition of its reflective component but not its complete suppression. Mentalization processes of obscure or explicit attribution of relatedness and intention are present from the beginning of life and never disappear. They always eventuate in the formation of complex and varied representational processes at many levels from somatic to fantasized imagery that are registered as memorial processes, mostly unconscious or preconscious, which are potentially retrievable in different modalities. Conscious articulation of such processes requires verbalization frequently in the form of complex metaphors. Such metaphors may also have pictorial form and imaginative organization. Their conscious elaboration with the help of parents, other people, and therapists permits the articulation of the *reflective* component of the mentalizing processes.

All this is to say that Olav did not lack the capacity to create powerful and rich representations and to attribute intentions to his internal objects. His powerful private imagery—the eyes of God, *the Committee*, the *crucified child*, the *Inner Wolf*—were for him compelling, even if pathogenic, *representations* of the divine being and of himself portraying powerful *interpretations* of his state of being as a self in relation to the intentions of his family and his God. He *believed* his own mental processes, thought they were objectively real, and was unable to submit them to critical examination. In other words, his mental operations in relation to his self functioned at many levels as "psychic equivalents" in the terminology of Target and Fonagy.[47] They became organizing convictions about his being Olav, a prisoner of the persecutory God he had created and found in the traumas of his growing up when competing with a perfect dead brother and parental harshness, disharmony, and abandonment. The powerful continuous presence of his God-favored dead brother and the absence of adults who could assist him in understanding his representational world did not permit him to articulate his memories, fantasies, and interpretations of them and the intentions of others into the kind of God he desired to have or into a was self acceptable to himself.

The VITA treatment offered him multiple avenues to articulate, evaluate, feel, and express in different modalities—drawings, writing, and personal and group participation—the dominant representational themes in the form of convictions, imagery, and metaphors that up to that point had dominated his experience of the world, God, and himself. He could not have changed without the constant invitation to give his internal representations external articulation to himself and to others in the visual and verbal forms. The most important aspect of the VITA program consisted in conveying to Olav in words and through the requisite participation in all aspects of the program that the staff wanted him to know himself and to know himself even as they also offered him all the support he needed to achieve such a difficult task.

From the theoretical point of view, all the required activities of the VITA program have something in common with Freud's original injunction to his patients to free associate, that is, to allow their minds to uncover what emerges in them, to capture it with their attention, and to articulate this into words or drawings shared with the therapist. The process of mentalization, in particular of the severe pathological and complex representations Olav harbored in his mind, *cannot* take place without the previous internal *revival* of imagery, thoughts, fantasies, sensations, and bodily experiences from the past and the present that form part of representational processes preserved as personal memories related to the self, be it in an obscure and inchoate manner or as explicit and overpowering images such as *The Committee* or the crucified child. The revival in the presence of others and the exposure of internal representations to the patient's view is the first step that makes it possible for the patient to create the necessary psychic distance to give these internal representations a second look and to experience these representations not in the isolation of the patient's own mind, but in the presence of the other. The benign therapeutic other and the VITA milieu of inquiry, acceptance, and persistent exploration of his representations offered Olav the possibility of giving a second look at his representational reality: himself, his God, his parents, and his helpers and fellow patients. In this manner he progressively developed the capacity to give most of them a new objective reality that permitted him to reconsider them, feel them anew, and, most importantly, to assume responsibility for his psychic productions as his own. He no longer needed to be the plaything of a representational world dominated by *The Committee* whose searching eyes gave him no rest.

In brief, I wanted to make explicit that the process of mentalization cannot occur unless the patient is able to attend to his own psychic representations and find a way of expressing them in one form or another. In the end for mentalization to occur the partners involved in the therapeutic process must find a way of articulating them verbally and reaching some shared understanding of their meaning and their connection, or lack thereof, within a jointly articulated actual reality.

Finally, Olav's case demonstrates with particular clarity the inseparable relation between the conception of oneself and the God one experiences as real. Olav said it very clearly when he was able to take some command of his psychic life and to look at himself and his God with the new eyes of his VITA experience: "Now I have the responsibility. The voices of *The Committee* are my own lack of mercy to me."

I thank the authors for sharing with us this fascinating case.

NOTES

1. Ana-María Rizzuto, "Metaphors of a Bodily Mind," *Journal of American Psychoanalytic Association* 10 (2001): 22–49; "Psychoanalysis: The Transformation of the Subject by the Spoken Word," *Psychoanalytic Quarterly*, LXXII (2003).

2. Rizzuto, "Psychoanalysis: The Transformation."

3. Andre Green, *On Private Madness* (London: The Hogarth Press Ltd., 1986) 295.

4. Rizzuto, "Psychoanalysis: The Transformation," 556.

5. "Olav" is a pseudonym. All identifying factors of the actual patient have been changed/removed in this narrative.

6. Stålsett, Gry, Leif G. Engedal, and Arne Austad. "Response to Commentaries on 'The Persecuting God and the Crucified Self,'" *Pragmatic Case Studies in Psychotherapy* 6, 2, 5 (2010).

7. Scott Richards, James Jones, and Max S. Malitzky. See *Pragmatic Case Studies in Psychotherapy,* http://libraries.rutgers,edu, 6, Mod.2.

8. Psychic equivalence refers to the phenomenon in which a person thinks that just because they are thinking something, it automatically is true. Flashbacks are an extreme example, and intolerance of alternative perspectives is a more ordinary one. (Anthony W. Bateman and Peter Fonagy, Handbook of Mentalizing in Mental Health Practice, American Psychiatric Association, 2012).

9. Gry Stålsett et al., "Existential Dynamic Therapy (VITA) for Treatment-Resistant Depression with Cluster C Disorder: Match Comparison to Treatment as Usual," *Psychotherapy Research* 22 (2012).

10. Stålsett et al. "Existential Dynamic."

11. The VITA project was developed in 1998, and Ana-María Rizzuto, John McDargh, David Wulff, James Jones, William Meissner, Donald Capps, Robert Dykstra, and Irvin D. Yalom were all consulted in the first phase.

12. Psychoanalytic object relations theories may be defined as those that place the internalization, structuralization, and clinical reactivation (in the transference) of the earliest dyadic object relations at the center of motivational formulations. The infant

internalizes the relationship between the self and the significant other (parental figure) in the form of a self-image (self representation) interacting with an object image (object representation). This internal structure replicates in the intrapsychic world both the real and fantasized relationships with significant others. See Otto Kernberg, *International Dictionary of Psychoanalysis* (New York: NY: MacMillan Reference USA, 2005.) According to the object relational perspective, we build experiences of new relationships upon earlier patterns of relatedness to our primary objects. The original contribution from Rizzuto is her research on the development and function of the God representation, a fantasized relationship entering the intrapsychic world of the child in the separation - individuation phase of development. Elaborating on this theory, Rizzuto is inspired from Donald Winnicott who regarded "*the transitional space* as *the locus where God comes to existence*. The process in therapy is thus to identify and differentiate the inner representation of God from its dynamic rootedness in other inner representations and to examine similarities and differences between self, parental and God representations." Donald Winnicott, "Transitional Objects and Transitional Phenomena," *International Journal of Psychoanalysis* (1953); Rizzuto, *The Birth of the Living God* (Chicago: The University of Chicago Press, 1979) 177; D. W. MacKenzie, "The Symbolic Parent Versus Actual Parent Approaches in the Examination of Similarities between Parent and God Concepts" PhD diss., United States International University, 1987.

13. Rizzuto. *The Birth* (Chicago: The University of Chicago Press, 1979).

14. The task in therapy, within the framework of *a culture of inquiry* (a core concept in VITA), is to explore how existential concerns in focus at a given moment are emotionally charged and often tied up with inner representations. Dynamically, inner conflicts around existential and religious issues—like affects—trigger anxiety, shame and guilt, and the need for defensive operations, i.e. projection and denial. In the Vita Treatment Model, we identify and share existential issues at the end of every week to apply a broad perspective or "bird's eye" view on the self and the therapy process. This weekly practice develops the art of "meta-reflection," creating distance from a patient's emotional turmoil and enhancing his or her coping and insight. Stålsett, Gry, Arne Austad, Torte Gude, and Egil Martinsen, "Existential Issues and Representation of God in Psychotherapy," *Psyche & Geloof* 21 (2010); Ludwig Binswanger, *Being-in-the-World: Selected Papers of Ludwig Binswanger* (New York, London: Basic Books,1963); Menard Boss, *Psychoanalysis & Daseinanalysis* (New York: Basic Books, 1963); Martin Heidegger, *Being and Time* (New York: Harper & Row, 1927); Irvin Yalom, *Existential Psychotherapy* (New York: Basic Books, 1980).

15. Affect regulation entails the capacity to control and modulate affective responses. A healthy affect regulation depends upon an integration of affects. The Vita program addresses how affects are organized toward the inner objects and how they are connected to existential concerns. In order to develop *affective capacity*, the Affect Consciousness Interview (ACI) is used to assess and help build the patient's consciousness, tolerance, and expression of nine basic affects. See Stålsett, Gry, Leif G. Engedal, and Arne Austad, "The Persecuting God and the Crucified Self," *Pragmatic Case Studies in Psychotherapy* 6 (2010): 55, appendix expanded version of the ACI Jon Monsen, et al., "Affects and Affect Consciousness: Initial Experience

with the Assessment of Affect Integration," *Journal of Psychotherapy Practice and Research* 5 (1996). Silvan Tomkins, "Script Theory," in *The Emergence of Personality*, ed. Jonathan Aronoff et al. (New York: Springer, 1987); Donald Nathanson, *Shame and Pride: Affect, Sex and the Birth of Self* (New York: Norton and Company, 1992; Allan Schore, *Affect Regulation and the Origin of the Self. The Neurobiology of Emotional Development* (Hillsdale, NJ: Lawrence Erlbaum Associates Inc. Publishers, 1994); Leigh McCullough-Vaillant, "The Next Step in Short-term Dynamic Psychotherapy," *Psychotherapy* 31 (1994): 642–654; Monsen et al., "Affects and Affect Consciousness," *Journal of Psychotherapy Practice and Research* 5 (1996): 238–249; Jon Monsen and Kristi Monsen, "Affects and Affect Consciousness: A Psychotherapy Model Integrating Silvan Tomkins's Affect- and Script Theory Within the Framework of Self Psychology," in *Pluralism in Self Psychology: Progress in Self Psychology,* ed. Arnold Goldberg (Hillsdale, NJ: The Analytic Press 1999).

16. At the core of the narrative approach in psychotherapy is the argument that human beings need to be understood, and to understand themselves, as creators of meaning. It is through narratives that the process of meaning making is found, developed, and changed. In narrative work, the aim is to detect and articulate key narratives, or repetitive life narratives, and monitor them for closer reflection. *Psychoeducation* about narrative work, that is information about affects and existential issues, precedes each repeated writing of the patient's life story. Patients are supposed to write narratives three times during the course of therapy, each time following a sequence of drawing inner images of self, father, mother, and God. Different ways of conceptualizing a life story elicit different emotional processes (e.g. grief, rage, and shame) and different existential concerns such as loneliness, guilt, meaninglessness, freedom, and more. If spirituality is understood as a search for the sacred, stories and *metaphors* may reflect the ways the person negotiates his or her search for the sacred. This can be longing, doubts, experiences of the role of God in personal strivings, etc. The religious beliefs of significant others may be interwoven, explicitly or implicitly, in the shared narratives and reflected in affectively loaded and culturally influenced representations and metaphors. Investigating narrative roots and meaning making, within the use of a metaphor, may illuminate a hidden symbolic message that is waiting to be understood. These narratives can illuminate a patient's life history, cultural background, and possible traumatic experiences that have contributed to the choice of language and metaphors they use. Jerome Bruner, 1986; Hubert Hermans, "Self-Narrative as Meaning Construction: The Dynamics of Self-Investigation," *Journal of Clinical Psychology* 55 (1999); James Pennebaker and Janel Segal, 1999; Donald P. Spence, *Narrative Trust and Historical Truth: Meaning and Interpretation in Psychoanalysis,* (New York: Norton, 1982); Michael White and David Epston, 1990.

17. William W. Meissner, "The Pathology of Beliefs and the Beliefs of Pathology," in *Religion and the Clinical Practice of Psychology*, ed. Edward Shafranske (Washington, DC: American Psychological Association, 1996); Jeffrey Young, 1990.

18. Jon T. Monsen et al., "Affects and Affect Consciousness;" Donald Nathanson, *Shame and Pride: Affect, Sex and the Birth of Self* (New York: Norton & Company,1996); Leigh McCullough-Vaillant, 1994; Allan Schore, *Affect Regulation and*

the Origin of the Self. The Neurobiology of Emotional Development (Hillsdale, NJ: Lawrence Erlbaum Associate Inc. Publishers, 1994); Silvan S. Tomkins, 1987.

19. Len Sperry and Edward Shafranske, *Spiritually Oriented Psychotherapy* (Washington, DC: APA, 2005).

20. Rizzuto. *The Birth* (Chicago: The University of Chicago Press, 1979).

21. Stålsett, Gry, Leif Engedal, and Arne Austad, "The Persecuting God and the Crucified Self," *Pragmatic Case Studies in Psychotherapy* 6 (2010): 49, 53, 69.

22. Ibid., 68.

23. James Masterson, *Psychotherapy of the Borderline Adult. A Developmental Approach* (New York: Brunner/Mazel Publishing, 1976); Allan N. Schore, "Affect Regulation."

24. Michael First et al. *Structured Clinical Interview for DSM-IV Axis I Disorders (SCID-1): Clinical Version.* Washington, DC: American Psychiatric Association, 1997.

25. Rizzuto, *Metaphors*, 556.

26. Ibid., 556–557.

27. Ibid., 556, 565–566.

28. Ibid., 554.

29. Rizzuto, *The Birth.*

30. Referred also to the Schreber case, William Meissner, "Pathology of Beliefs and the Beliefs of Pathology," in *Religion and the Clinical Practice of Psychology,* ed. Edward Shafranske (Washington DC: APA, 1996): 241–267.

31. James Masterson, *The Search for the Real Self: Unmasking the Personality Disorders of Our Age* (New York: The Free Press, 1988).

32. Sigmund Freud, "The History of an Infantile Neurosis," in *The Freud Reader*, ed. Peter Gay (London: Vintage, 1995).

33. Rollo May, "Freud and the Wolf Man," *Psychoanalytic Psychology* 7 (1990).

34. See George Lakoff and Mark Johnson, *Metaphors We Live By,* (Chicago: University of Chicago Press, 1980) on how new metaphors may create new reality.

35. Rizzuto, *Metaphors,* 49.

36. Max S. Malitzky, "Dissolution of 'The Committee': Mentalization and Psychic Transformation in the Case of Olav," *Pragmatic Case Studies in Psychotherapy* 6 (2010): 121.

37. Robert Elliot, "Hermeneutic Single-Case Efficacy Design," *Psychotherapy Research* 12, (2002).

38. Malitzky, "Dissolution of 'The Committee'", 121.

39. Rizzuto, *Metaphors*, 566.

40. Ibid., 556.

41. Ibid., 556.

42. Ibid., 556–557.

43. "The Persecuting God and the Crucified Self: The Vital Role of Metaphors in Psychotherapy."

44. Gry Stålsett et al., "The Persecuting God and the Crucified Self: The Case of Olav and the Transformation of his Pathological Self-Image," *Pragmatic Case Studies*

in Psychotherapy, 6, Mod. 2, Art. 1(2010): 49–100, accessed May 4, 2016, http://pcsp.libraries.rutgers.edu

45. Max S. Malitzky, "'The Committee': Mentalization and Psychic Transformation in the Case of Olav," *Pragmatic Case Studies in Psychotherapy*, 6, Mod. 2, Art. 4 (2010): 118–125, accessed May 4, 2016, http://pcsp.libraries.rutgers.edu

46. Efrain Bleiberg, "The Psychoanalytic Understanding of Mental Disorders: The Developmental Perspective," in *Textbook of Psychoanalysis,* ed. Ethel S. Person et al. (Washington, DC: American Psychiatric Publishing Inc., 2005): 182.

47. Peter Fonagy and Mary Target, "Playing with Reality: II. The Development of Psychic Reality from a Theoretical Perspective," in *International Journal of Psychoanalysis*, 1996), 77: 459–479. Retrieved April 13, 2016, from http://www.pep-web.org/document.php?id=ijp.077.0459a&type=hitlist&num=2&query=zone1%2Cparagraphs|zone2%2Cparagraphs|whocitedthis%2Capa.039.1015a

BIBLIOGRAPHY

Binswanger, Ludwig. *Being-in-the-World: Selected Papers by Ludwig Binswanger.* Translated by Jacob Needleman. New York, London: Basic Books, 1963.

Borbely, Antal F. "A Psychoanalytic Concept of Metaphor." *International Journal of Psychoanalysis* 79 (1998): 923–936.

Boss, Menard. *Psychoanalysis & Daseinanalysis.* New York, NY: Basic Books, 1963.

Bruner, Jerome. *Actual Minds, Possible Worlds.* Cambridge, MA: Harvard University Press, 1986.

Elliot, Robert. "Hermeneutic Single-Case Efficacy Design." *Psychotherapy Research* 12 (2002): 1–21.

Emmons, Robert. "Purposeful Action and the Striving for the Sacred." *Psyche & Logos* 28 (2007): 794–804.

First, Michael, B., Spitzer, Robert L., Gibbon, Miriam, and Williams, Janet B. W. *Structured Clinical Interview for DSM-IV Axis I Disorders (SCID-I): Clinician Version.* Washington, DC: American Psychiatric Association, 1997.

Fonagy, Peter, and Anthony Bateman. "Mechanism of Change in Mentalisation Based Treatment of Borderline Personality Disorder." *Journal of Clinical* Psychology 62 (2006): 411–430.

Freud, S. (1918). "From the History of an Infantile Neurosis." In *The Freud Reader* edited by Peter Gay, 400–426. London: Vintage 1995. Originally published in *The Standard Edition of the Complete Psychological Works of Sigmund Freud*, 17 (London: The Hogarth Press, 1918) 1–122.

Gilbert, Paul, Gilbert, Jean, and Irons, Chris. "Life Events, Entrapments and Arrested Anger in Depression." *Journal of Affective Disorders* 79, no. 1–3 (2004): 149–160.

Gottschalk, Louis A. "On Shame, Shame-Depression and other Depressions." *Psychiatry* 64, no. 3 (2001): 225–227.

Green, Andre. "Sources and Vicissitudes of Being in D.W. Winnicott's work." *The Psychoanalytic Quarterly* 79 (2010): 11–35.

Green, Andre. *On Private Madness.* Madison, CT: International Universities Press, Inc., 1986.

Heidegger, Martin. *Being and Time.* Translated by J. Macquarrie and E. Robinson. New York, NY: Harper & Row, 1927.

Hermans, Hubert J. M. "Self-narrative as Meaning Construction: The Dynamics of Self-Investigation." *Journal of Clinical Psychology* 55, no. 10 (1999): 1193–1211.

Hill, Peter C., Pargament, Kenneth I., Hood, Ralph W., McCullough, Michael E., Swyers, James P., Larson, David B., and Zinnbauer, Brian J. "Conceptualizing Religion and Spirituality: Points of Commonality, Points of Departure." *Journal for the Theory of Social Behavior* 30, no. 1 (2000): 51–77.

Johnson, Mark. *The Body in the Mind: The Bodily Basis of Meaning, Imagination and Reason.* Chicago, IL: University of Chicago Press, 1987.

Jones, James W. "Commentary on The Persecuting God and the Crucified Self: The Case of Olav and the Transformation of His Pathological Self-Image. Psychotherapeutic Change and Spiritual Transformation: The Interaction Effect." *Pragmatic Case Studies in Psychotherapy* 6, mod. 2, article 3 (2010): 109–11, accessed April 25, 2016, *http://pcsp.libraries.rutgers.edu/index.php/pcsp/article/view/1026/2421*

Kernberg, Otto. *International Dictionary of Psychoanalysis.* New York, NY: MacMillan Reference USA, 2005.

Lakoff, George, and Johnson, Mark. *Metaphors We Live By.* Chicago, IL: University of Chicago Press, 1980.

Malitzky, Max S. "Dissolution of 'The Committee': Mentalization and Psychic Transformation in the Case of Olav," *Pragmatic Case Studies in Psychotherapy,* http://libraries.rutgers,edu Volume 6, Module 2, Article 4, (2010): 118–124, 07–11–10.

Masterson, James F. *The search for the Real Self: Unmasking the Personality Disorders of Our Age.* New York, NY: The Free Press, 1988.

Masterson, James F. *Psychotherapy of the Borderline Adult. A Developmental Approach.* New York, NY: Brunner/Mazel Publishing, 1976.

Mathes, Eugene W., Adams, Heather E., and Davies, Ruth M. Jealousy, Loss of Relationship Rewards, Loss of Self- Esteem, Depression, Anxiety and Anger. *Journal of Personality and Social Psychology* 48 (1985): 1552–1561.

May, Robert. "Freud and the Wolf Man," *Psychoanalytic Psychology* 7, no. 2 (1990): 163–183.

MacKenzie, D.W. The Symbolic Parent versus Actual Parent Approaches in the Examination of Similarities between Parent and God Concepts. *Dissertation Abstract International,* 48 (1987): 1156B.

McCullough-Vaillant, Leigh. "The Next Step in Short-term Dynamic Psychotherapy: A Clarification of Objectives and Techniques in an Anxiety-regulating Model." *Psychotherapy* 31 (1994): 642–654.

Meissner, William W. "The Pathology of Beliefs and the Beliefs of Pathology." In *Religion and the Clinical Practice of Psychology,* edited by Edward P. Shafranske, 241–267. Washington, DC: American Psychological Association, 1996.

Monsen, Jon T., and Monsen, Kristi. "Affects and Affect Consciousness: A Psychotherapy Model Integrating Silvan Tomkins`s Affect and Script Theory Within the Framework of Self Psychology." In *Pluralism in Self Psychology: Progress in Self*

Psychology 15, edited by Arnold Goldberg, 287–306. Hillsdale, NJ: The Analytic Press.

Monsen, Jon T., Eilertsen, Dag E., Melgård, Trond, and Ødegård, Pal. "Affects and Affect Consciousness. Initial Experience with the Assessment of Affect Integration." *Journal of Psychotherapy Practice and Research* 5 (1999): 238–249.

Nathanson, Donald L. *Shame and Pride: Affect, Sex and the Birth of Self.* New York, NY: Norton & Company 1992.

Pennebaker, James W., and Janel D. Seagal. "Forming a Story: The Health Benefits of Narrative." *Journal of Clinical Psychology* 55 (1999): 1243–1254.

Rector, Lallene J. "Developmental Aspects of the Twinship Self object Need and Religious Experience." In *Pluralism in Self Psychology: Progress in Self Psychology* 16, edited by Arthur Goldberg, 257–276. Hillsdale, NJ: The Analytic Press, 2000.

Richards, Scott. (2010). "Commentary on The Persecuting God and the Crucified Self: The Case of Olav and the Transformation of His Pathological Self-Image. The Role of Religion and Spirituality in Olav`s Treatment and Recovery: Commentary on an Exemplary Case Report" *Pragmatic Case Studies in Psychotherapy* 6, 2, 2 (2010): 101–108. http://pcsp.libraries.rutgers.edu.

Rizzuto, Ana-María. "Psychoanalysis: The Transformation of the Subject by the Spoken Word." *Psychoanalytic Quarterly*, LXXII, 2003. Chicago: IL.

Rizzuto, Ana-María. "Metaphors of a Bodily Mind." *Journal of American Psychoanalytic Association*, 10 (2001): 22–49.

Rizzuto, Ana-María. *The Birth of the Living God.* Chicago: The University of Chicago Press, 1979.

Schore, Allan N. *Affect Regulation and the Origin of the Self. The Neurobiology of Emotional Development.* Hillsdale, NJ: Lawrence Erlbaum Associates Inc. Publishers, 1994.

Shafranske, Edward P. "God-representation as the Transformational Object." In *Object Relations Theory and Religion. Clinical Applications*, edited by Mark Finn and John Gartner, 57–72. Westport, CT: Praeger, 1992.

Spence, Donald P. *Narrative Truth and Historical Truth: Meaning and Interpretation in Psychoanalysis.* New York, NY: Norton, 1982.

Sperry, Len, and Edward P. Shafranske. *Spiritually Oriented Psychotherapy.* Washington, DC: American Psychological Association, 2005.

Stålsett, Gry. *Existential and Religious Issues in Psychotherapy: Development and Evaluation of a New Integrative Treatment Model (VITA) for Comorbid Depressive Disorders.* PhD diss., University of Oslo, 2012.

Stålsett, Gry, Tore Gude, Michael H. Rønnestad, and Jon T. Monsen. "Existential Dynamic Therapy ('VITA') for Treatment-Resistant Depression with Cluster C Disorder: Match Comparison to Treatment as Usual." *Psychotherapy Research,* 22, no. 5 (2012): 579–591.

Stålsett, Gry, Leif G. Engedal, and Arne Austad. "The Persecuting God and the Crucified Self: The Case of Olav and the Transformation of His Pathological Self-Image." *Pragmatic Case Studies in Psychotherapy,* http://libraries.rutgers,edu 6, Module 2, Article 1 (2010): 49–100.

Stålsett, Gry, Leif G. Engedal, and Arne Austad. "Response to Commentaries on The Persecuting God and the Crucified Self: The Case of Olav and the Transformation of His Pathological Self-Image. Reflections on Olav's Therapy: The Roles of Religious Experience, Self Psychology, and Mentalization." *Pragmatic Case Studies in Psychotherapy* 6, no. 2, http://libraries.rutgers,edu 6, Module 2, Article 5, (2010): 126–133.

Stålsett, Gry, Arne Austad, Tore Gude, and Egil Martinsen. "Existential Issues and Representation of God in Psychotherapy: A Naturalistic Study of 40 Patients in the VITA Treatment Model." *Psyche & Geloof* 21 (2010): 76–91.

Tomkins, Silvan S. "Script Theory." In *The Emergence of Personality*, edited by Jonathan Aronoff, A.I. Rabin, and Robert A. Zucker. New York, NY: Springer, 1987.

White, Michael, and David Epston. *Narrative Means to Therapeutic End*. New York, NY: Norton, 1990.

Yalom, Irvin D. "On Psychiatry and Religion." *American Journal of Psychiatry* 56, no. 3 (2002): 300–309.

Yalom, Irvin. D. *Existential Psychotherapy*. New York, NY: Basic Books, 1980.

Young, Jeffrey E. *Cognitive Therapy for Personality Disorders: A Schema Focused Approach*. Sarasota, FL: Professional Resource Exchange, 1990.

Zuckerman, Miron. *Vulnerability to Psychopathology: A Biosocial Model*. Washington, DC: American Psychological Association, 1999.

Chapter 4

The Healing Factor in Psychotherapy

An Encounter with Ana-María Rizzuto

Anthony Stern

I had a memorable meeting with Ana-María Rizzuto at the American Academy of Psychoanalysis winter 1995 meeting in Cambridge, Massachusetts, where I chaired a panel on psychoanalysis and spirituality. The next day Rizzuto gave an informal case discussion that a few of us from the panel attended. After her presentation we joined her for lunch. Meeting this petite, pleasant-looking woman in her sixties was a thorough delight, both personally and intellectually. The fact that she has sometimes been mistaken for being a nun is not surprising; she has a bit of that no-nonsense air about her, combining a serious incisiveness and a fine sense of humor.

Over lunch, we quickly found ourselves discussing the subject of what heals in psychoanalysis and psychotherapy. Rizzuto stated that there is a common misconception that the answer is love. But the main thing that cures, she said emphatically, is not love, but rather self-understanding[1] that grows out of the process of free association that leads to a growing awareness of one's fantasies in the context of therapy.

We were taken aback by Rizzuto's position. She was taking a traditional stance on a long-simmering controversy in the field. In the last thirty years or more, even quite a few diehard analysts have turned away from a central focus on "insight" and "interpretation" to a fuller appreciation of "the relationship" and its intangible elements.[2] Perhaps Rizzuto's own stance also has softened over the last few decades. But in this moment she was relishing in being old-fashioned, and it appeared that she believed passionately in what struck us as a somewhat outmoded view.

I don't think I was alone in wondering how her viewpoint could fit with her own devoted Christian position. I asked, "What's the saying in the Gospel of John . . . about how God is love and where there is love there is God . . .?" "No," Rizzuto corrected, "it's the First Epistle of John, Chapter

Four." She proceeded to give a precise quote: "God is love; and he who dwells in love dwells in God" (verse 16). But she also stood her ground. No doubt love informs the work of the psychoanalyst or therapist, she said. But it's self-understanding, not love, which makes the real difference in someone's life. And when Rizzuto spoke of understanding, she was not referring to deep spiritual insight; rather, she was speaking of learning about oneself in a psychological vein—about one's own unconscious wishes and fears and how we defend against them.

Like any engaging dialog, this one got us all to thinking. In those few minutes, Dr. Rizzuto not only championed the power of free association but also prompted us in that direction. In my case, this unfolding encounter brought my own associations back to another unexpectedly enriching encounter I had had more than twenty years earlier.

It was early May 1972. I was all of seventeen years old and completing my senior year in high school. Natalie Shapiro, a cousin of a friend, heard of my interest in spirituality and suggested that, if I ever found myself in her old teacher's neighborhood, I might like to meet him. She was an ex-student of a man nicknamed "Rudi" (aka Albert Rudolph, aka Swami Rudrananda), and she spoke warmly about him. He had an Oriental art store in downtown Manhattan, she said, and it would be worth my while dropping by just to see the first-rate art in the place. She also related that he had been born and raised in Brooklyn and had had profound contact with several teachers from the East, including Hindu swamis and Tibetan lamas.

Natalie went on to describe how Rudi had had a number of extraordinary mystical experiences, and that he taught a form of "kundalini yoga" whose purpose is to activate subtle spiritual energies within the body, in particular a powerful energy stored at the base of the spine known as "kundalini."[3] With this brief account, Natalie had fully succeeded in arousing my interest.

MEETING RUDI

A week or two after talking with Natalie, I found that I had no particular plans one balmy, leisurely Saturday. So at elevenish that morning, I took the Lexington subway down to the Astor Place stop, figuring I'd go to one or two of the spiritual book stores in the area, maybe try a macrobiotic meal at "Paradox" or "The Cauldron," and, before or after lunch, drop by Rudi's shop to meet him.

I browsed at Samuel Weiser's and East/West Books, making a few purchases, then proceeded over to Rudi's Oriental art store on 10th Street and 4th Avenue. Entering the store was like going into another world, but I can't say I took much of it in at first. I could detect a pleasing fragrance of incense within a few seconds of being there. Rudi's desk was almost all the way to the back of the large interior. I walked along an aisle crammed on either side with statues of Buddhas, bodhisattvas, and various Hindu deities. The walls displayed mountainous Chinese landscapes, Japanese drawings, elaborate Tibetan "thanka" hangings, and Persian miniatures. I wasn't surprised to learn later that this was one of the premier shops for Asian art in this country.

As I made my way to the back of the store, I saw a man with a shaved head whom I guessed was Rudi. He was wearing a light orange tee shirt, khakis, and sandals. He looked to be about 5'10" and in his early or mid-40s. He had a pronounced "Buddha belly"; his face was round and kind looking and serious, with big ears sticking out, strikingly dark eyebrows, and dark brown eyes. These eyes had a calm, clear, soft quality to them. Although I know it's silly and clichéd to say, they did twinkle. There were a few people around Rudi, including a short, old lady who turned out to be his mother.

Rudi turned and looked at me as I approached. I introduced myself and explained that Natalie had spoken of him. He noticed that I'd bought a few books, including *Meditation in Action,* by the Tibetan Buddhist teacher Trungpa Rimpoche. A few moments later I suddenly found myself blurting out, "You know you look like one of those old Zen masters in paintings." He replied, "Not Zen masters in particular, just Buddhas in general. Because I am a Buddha."

The thoughts began to form in my mind—"What an egotistical idea! No real Buddha would ever . . . ." But before this judgment-in-the-making had any chance to coalesce, Rudi proved himself to be a Buddha, at least in that living moment. He already somehow had approached a few steps in a flash; he was stroking the stubble on my chin; and he had a disarmingly humorous cross-eyed look on his face as he remarked, "*You* look like a chipmunk." We both laughed.

I asked, "What's a Buddha?" Rudi responded, "Someone who's enlightened. But of course there are degrees of enlightenment. A friend can tell you come on over, I've just cleaned my place. For him maybe it's clean, but you go and there's three inches of dust in the corners." Rudi spoke with a casual calm and a heavy Brooklyn accent. The resulting voice was interesting and appealing.

I had been meditating for an hour or more each day for the three weeks before meeting Rudi. At times while meditating I'd begun to feel buttery sensations in my chest, like quick little flows or spurts of a warm liquid. It was pleasant and a bit intriguing. (Wilhelm Reich had described this phenomenon as "streamings.") Now, standing and talking with Rudi, I was feeling these same sensations. I asked him what they meant. "It's your heart opening. First you feel the ocean, and you see it, hear it, taste it, and smell it. Then you become it." Rudi smiled. After a pause he recommended that I take a walk around to have a look at the art, and he turned his attention to one of his other visitors.

As I did what he advised and began to wander the store, the kinesthetic buttery experience in my chest intensified, both in sheer activity and in how increasingly delicious it felt. Within a minute or two I was standing still, looking down at the brick floor, and wondering at what was happening: the wonderful streaming sensations in the chest were going wild. It all but felt as if my whole chest was melting down to the floor in one big, happy, buttery puddle. It was almost too much; I was amazed and on the verge of feeling alarmed. One apt way of characterizing the moment would be to cite the apostle Paul: "It is a terrifying thing to fall into the hands of the living God" (Hebrews 10:13). And then I felt an arm around my shoulders. It was Rudi. As he looked at me he smiled and stated matter-of-factly, "It's all a matter of surrender to this energy."

It would have been reasonable for me to wonder how Rudi knew what I was going through in those moments—and how much he did know. I can't say these questions came to mind at the time. I think my answer then would have been about the same as it is now: Rudi sensed the essence of my experience through his own highly developed intuitive awareness. That I'd frozen in my tracks with who-knows-what expression on my face must have been a bit of a tip-off, too.

"It's all a matter of surrender to this energy." That had the ring of truth to it. Over the next decades between meeting Rudi and Rizzuto, I tended to debate in my own mind which was truer: that it's all a matter of surrender to this energy, or that it's all a matter of being quietly aware of the present moment. I did suspect that the two more or less boiled down to the same thing. But it's taken a long time to get somewhat clearer about the fact that these two are intimately related aspects of the same basic work.

As one direction of a two-way process, an attention to the present opens us to a deeper flow of subtle energy in the body. In the other direction, the flow of energy brings us to a fuller attention to the present. We habitually resist this flow, but we can consciously surrender our resistance and allow it. When we let it penetrate, the inner energy unearths and dissolves tensions that otherwise keep us caught in being busy—caught in agendas of past and future. The release of tensions enlarges our awareness of the present. In the West, perhaps "the Holy Spirit" is one name for the energy that melts these obstructions.

My meeting with Rudi was my first distinct experience of a transmission of spiritual energy between two people. I've slowly become convinced that some such transmission happens among people (and indeed between all beings) much if not all the time, if only in mild, subtle, usually imperceptible ways. But here was an unmistakable example. Something in me came alive through Rudi's presence. Something in me opened through contact with a person who had done inner work on himself over many years. It was an unusual moment of resonance, and it changed me. It was the most striking of several incidents in this period that shifted me in the direction of a deeper joy as well as toward a renewed dedication to the spiritual path.

I asked Rudi several more questions as my experience was subsiding, none of them noteworthy. I was clearly jabbering to protect myself from the continued sense of intensity, and Rudi stopped me after a few minutes by saying, "You ask too many questions, Tony. To stick two pieces of paper together, you only need a dab of glue. Apply any more and it creates a mess. And it's unnecessary."

Inwardly we need only know enough to apply what we know to the next leg of the journey—this next hour, this next day. Knowing more can interfere. It's wisdom that I often have forgotten on a true gut level and then eventually have remembered again. For most of us, these things can take a long time to sink in.

INTERPERSONAL CONTACT AND SELF-KNOWLEDGE

As I emerged from my free association and became aware once again that I was seated at a table, eating lunch with Rizzuto, it occurred to me that it would be interesting to hear what she thought of my first meeting with my teacher. It had been an especially dramatic moment that seemed to go against the view that Rizzuto was espousing. I described to her this first meeting with Rudi, my inner experience after a few minutes in his store, and how it had altered me. It seemed to have nothing really to do with understanding, but much to do with relationship, contact, and love. What would she say about that?

Rizzuto responded with interest. She acknowledged that there are holy people like Mother Teresa whose very presence can be uplifting. She also pointed out that there can be very intimate and intense experiences of non-verbal dialog between two people. This one between Rudi and me was such a dialog, she said. You two were deeply attuned to each other. What allowed for that? She wondered. What, for one thing, led you to be so receptive?

She was bringing the focus back to the individual psychological factors at play. Of course there were such factors, as there always are. But how fully do they explain matters of the spirit? My basic reply to Rizzuto still rings true to me: at the heart of such occasions lies the mystery of grace. By "grace" I meant all the unexpected gifts we receive—all the life of blessing that cannot be controlled or explained.

I think Rizzuto agreed, at least partially. She told us that we might be interested to know that the Catholic Church is currently revising its theology of grace to account more for such experiences—to stress the importance of the relationship between human beings as the medium of grace.

Clearly, my own receptivity to Rudi was crucial. The majority of folks walking into his store felt nothing unusual. At the same time, countless people did—these kinds of openings were commonplace around Rudi, suggesting that such receptivity was fairly ordinary among people of varying backgrounds. Some, like myself, became students of Rudi. Others did not. Nonetheless, they were affected.

For example, one of these unsuspecting visitors to the store was a well-known Reichian psychiatrist named Barbara Koopman. I met with her in 1978 to discuss a conference on chronic muscular tension ("armoring") in children that I was trying to get off the ground. It turned out she'd known Rudi. She'd never studied with him, but she'd been powerfully impressed by his presence. When the conversation turned to her describing her own first meeting with him in his shop, she was overcome with tears.

I didn't expect that. Nor did she. Speaking through her unexpected tears, she said, "It's hard to believe that any person could be surrounded by the remarkably fresh, renewing atmosphere that was around him. I just didn't know it was possible that a human being could generate an energy like that."

AN UNEXPECTED FACIAL

That first day, after meeting Rudi, I hung around in his store for an hour or so as he went about his business of unpacking art and shmoozing with clients, friends, and students. I finally left to have lunch. It was the first time I'd had a whole meal of macrobiotic food. As I was eating I had the experience of a sweet and ever-so-gentle cleansing energy streaming out of every pore in my face. It was like a divine facial. Delighted and a little perplexed, I confess that I reflected, "Boy, this macrobiotic food really is something! It's everything folks have claimed for it, and then some!"

Only after getting to know Rudi more over the next year did it fully dawn on me that the sense of cleansing energy I experienced over lunch had had little, if anything, to do with the food. Rather, it was one of the direct lingering effects of meeting Rudi.[4]

METAPHOR AND THE PROCESS OF HEALING

In the years that have passed since my conversation with Rizzuto, I have thought about it in relation to Rudi, my own inner work, and the work I do as a psychiatrist. Like most psychotherapists, I am fascinated by the questions Rizzuto raised. What is "the healing factor"? Is it love? Is it insight that comes from self-understanding? Or is it perhaps a source that lies behind both?

In order to investigate these questions more deeply, Rizzuto's 2001 paper, "Metaphors of a Bodily Mind," proves fruitful in two ways. First, in this essay, she makes a strong argument for how and why healing hinges so crucially on the fantasies that emerge out of the process of free association. She describes how fantasies emerge from the sharing of associations with the therapist, and how these metaphors are alive; they literally embody one's layers of self and one's feelings about self and other, and they serve as a bridge for further self-encounter and sharing in therapy.[5]

Second, Rizzuto describes two cases as illustrations that push the boundaries of our exploration. In the first case study, Mr. H begins to imagine himself living in a castle a year or so into his analysis. He has hidden himself in a windowless, remote room in the castle, and he prefers it that way. In the second case, Ms. T discovers well into the process of therapy that "I have never lived in my own castle"; she finds herself hidden *from* a castle, rather than hidden *within* it. Mr. H is terrified at the prospect of anyone coming near him yet also despairs of his own self-isolation. Ms. T's challenge is to gain access to her own dwelling-place and to come to grips with what she finds there: the power of her denied feelings about deceased family members. Most centrally, this includes her mother, who had never loved or wanted her, and Ms. T's continued sense of fear and rage about her.

The castle in each instance is a metaphor for the embodied self. In Mr. H's predicament, he discovers that he is hiding *within* his self; in contrast, Ms. T comes to imagine the scenario of hiding *from* herself. In both cases, the walls of a castle represent the inner situation of being barricaded from self and other. Their therapeutic sessions with Dr. Rizzuto slowly free each of them to inhabit their own self more fully, flexibly, and openly, less shut *in* and less shut *from* their own lives.

My summary does little justice to the beauty and wisdom of these case descriptions, but I want to underscore a key point. In both of these situations, the metaphor of a castle arises well into the therapeutic process and gels as a way for Mr. H and Ms. T to speak to another about themselves. Returning to the original controversy over our luncheon, it is easy to concede that, four years prior to our time together, Rizzuto makes a compelling case in her essay for how fantasy is a medium for the process of self-understanding as well as for how vital this process of insight is for healing. I would offer one response that takes nothing away from this truth. I want to emphasize the word *process*. This process involves contact with another, the analyst/therapist, and contact with oneself.

The formation of the castle metaphor for both Mr. H and Ms. T is a landmark, or icon, in that process for them; nevertheless, ultimately it is no more important than the interstitial dialog with Dr. Rizzuto that gave birth to it. The image of the castle can be likened to an apple growing on a tree—it is visible, and we can hold it, prize it, and share it. We can even eat it and eventually digest it. But the leaves and branches, the trunk and roots, as well as the soil, air and sunlight all have brought it into being.

While formal therapy is one major venue for the process of growth and healing, informal encounters, spiritual moments, and contact in other arenas are also of significance. For instance, I believe that my own chest-melting experience with Rudi was one opening in what can be seen to be the same multidimensional process, as are the ongoing reflections about it, both unconscious and conscious, that continue in my life, and indeed are embodied in this chapter. It is a process that exposes and cleanses layers of tension and self-rejection in oneself and others. My first meeting with Rudi is an example of a spiritual experience that involves a letting go of old assumptions and tensions. The therapeutic/analytic process does the same, though more clearly on the level of the personal self. Is all of the above, seen differently as spiritual and therapeutic, perhaps a single grand process of healing?

Could it be said further, perhaps, that this process involves a light of awareness that allows for both contact and understanding, the unfolding of love and truth? If so, this "light" not only leads to such gifts, but also grows out of them. It grows stronger, in other words, as we let go of old assumptions and tensions, make real contact with others, and learn more deeply about ourselves. It shines into surprising nooks and crannies as we meet others and as we meet ourselves anew.

Admittedly, to pose such questions and to consider their implications are acts of glaring over-reaching for a strict academic discourse. Here I reveal myself as neither a scholar nor a full-fledged psychoanalyst, but rather an amalgam of a spiritually oriented thinker and a clinical psychiatrist. Therein lies the obvious weakness of my contribution, as well as its potential strength.

Unitary process or not, I would suggest that sooner or later everyone's journey as a whole has engaged both the individual self and the larger life of blessing underlying and transcending the self. There is a mystery of connection between each of us as individuals and the reality encompassing all. "The other," whether in the form of the analyst or the spiritual teacher, serves not only as a guide to hidden or half-hidden truths, but also as an emissary from a growth-promoting power of life that bids us to live it more fully.

It is the nature of being human to have hidden to one degree or another from this life that which lies beyond the castle of the self. It is also simply human to be sealed off from the castle of the self we have not yet learned to inhabit. The fear of life's intensity and immensity that has established itself in someone needing help is a challenge for any inner guide. One of the most poignant moments in Dr. Rizzuto's description of Mr. H is her recognition of what exquisite care was required as she slowly helped him to see his fortified self-isolation, and to what a deep sense of compassion this brings her.[6] In one form or another, every healer learns to approach the reality of self-enclosure with painstaking caution and a respect for the power of fear. Hiding within the Self, Hiding from the Self.

Mr. H has a desperate moment in the course of his analysis when he inquires, "Where am I?"[7] Over a lifetime he has so enclosed himself, so hidden himself in his castle of fears and defenses, he cannot find himself. In one of his great essays, Martin Buber describes the moment when God asks Adam, "Where are you?"[8] Like other Jewish teachers before him, Buber points out that we are all Adam, and that the holy one of being is always asking us this one question. (This makes God the very first psychotherapist!) Like Adam, we all have hidden from the source of life, and, in the process, we all have hidden from ourselves.

Buber suggests that everything depends on whether we truly face the question, "Where are you?" Mr. H does this, with Dr. Rizzuto's assistance. Whatever it is deep in our interior that imparts life and consciousness asks us anew each day, "Where are you?" This question can test the solidity of the castle walls that encase us and exclude us, that shield us from the larger life outside us and keep us from the life of authentic feelings inside us. Only a caring stand against those seemingly cold and impenetrable walls that keep us hidden can begin to free anyone. These are walls all human beings to one extent or another have built to protect themselves from pain. Their rigidity may have served a purpose at one time, but they bar us from the fullness of life in the present.

THE CASTLE OF THEORY

As thinkers and clinicians, what should we think about the castles we have erected to explain these inner dynamics? Rizzuto's paper about metaphor considers more broadly the role of *language* in our castle creation processes. Following in the spirit of her insights, we might posit that language always functions fundamentally like a barely noticed substratum of metaphor. That is, like all human creations, the words we use to talk with each other inevitably serve as both walls and windows—walls that shut light out, windows that let light in—concealing and revealing our truest feelings and the very stamp of individual identity.

How do we speak of human suffering? Dr. Rizzuto has remained within the castle of technical language throughout her effort to integrate psychoanalytic understanding with the findings of neuroscience. (When her language shifts to describe her process with patients, it seems we have moved to a different set of rooms, with refreshing breezes from outside wafting through the space.) In contrast, I have intended to venture beyond the castle and therefore beyond the confines of formal, academic discourse, in an attempt to take a step toward integrating the lexicon indispensable to psychology and religion.

Buber has proposed that all of our systems and categories belong to the I-It world of relations, which is yet limited. Only when we enter the world of I-Thou relation through real meetings with others do we open ourselves to the unknown and unexpected and hence to the possibilities of more core healing.[9] We often miss the potential meetings in our midst as we hide behind castle walls of our own making. Yet, it should be added, we do not necessarily gain entry to the mystery of I-Thou by leaving the castle.

One of Buber's close associates, the psychoanalyst Leslie Farber, has written in greater detail on how Buber's language of I-Thou can help in the quest to appreciate what it means to be human. As it happens, the beginning of Farber's essay calls the various terms of psychoanalytic theory into question through using the metaphor of the moment, the castle. Alluding to Kierkegaard's and Kafka's own visions of the castle, Farber submits that the mental health field has yet to build a castle "fit for human habitation."[10] He invites us to imagine together a more hospitable castle of theory. Similar to our work with patients who face the thickness of castle walls, these efforts need to proceed at a careful pace, and for the same reason as in patient care: the weight of the past and the human attachment to it make this process fraught with a sense of peril.

REMAINING QUESTIONS

I suggested earlier that perhaps both spiritual experiences and therapeutic dynamics are expressions of the same process, the same light, the same basic awareness. I am keenly aware that there is no way of proving or disproving this idea! I have also referred to distinctions in the spiritual and psychological orientations of healing. In particular, "the life of the spirit" has more of a focus beyond the personal self, the psyche, whereas psychoanalysis and psychotherapy are more fully centered on the individual self in the world. I continue to wonder about the proper role of the personal self in the larger picture. In my own role as a psychiatrist and therapist, I am concerned with the welfare and growth of my patients as selves in the world. Yet in the long run, to have such a focus without a connection to the whole is both counterproductive and impossible. It would be like asking for a foreground without a background, a cloud without a sky, a flower without the earth from which it grows. Such a one-sided focus parallels a strong wish that each of us has—to be a wave, as it were, without the ocean below it. If I could be a self-enclosed wave or an airtight castle, perhaps I could even shut out the threat of death herself from lapping at my feet or tap-tap-tapping on my door. Most spiritual traditions propose in one way or another that we need to turn in the unfamiliar opposite direction: that only by opening ourselves radically to the uncertainty of life do we discover that death has no dominion. According to Buddhism, the rigid clinging to individual selfhood is our central problem. Rizzuto and other seasoned psychoanalysts reveal how much the *avoidance* of selfhood, of being fully one's self, is one major expression of this same clinging. Being imprisoned within the castle of selfhood or being unable to enter into it can both be seen as the same ultimate difficulty. In Mr. H's case, he has locked himself away from others partly due to the fear and the conviction that he has no real self to offer anyone else.[11] To some extent, this anxiety over having no self is likely true for many people, and this factor complicates the discussion about self and no self. This is one small hint at how the topic of selfhood is subtle to an intricate degree; perhaps such intricacy is one of the reasons that, following his enlightenment, the Buddha came to the initial conclusion that the truth about these matters was simply too deep to convey to others.

In this light, at the end of my lunch with Ana-María Rizzuto, I told her that I had one pressing question. Spiritual teachers like St. John of the Cross, Meister Eckhart, and many Buddhists point us in the direction of letting go of thoughts, musings, and fantasies. The purpose of such actions, ultimately, is to let go of oneself. Psychoanalysts beginning with Freud point in the direction of more thinking, musing, and fantasy. The purpose, they say, is to get know oneself in greater depth.

Both of these directions are valid. And to learn both approaches is wise. But, I asked Rizzuto, when is it best to take each respective path? When is it best to let go of thoughts and fantasies, and when is it best to connect to them more completely? Rudi rightly had rebuked me for asking so many questions. Nonetheless, a host of closely associated questions arise now: When is thinking a defense, and when is it an opening? Is it sometimes both? When is it best to direct one's attention to the sense of being conscious (for instance, by praying with St. Francis, "Who are you, God, and who am I?"), and when to the contents within one's consciousness? When can we safely aim to be alert, as is often recommended by teachers of meditation or prayer, and when do we risk suppressing something by this very work of alertness? In contrast, when should we allow the mind to drift? When to provide a feeling or a daydream or a train of free associations a bit of room to breathe and grow? When to go further and allow it endless room, following its momentum of musings to the end, with the risk of avoiding the discomfort of being more quietly in the present moment, or with the risk of hiding in my castle, of reinforcing the sleepy and distracted "me"? Is there a stance that truly is in the middle, that let go of thoughts and also embraces them, all at once? What would a life poised between these two approaches look like? How widely would it differ from person to person? And how is some comprehension of these choices best communicated to my patients? All of these questions, among others, spring up as immediate offshoots of my single question to Rizzuto.

In response to my direct question—when to let go of thoughts and when to embrace them—Rizzuto smiled and replied, "If I could answer that, I would win the Nobel Prize for Spirituality!" Yes, it is indeed a vexing question to answer. But answer it we must. And answer it we do. Every day, without the benefit of a Nobel Prize level of intellect or attainment, each of us faces this question, and each of us answers it for ourselves, however tentatively or even unknowingly.

Whether we realize it or not, the way we relate to ourselves in each hour is itself an answer to the question. Like an elephant in the living room, its challenge is unavoidable. As spiritual seekers, as therapists, or simply as people trying to live and to help others, we are constantly making subtle choices in relation to this challenge. At the same time, this vision of never-ceasing choice is only half of the story, as I explain below.

LETTING THE MIND BE

Personally, I respond to the challenge of the choice partly by falling back on tried and true routines of scheduling: set times for meditation in the morning and evening, set hours in therapy each week, and set retreats for longer periods of inner work one or more times each year. Such a cut-and-dried approach doesn't address the question of focus or inclination "the rest of the time," even while immersed in work tasks and other outer activities. Here my main response is experimental trial and error.

The vision of unceasing inner choice is incomplete in any case. To entertain such a notion as our exclusive model is an artifact of seeing inner growth only as the outcome of techniques that we apply to ourselves, and it suggests a busy pursuit of inner goals that would rival our more usual pursuit of outer goals. How easily we get caught in keeping busy! In the midst of all my doing, all our diligence and enterprise, Buddha comes along with the subversive statement, "You are not the doer."

What could it mean simply to allow the mind to be? Perhaps this question begins to answer the question I asked Rizzuto. The less we try to be anyone or to impose an agenda on the present moment, the more an answer steps forward on its own. At the same time, how often we need to exert the utmost focus to counteract the sway of old tensions! The thirteenth-century Zen teacher Dogen emphasized how nothing needs to be done; yet, he also said that the Way takes sweat, tears, and sometimes blood.

The answer that steps forward and meets us is the mind finding its own way. This way is natural, living, and ongoing. It includes the mind and the body and all to which they are connected. It presents and it bears with the flow of metaphor, with a river of images and the feelings and interactions that feed them. It includes castle walls and the oxygen within and beyond those walls; solid earth and sunlit skies; apples on a tree and all the sources that have nourished them. It encompasses both rigor and ease, muddled fantasy and diamond clarity, the personal self and the breeze of utter transcendence. As we grow over the years, less dominated by fear and less inclined to hide, we can learn to *be* the mind in all of its modes.

In other words, when we allow our thoughts and feelings to be, the mind is free. This includes learning to let the imagination run free and settle into fantasies that are launching off points for further inner exploration. These associations cluster around metaphors for the self that are keys to the dynamic of healing, as Dr. Rizzuto has shown with compelling clarity and subtlety.

DISCUSSION

Ana-María Rizzuto

At our encounter at the American Academy of Psychoanalysis winter 1995 meeting in Cambridge, Massachusetts, I shocked Anthony Stern when I asserted, emphatically he says, that the main curative factor in treating patients is not love but their *self-understanding*, resulting from free association and interpretation. Stern told me about his first encounter in 1972 with Rudi, the man who later would become his spiritual teacher, during which Stern felt that he was "overwhelmingly in the hands of the living God." He presented the dramatic encounter with Rudi as an event that seemed to go against the view that I was espousing. Stern asks, "What is the relation between our individual psyches and the reality of an other, or Other, beyond them?" In his paper he reminds me that analysts have turned away from a central focus on "insight" [I had said self-understanding, a concept that goes beyond insight] and "interpretation" to a fuller appreciation of "the relationship" and its intangible elements. He clarifies in his paper that when I was speaking of understanding, I was not referring to deep spiritual insight, but rather about learning about oneself in a psychological vein.[12]

Stern describes his encounter with Rudi as his first distinct experience of a *transmission* of *spiritual energy* between two people and suggests that "such transmission happens among people (and indeed between all beings) much, if not all the time, if only in mild, subtle, usually imperceptible ways." In other words, not only contemporary analysts but also ordinary and extraordinary relational encounters with people offer a "transmission" of *energies* that in his view is absent from self-understanding and interpretation. Stern felt that "something in me came alive through Rudi's presence . . . something in me opened through contact with a person who had done inner work on himself over many years . . . an unusual moment of resonance, and it changed me." The encounter resulted in his "dedication to the spiritual path." Stern concludes that I have remained within the castle of technical language while he has ventured beyond the castle in his attempt toward integrating the lexicons of psychology and religion.[13]

Integrating the lexicons of psychology and religion appears to me not only as a monumental task but also as an impossible one. Religion, as an organized institutional structure, belongs to the culture and calls for a lexicon of socially collectively conceived deities and cultic prescribed activities that exist before the individual encounters it during development. Religion that involves personal faith and the emotional involvement of the person *must* encounter in the psychical disposition of the individual the conditions for *belief*[14] in what appears as a religious experience of significance for him or her. In other words, any religious experience is by its very nature also a psychical experience. They cannot be separated because, even when they are part of a very meaningful personal encounter such as the one of Stern with Rudi, it becomes a spiritual/religious experience when Stern becomes *subjectively convinced* that he has received his *energy* and describes the moment as being "in the hands of the living God." I point out that such beautiful and powerful description is Stern's manner of *interpreting* to himself a *subjective* experience by the mediation of the metaphor of the *hands* of a God who, by definition has no hands.

Stern uses my paper *Metaphors of a Bodily Mind*[15] to reflect on the function of metaphor in treatment and also in our relationships with others, including the Other, as real beings we encounter in our life journey. In that paper I said, "metaphor gives voice and meaning to otherwise ineffable experiences of being a bodily human being dependent on others to be psychically alive and to own oneself. Personal metaphors are over-determined linguistic creations by which we objectify ourselves as feeling beings in order to know ourselves and make ourselves emotionally available to others. We do not only live *by* metaphors; we find ourselves *in* metaphors."[16]

The description involves the use of spontaneous metaphors [Aristotle said that they "cannot be learnt from others"] as *interpretations* of personal experiences bodily registered in the context of being *dependent on others* and needing to make ourselves *emotionally available* to ourselves and others. This description clearly shows that there are no metaphors that do not include others—even the Other—in a type of emotional relationship with them. The metaphors of the castles, one to hide from others out of fear and the other to avoid a painful maternal encounter, clearly illustrate the presence of these three components of a personal metaphor.

So, when Stern asks, "What is the relation between our individual psyches and the reality of an other, or Other, beyond them?"[17] I am inclined to respond that in our efforts to objectify ourselves as experiential beings we cannot help but to include them, metaphorically or not, in our *affective interpretation of ourselves* as experiential beings.

Stern's experience with Rudi in their intense first encounter clearly illustrates these concepts. He tells that during his meditating prior to his meeting Rudi he had "begun to feel buttery sensations in my chest." "Now standing and talking with Rudi I was feeling these same sensations. I asked him what they meant." Rudi responded with an *interpretation*: "It's your heart opening. First you feel the ocean, and you see it, hear it, taste it, and smell it. Then you become it," and he smiled.[18] Stern's bodily sensation in the presence of Rudi was also described to himself as 'buttery,' a metaphoric description that corresponds to no objective physiological event. Rudi's response also made use of a metaphoric heart opening to an ocean that once tasted and smelled makes you to *become* it. The whole exchange occurred in the realm of a reality and personal encounter that could only be articulated metaphorically.

Soon Rudi put his arm around Stern's shoulders, looked at him, smiled, and stated matter-of-factly: "It's all a matter of surrender to this energy." Rudi was a "kundalini yoga" mystic. The purpose of such yoga is "to arouse subtle *spiritual* energies *within* the body, in particular a powerful energy *stored* at the base of the spine known as "kundalini."[19] Obviously, this stored energy is physical, but it has spiritual power. In my way of thinking, body and mind are of one cloth, that is, a bodily mind constantly *interpreting* the person's *total simultaneous experience of a given moment:* physical, affective, relational, and cognitive in the context of a particular experiential moment.

In the paper Stern reflects that between meeting Rudi and Rizzuto he debated in his own mind "which was truer: that it's all a matter of surrender to this energy, or that it's all a matter of being quietly aware of the present moment. I did suspect that the two more or less boiled down to the same thing."[20] I find the question and the response to it intriguing because of the conceptual distance between "energy" (supposedly stored in the spine) and a person existentially and psychologically being present to him/herself, attempting to capture in a metaphoric way a particular experiential moment. To me, conceptually it is like comparing apples and oranges, or, using widely diverging metaphors.

Next Stern introduces the "mystery of grace" and offers his own definition of it: "All the unexpected gifts we receive."[21] "Grace" is a theological term that implies a divinity dispensing it to his creatures. By definition it does not belong to the psychological realm but to the sphere of a divine being relating to human beings. It is here that I believe it is not possible to create a lexicon that integrates religion and psychology. The best we can do is to explore the psychical processes of those who believed themselves to have been favored by grace or to explore at the theological level what we mean by divine grace and its being given to us.

Stern calls on Martin Buber to remind us that our systems and categories belong to the I-It world of relations, which is indispensable yet limited. He suggests that only when we enter the world of I-Thou relationships are we able to meet others. I have profound respect for Buber's thinking and I agree with him. However, we must remember that one has to become an "I" in one's own right before we are capable of recognizing another as a "Thou." Most of the people who come to me as patients are lost and confused about themselves and deeply concerned about their value to others. They don't arrive with an "I" capable of encountering a "Thou." It is the therapist's task to help them move in that direction and find in the encounter with the analyst the respect, tact, and interpretation of their experiences that would make possible for them to take some possession of themselves as an experiential "I" progressively opening to deeper and more meaningful encounters with others.

During our conversation the key questions emerge: What is "the healing factor"? Is it love? Is it insight? Or is it perhaps a source that lies behind both? Stern portrays my approach as an understanding that grows out of the process of free association leading to a growing awareness of one's fantasies in the context of therapy. Such description is a dry and limited presentation of the richness of the analytic approach conceived as a metaphoric process.[22] Stern acknowledges that "the fantasies that emerge out of the process of free association, . . . embody one's layers of self and one's feelings about self and other." He concludes that the two cases about castles do represent a metaphor for the embodied self and underscores that "Rizzuto makes a compelling case for how fantasy is a medium for the process of self-understanding, and how vital this process of insight is for healing." I would have preferred to use the term "experiencing oneself" instead of "insight" to describe the process that took place in those treatments.[23]

Stern claims that in his first encounter with Rudi there was a "letting go of old assumptions and tensions." He continues, "The therapeutic/analytic process does the same, though more clearly on the level of the personal self. Is it perhaps a single grand process of healing?"[24] I propose that analytic psychotherapy is the particular application of human relatedness mediated by speech, metaphors, and bodily stances that we continuously use to assist our patients to become more themselves. After all, mothers and fathers in their relational capabilities offer the foundation for becoming who we are. They also provide "buttery" feelings of a moderate nature that are foundational for being oneself. All this is in the order of being, not of doing. In the same way that there is not such a thing as a baby, there is not such a thing as an isolated human: we are always with others internally and externally; humans cannot be islands. Freud discovered it when in his scientific therapeutic method he encountered the transference. Macrobiotics are not our food: others are our food and vitamins.

Stern proposes that "life . . . lies beyond the castle of the self."[25] I disagree; life finds its center in the self in relationships, a self that does not need to be in a castle but simply inhabit itself in the act of being with others and with himself in the privacy of his/her experience. In that situation the person may sense the need for a transcendent reality, something meaningful beyond the self but not without a relationship with it. That need, already in germ during development, is the source of the religious and spiritual quests for a transcendent reality or being that could offer a broader universal context of meaning beyond already meaningful human relations.

Stern continues, "I suggested earlier that perhaps spiritual experiences and therapeutic dynamics are both expressions of the same process, the same light, the same basic awareness."[26] I prefer to say that spiritual experiences search for what transcends and encompasses our being and that of others; therapeutic dynamics helps us to get internal organization to become available to ourselves, others, and the transcendent. They complement each other but they have a hierarchy.

Finally, Stern brings the teachings of Buddha to focus reminding us that according to Buddhism, the rigid clinging to individual selfhood is our central problem. He suggests that psychoanalysts show how much the *avoidance* of selfhood, of being fully one's self, is one major expression of this same clinging. The Buddhist suggestion is to let the mind be. In that context Stern asked me, "When is it best to let go of thoughts and fantasies, and when is it best to connect to them more completely?"[27] This question ignores an obvious fact: a large number of people live with minds that don't let them be. When they arrive as patients they bring with them a mind that does not make room for *them* to be. The narcissist, the obsessed, the depressed, the perversely compelled cannot let their minds be because they are pathologically compelled by a mind that gives them no rest. Their minds are not free to be. They need psychic help because they are not free. They need the presence of a skillful therapist that accompanies them to let their dreaded fantasies and feelings emerge into the psychoanalytic playground where they are welcomed with empathic equanimity until they are able to make sense of them and of themselves with them. And this is not a matter of letting their mind be, but a most arduous work of confronting pain, terror, shame, and fear of rejection. When they entrust their analyst/therapist with all of these experiences, they are *beginning to let themselves and their minds be.* Only in this sense can I agree with Stern when he says, "When we allow our thoughts and feelings to be, the mind is free. This includes *learning* to let the imagination run free and settle into fantasies that are launching off points for further inner exploration" (my italics). He concludes, "These are metaphors for the self that are keys to the dynamic of healing as Dr. Rizzuto has helped us to appreciate it."[28]

In brief, I hope to have clarified beyond doubt that my model of free association and interpretation is not an arid "artifact of seeing inner growth only as the outcome of techniques," about which Stern has expressed concern, but a deeply engaged process of self-discovery in which patient and analyst are engaged as two people committed to the same task—to help patients to become as much themselves as their pathology at the start of the treatment permits them.

In this context the search for a transcendent being and reality and the need to relate to them may emerge at any level. Mental health is not a requisite to need a spiritual encounter with the world and its transcendent dimensions.

NOTES

1. Quotations in this chapter are based on memory and are not verbatim quotes drawn from transcribed recordings or interview notes.

2. This was true for most of the psychiatrists at Cornell where I trained, including Dick Munich, Bob Michels, Arnold Cooper, Ted Jacobs, and probably even to some degree Otto Kernberg and Paulina Kernberg. Merton Gill and James Grotstein are two prominent psychoanalysts who have led in this shift of emphasis. But most psychoanalytic thinkers have moved at least somewhat in this direction. That they have done so becomes strikingly clear, for instance, in reading the autobiographical contributions in the special millennial issue of *Psychoanalytic Inquiry* (vol. 22, no. 1, 2002).

3. For more on kundalini, see Mircea Eliade, *Yoga, Immortality and Freedom* (Princeton: Bollington Foundation, 1969). Ajit Mookerjee, *Kundalini: The Arousal of the Inner Energy* (Rochester VT: Destiny Books, 1982) and Philip St. Romain, *Kundalini Energy and Christian Spirituality* (New York: Crossroad, 1991). See also the excellent annotated bibliography at the end of St. Romain's work. Rudi studied for twelve years with the well-known kundalini yoga teacher Swami Muktananda and had brief, but significant, contact with Muktananda's own teacher, Nityananda.

4. Rudi died in a plane crash the following February, three months after I had begun to study with him formally. See John Mann, *Before the Sun: Meeting Rudi* (Lummi Island, WA: Portal Press, 2014). See Swami Rudrananda, *Rudi: In His Own Words* (Portland Oregon: Rudra Press, 1990) for a good introduction to his teachings.

5. Ana-María Rizzuto, "Metaphors of a Bodily Mind," *Journal of the American Psychoanalytic Association* 49 (2001): 535.

6. Rizzuto, 561.

7. Ibid, 560.

8. Martin Buber, *Between Man and Man* (London: Routledge, 1947), 197; Kenneth Paul Kramer, *Martin Buber's I and Thou: Practicing Living Dialogue* (Mahwah, NJ: Paulist Press, 2003), 99.

9. Martin Buber, *The Way of Man according to the Teaching of Hasidism* (New York: Citadel Press, 1964), 9–12. Martin Buber, *I and Thou* (New York: Scribner, 1958); Leslie Farber, "Martin Buber and Psychotherapy," in *The Philosophy of Martin Buber*, ed. Paul Shilpp and Maurice Friedman (LaSalle, IL: Open Court, 1967), 577–579.
10. Leslie Farber, "Martin Buber and Psychotherapy," in *The Philosophy of Martin Buber*, ed. Paul Shilpp and Maurice Friedman (LaSalle, IL: Open Court, 1967), 577–579.
11. Rizzuto, 560.
12. Anthony Stern, "The Healing Factor in Psychotherapy."
13. Ibid.
14. Ana-María Rizzuto, "Believing and Personal and Religious Beliefs," *Psychoanalytic Contemporary Thought* 25 (2002): 433–463.
15. Ana-María Rizzuto, "Metaphors of a Bodily Mind," *Journal of the American Psychoanalytic Association* 49 (2001): 535–568.
16. Ibid., 565.
17. Anthony Stern, "The Healing Factor in Psychotherapy."
18. Ibid.
19. Ibid.
20. Ibid.
21. Ibid.
22. Ana-María Rizzuto, "Metaphoric Process and Metaphor: The Dialectics of Shared Analytic Experience," *Psychoanalytic Inquiry* 29 (2009): 18–29.
23. Anthony Stern, "The Healing Factor in Psychotherapy."
24. Ibid.
25. Ibid.
26. Ibid.
27. Ibid.
28. Ibid.

BIBLIOGRAPHY

Bornstein, Melvin, ed. Millennial Special Issue. *Psychoanalytic Inquiry* 22 no. 1 (2002).

Buber, Martin. *Between Man and Man.* London: Routledge, 1947.

———. *I and Thou.* New York, NY: Scribner, 1958.

———. *The Way of Man according to the Teaching of Hasidism.* New York, NY: Citadel Press, 1964.

Eliade, Mircea. *Yoga, Immortality and Freedom.* Princeton, NJ: Bollington Foundation, 1969.

Farber, Leslie. "Martin Buber and Psychotherapy." In *The Philosophy of Martin Buber,* edited by Paul Shilpp and Maurice Friedman, 577–579. LaSalle, IL: Open Court, 1967.

Kramer, Kenneth Paul. *Martin Buber's I and Thou: Practicing Living Dialogue.* Mahwah, NJ: Paulist Press, 2003.

Mann, John. *Before the Sun: Meeting Rudi.* Lummi Island, WA: Portal Press, 2014.

Mookerjee, Ajit. *Kundalini: The Arousal of the Inner Energy*. Rochester, VT: Destiny Books, 1982.

Rizzuto, Ana-María. "Believing and Personal and Religious Beliefs." *Psychoanalytic Contemporary Thought* 25 (2002): 433–463.

———. "Metaphors of a Bodily Mind," *Journal of the American Psychoanalytic Association* 49 (2001): 535–568.

———. "Metaphoric Process and Metaphor: The Dialectics of Shared Analytic Experience," *Psychoanalytic Inquiry* 29 (2009): 18–29.

Rudrananda, Swami. *Rudi: In His Own Words.* Portland, OR: Rudra Press, 1990.

St. Romain, Philip. *Kundalini Energy and Christian Spirituality.* New York, NY: Crossroad, 1991.

Chapter 5

Birth of a Living Monster

Rizzuto and the Religious Imagination

Martha Reineke

In her groundbreaking work, *The Birth of the Living God*, Ana-María Rizutto links the quest for religious ultimacy with the emergence of the imagination.[1] Employing the metaphor of a theatre stage to illustrate this phenomenon, Rizzuto observes that young children's lives are filled with a "colorful cast of characters": monsters, devils, heroes, superheroes, witches, gnomes, fairies, and many others.[2] God arrives on this theatre stage together with this lively crowd; however, as children develop, monsters play increasingly smaller roles in children's lives even as God looms as an ever larger presence. Rizzuto argues that, because parents treat God differently from gnomes, fairies, and monsters, children learn to discriminate between God, who holds favor with their parents, and these other characters, which do not.[3] Eventually, but for a few bit parts played by the Devil, monsters, and their kin retreat from children's lives.

What would happen if we tracked and kept in view that colorful crowd that Rizzuto claims slips away as children reach maturity? Building on Rizzuto's work in hopes of expanding its range of influence, I answer this question. Revisiting Rizzuto's assumption that witches and monsters exit stage right and stage left as children develop, I suggest that the theatre stage on which humans live out our lives remains more crowded than Rizzuto has thought—not only for growing children but also for adults. Moreover, if we remain attentive to the work that monsters and their kin do on stage—personifying otherness, embodying the uncanny, and filling us with wonder and dread—we can observe that, even when these monsters exit, the work they have done while on the stage of human experience falls to other characters, even to some who are not recognized initially as monstrous.

I draw, as does Rizzuto, on the insights of D. W. Winnicott and object relations theory. With the term "mythic imagination," I refer to experiences

Winnicott describes as transitional phenomena, midpoint in a developmental cycle between an infant's subjective experience and childrens' and adults' objective perceptions that are subject to reality testing in the larger world. Human cultural activity and creativity originate in the human capacity for experiencing transitional phenomena. Among the most important of these achievements are art and religion, home to the founding stories—myths—through which humans describe and inscribe fundamental meaning in their lives. Central to my line of inquiry also are symbols that attest to the human capacity to create shared meanings in communal contexts oriented toward ultimacy. Beliefs in monsters are symbolically articulated in sacred scriptures and ritual practices. As Timothy Beal demonstrates in *Religion and Its Monsters,*[4] monsters regularly take center stage in the world religions. Moreover, as Beal also explains, despite the averred secularism and sophistication of our time, monsters continue with the work they did in a religious universe. Persisting as disturbing forces, they frequent our dreams and lurk in the shadows of our art and literature.

In this essay, as I draw on Beal and on the psychoanalytic theory of Julia Kristeva, I uncover a matrix of meaning that demonstrates how dramas created by the mythic imagination feature diverse casts, inclusive of gods *and* monsters. Adult lives remain haunted by the creatures who filled our dreams and nightmares as children, shaping who we were then and who we are now as religious and cultural beings. In suggesting ways in which Rizzuto's pioneering explorations of the theatre stage of the religious imagination can be augmented, I highlight the significance of Rizzuto's work in new contexts, thereby extending the legacy of *The Birth of the Living God.*

DEVILS AND MONSTERS IN RIZZUTO'S WORK

In *The Birth of the Living God*, Rizzuto adopts Goldings's view of the developmental trajectory whereby monsters and their ilk appear in a child's life: monster, devil, hero, and superhero. The earliest entrants into the child's life—monsters and devils—play two roles. They "help the child tolerate his own badness, impulses of rage, frustrations, and deceptions," and they provide "narcissistic reassurance of the child's own power," responding well to the child's magical control over them.[5] However, as the child moves on to the Oedipal stage of development, even as the child notices that monsters and their kin have no standing in his parents' lives, so also does the child perceive that the parents far outrank the child. Heroes and superheroes now enter the child's life to mediate the child's frustration and object loss.[6] As the child's developing vocabulary and burgeoning social relationships empower the child to traverse an ever-expanding world, the child's God representations persist because they are sustained linguistically and socially. By contrast, the monsters of early childhood fade from view. If a devil appears now in a child's life, it derives from a new source: rather than emerging out of the child's self-representation of its own badness, as did the younger child's devils, this Devil originates in the "sadistic, phallic components of the parental representation."[7]

Rizzuto does not develop a full portrait of the Devil and his monstrous kin in *The Birth of the Living God*. Noting that the phallic power of the Devil, visible in cultural symbols, is exclusively male, Rizzuto suggests that representations of maternal destructiveness are associated with witches who participate with the Devil in sexual orgies. But Rizzuto does not explain further how witches might figure in ongoing work the child does with his/her parental representations. She notes that, because belief in the Devil is "unsupported by the general culture," it largely is a private experience for specific individuals and within a few religious communities. Rizzuto concludes that the archaic origins in earliest childhood of the devil, overlain by the growing child's diverse representations of parental destructiveness, make the child's Devil a "less elaborate and less necessary representation than God."[8]

Elsewhere in *The Birth of the Living God*, Rizzuto does discuss the development of Devil representations in Freud's work,[9] echoing insights she offers in her 1976 essay, "Freud, God, the Devil and the Theory of Object Representation." Rizzuto notes that God and the Devil share a common history in the parental and self-representations of a child. She argues that Freud describes two sources of the Devil: the child's father and the child's own self-representation. The former is based on splitting of an ambivalent paternal representation and the latter on the splitting of a good-bad self-representation.[10] In turn, the paternal image has a two-part origin: one emerges in a child's participation in the archaic history of humankind, which is a source for inherited memory traces of the primal father about which Freud writes in *Totem and Taboo;* the other arises from the child's personal history with a father.[11] Rizzuto points out that, for Freud, the primal Father and the Devil are one, for a single figure possesses for archaic humanity all attributes of a towering and terrifying paternal presence. This entity becomes two in the history of humankind, as religions duplicate on a cultural scale the splitting that occurs in a child's own history with its father.[12] Indeed, according to Freud, splitting accounts for the profound emotional investment adherents of monotheism make in their devotion to a "single, great God" as well as for the intellectualization of belief and the emergence of a God concept.[13]

Significantly, Freud does not discuss maternal representations of divinity, whether good or evil, prior to this point in his exposition, and they emerge here only in the context of his discussion of the "victory" of a patriarchal order and its intellected God over a matriarchal order governed by sensuality.[14] Monsters are bypassed altogether in this account. In a 2002 essay,

Rizzuto delineates devils from the Devil as she has in earlier work, attributing the former to the child's sense of badness and the latter to the bad father. She elaborates also on the processes through which other magical beings emerge in the child's life. Monsters with "mean intentions" derive, as have devils, from the child's or its parents' "hostile dispositions."[15] Ogres are linked with projections of alimentary desires and fears. Witches and fairies emerge as representations of the bad and the wished-for good mother. Rizzuto asserts that monstrous beings "disappear spontaneously before puberty, leaving no traces of their frightening or exhilarating presence."[16] Her assertion that these beings play only a "transient function" in a child's development echoes her claims about monsters in *The Birth of the Living God*: adults affirm the reality of God when they build for God "the best and biggest houses in town; by contrast, adults deny the existence of witches, leaving them homeless."[17]

Rizzuto's most extensive and nuanced discussion of monsters, describing their origins, role in children's lives and legacy in adult life, is found in a 1985 essay: "Eating and Monsters: A Psychodynamic View of Bulimarexia." Rizzuto acknowledges that humankind has not always viewed monsters and their kin with skepticism. Devils, spirits of the dead, and monsters abound in the premodern world. Indeed, they perform an important function, enabling persons who feel evil, bad, or dirty to locate the source of their discomfort outside of their own being, thanks to the "gracious availability" of creatures who not only bear evil but also are believed to be evil's source.[18] Today, when beset by a sense of ugliness and evil, we contain it in our own individual being. Moreover, in an increasingly atomized world, many of us lack community and family support that could mitigate some of the psychic discomfort associated with our disordered state. Even so, and notwithstanding our impoverished relationship with monsters, especially when compared with that of our ancestors, most of us muddle along and attain key developmental milestones. However, when we encounter obstacles in our development, including those that emerge from our interactions as young children with the maternal object, we may have unbearable feelings. Absent the special resources afforded to our premodern kin by their belief in monsters, we may resort to extreme measures—for example, bulimarexia—to assuage our pain.[19]

Seeking to understand such measures, Rizzuto examines closely how the developmental trajectory of children intersects with the life-history of monsters. She focuses her attention on the "primal cavity": the origin of the self in the infant's oral experience.[20] Citing the work of Spitz, she remarks on how the boundaries of being—inside/outside, self/objects, incorporation/rejection—are initially worked out by the infant within the primal cavity. These experiences can result in feelings of well-being or discomfort, which are antecedent to the formation of the self.[21] Further, because oral play pre-dates a child's acquisition of language, the "mnemic traces" of these experiences are not directly available in adult life.[22] Rizzuto notes the significance of the maternal face to this play. While feeding, the infant discovers the maternal face, which becomes for it a mirror of its own being. Quoting Winnicott, Rizzuto writes; "When I look I am seen so I exist."[23] The infant integrates apperceptively its experience of the maternal face and its coenesthetic gastrointestinal state of fullness or emptiness. Thus, the self emerges, for better or worse, in the context of seeing and being seen, fullness or frustration.[24]

Alimentary experience unites the mother and child until, around the age of two, the child begins to use language to demarcate the boundaries of its own proper being. On the cusp of language, the growing child expresses fears of monsters; however, Rizzuto believes that language only makes visible to others what is already part of the child's experience. The child's fears about completeness and incompleteness, fusion and separation, aggression and defense, now explicitly attested to when the child speaks about monsters, have their origin in the primal cavity. Most important to Rizzuto are the *visual components* by which the child's evocation of monsters recalls its archaic encounters with the maternal face. The monster's face has "sadistic (wish to inflict fear and suffering) and perverse (exhibition of something horrifying) aspects."[25] Thus, the mythic imagination of the growing child forces its monsters to "wear the projected looks of intolerable self-representations (the ugly, messy, angry, revengeful child)."[26] Moreover, monsters enable the growing child to displace maternal traits that are intolerable to it, in order to preserve a nurturing and supportive maternal presence in its life. The child's fears alternately turn on the horror of being invaded by a bad object or taken over by a hungry, maternal monster.[27] Writes Rizzuto:

> These monsters are voracious, uncontrollable; their appearance is repulsive to the eye and their bodily surface is repulsive to touch. They are angry, vicious, and mean; therefore they must be controlled at any price. Their meanness is represented by their large and deformed size, and their unsightly faces make them horrifying to look at. Sometimes they make frightening noises. Indeed, they must not be seen; indeed, that explains why they lurk in dark and hidden places, always avoiding open spaces and the light of day. Some monsters may lose their life if seen by a person. The destiny of a monster, in short, is to live in hiding, away from the maternal eye and the awareness of its creator.[28]

Capturing decisive moments of the monster-making process in freeze-frame, Rizzuto describes how the alimentary relationship between mother and child determines the significance of food at conscious and unconscious levels and establishes for the child the preferred routes to oral satisfaction. She also describes how the maternal gaze is critical to the child's experience of the monstrous.

According to Rizzuto, the child's developing psychic resources normally keep pace with its maturing relationships with its parents, especially its mother, and the safety net afforded to the child by monsters eventually falls into disuse. However, if the child's needs are not met by its mother, "active maneuvers will be required to rid oneself of the 'bad' internal mother": refusal of food, vomiting, or voracious eating.[29] Moreover, if monsters prove inadequate to the task of assisting the child in managing its badness, the child's psychic isolation will grow. The child will develop "a compelling need not to be seen, psychologically, and in real life," lest its hidden voracious and monstrous self-representation be seen by others, leading to rejection.[30] The child may offer to the world a façade that gives no inkling of the turmoil that lies within; however, in adolescence, when the child typically separates from internal representations of primary objects, monsters that were deeply buried may emerge anew. For Rizzuto, the hunger for oral mothering may issue in early sexual relations, frantic activity, or the binging and purging cycles of bulimarexia.[31]

THE WORK THAT MONSTERS DO

Rizzuto and I concur that monsters in the premodern world have a viable existence. Certainly, the world religions offer powerful testimony to that effect. Writing in *Religion and its Monsters*, Timothy Beal tracks monsters across the global religious landscape. Among the creatures to which Beal calls our attention are the chaos gods of the ancient Near East, the sea monster gods of the Hebrew Bible (most notably Leviathan), the great dragon of John's apocalypse in the Christian New Testament, and Kali, the Hindu monster goddess.

But Beal also gives us reason to reassess Rizzuto's assertion that monsters have no home in the modern world. When Beal tracks the ongoing work of monsters in modern literature[32]—the creature in *Frankenstein* and the count in *Dracula*—and describes their monster and vampire progeny, which still haunt contemporary culture, he links these monsters with their ancient counterparts. He provides compelling evidence that monsters live, and not only for those mired in problematic developments such as the young women described by Rizzuto in her study of bulimarexia. In emphasizing how monsters do work that enables them to persist in every era, notwithstanding a change of habitat from the formally religious to the broadly cultural, Beal demonstrates that monsters continue to shape our lives. In this way, Beal offers insights which suggest how Rizzuto's discussion in *The Birth of the Living God* of monsters, devils, and their ilk may be augmented, thereby further enriching the explanatory power of her work.

Complementing Beal in his attentiveness to the cultural role of monsters, Julia Kristeva illuminates the monstrous from a psychoanalytic perspective. As a consequence, she draws close to Rizzuto even as Kristeva's distinctive insights on the monstrous attest to her background in Lacan rather than in object relations theory. Together, Beal and Kristeva suggest productive avenues Rizzuto might pursue were she to give further attention to monsters. Rizzuto has claimed that communities in the premodern world locate the source of their problems in devils and monsters because their naïve beliefs enable them to affirm these creatures' "gracious availability." By contrast, the savvy inhabitants of today's world cannot believe in monsters. But I suggest that the untutored imaginary of the premodern world actually exposes the bankruptcy of our own naïve belief in an autonomous "self." Kristeva views human experience through a Lacanian lens and sees that the human subject is haunted by *méconnaissance* in *any* era, belying the human claim to independent self-governance. Her sensitivity to the precarious standing of the subject in the world helps bring to light ways in which monsters still live for us, and not only for young women caught in the throes of a developmental crisis. Kristeva shows us that the work that monsters do for all of us, originating not with early object relations but with the abject, stands as evidence of a fragility endemic to human being.

For Kristeva, the first chapter in the history of human subject creation is preceded by a prefatory experience of abjection. When the human infant enters the world, it has no sense of existing separate from others. Kristeva describes as "abjection" that process through which a boundary eventually is raised between an "I" and others. The "abject" is that which is rejected and ejected—sour milk, bodily waste, even a mother's caress—in order that the "I" exist.[33] But that which is abjected is never definitively gone. The fragile borders of the subject can and will be breached. Thus, at the zero degree of being, abjection "is the avant-garde of the future oedipal revolt."[34] In the throes of abjection, careening between hatred *and* love, the proto-subject is divided *and* overwhelmed. Objects that will appear later, "caught in the fragile web of desire," are unknown to the abject, which pulls the not-yet-a-subject to a place where meaning collapses.[35]

On Kristeva's understanding, monsters emerge out of this proto-subject's boundary work with abjection. Where Freud has called our attention in his discussion of the primal father to the doubling of the paternal function in God, Kristeva has us observe a like doubling, this time monstrous, along a maternal axis. She argues that on the other side of the primal father's death is a maternal death. Kristeva claims that, no matter the era in which we live, all of us must negotiate this maternal death, for "matricide is our vital necessity."[36] Along this primal, maternal axis monsters arise and offer themselves for our analysis. Let's look in more detail at Beal's descriptive commentary on monsters and consider as well Kristeva's illuminating insights into figures of an uncanny sacred that lurk along a primal, maternal axis.

AN ENHANCED JOB DESCRIPTION FOR MONSTERS

Beal offers a "job description" for monsters that, in adding to Rizzuto's own description, enables us to see monsters we otherwise would not notice. Rizzuto depicts monsters with broad-brush strokes: they are hostile, mean, and ugly. But these pat descriptions are more reminiscent of monsters brought to us by Disney (e.g., Cinderella's step-mother) than of monsters that, across millennia, retain their power to terrify humans. These descriptions work against Rizzuto's intent that we take monsters seriously. The monsters that still shake us to our core defy ready labeling: ambiguous and unstable, they will not stay put. Beal identifies five features of monsters that unsettle and disturb us.

At their point of origin, monsters trouble us because their creators are typically problematic in their own right. As a consequence, on first acquaintance with a monster, we are caught off-guard: Is the monster or its creator the more monstrous? We are precluded from answering this question by an irresolvable ambiguity that is the monster's birthright.[37] In addition, monsters "personify otherness within sameness." They are in the world but not really of the world. Thus, the defining feature of the monster is its embodiment of the uncanny (*unheimlich*). That which is uncanny threatens our sense of "at-homeness" from the inside rather than from the outside. Monsters are horrifying because, when we encounter them, we are subjected to an unhomely experience in the home: that which should be outside is inside. We fear them because what we thought was bounded outside of us as wholly other threatens to become the same.[38] Moreover, monsters evoke an undomesticated sacred. The uncanny monster both threatens our sense of order and well-being, which leads us to demonize it, and acts as an envoy of a sacred, which leads us to deify it.[39] In our ambivalence, both demonizing and deifying our monsters, we confront accentuated uncanniness. Monsters in these ways participate in what Rudolph Otto called the *mysterium tremendum*: both fascinating and repulsive, they fill us with wonder and dread.[40] An other who was truly other would not summon from us such fear. The uncanny otherness of the other—an otherness within the same—shakes us to the core of our being. We fear that, because of monsters, we will die.

Monsters and the Maternal Body

Kristeva enables us to see how adults' uncanny encounters with monsters, in art, literature, and the world religions, so well described by Beal, duplicate the dynamics of the material, maternal dialectic of earliest childhood. Monsters' ambiguous boundaries, uncanny powers, and life-threatening power to fascinate and repel in the *cultural* unconscious replicate macrocosmically what transpires microcosmically in an *individual* unconscious. Well before the child begins to speak, its first efforts to create bounded identity take place in the maternal matrix, which Rizzuto calls the primal cavity. For the nascent human subject, separation from its maternal origins is prerequisite to its attaining full status as a subject. However, a threatening mimeticism haunts its efforts: with its maternal origins, sameness suggests to the subject a potential dissolution in being. Moreover, Kristeva shows us how the dynamic work that monsters do persists in later life. Others can appear to us as "monsters" whenever we find ourselves in the throes of a conflict with another person or group that we feel threatens our very being. The sounds, smells, and fluids of such encounters turn on primary repression. In the grip of crisis, we find ourselves before a monstrous menace that recalls our formative encounter with sameness and difference.[41]

Beal identifies these crises as cultural; but they also can originate in an individual's life. In all these cases, when an adult subject is about to lose its bearings in the world, the monstrous face that the subject encounters in a potentially deadly play of mirrors does not belong to the mother-object of childhood. Explaining this process, Ewa Ziarek states that it hearkens back to a more archaic encounter. The force present at the height of the conflict is like the "tain" in a mirror: the lining that produces a specular representation without appearing in it.[42] Experienced only at the limit, as an unbreachable alterity in being that is at once absolute promise and absolute threat, this prespecular encounter lends a maternal cast to the crisis. Less stable than a god representation, this monster "representation" remains a shadowy presence that seemingly rises forth from the tain of mirrored being only to fall back, ungraspable and unfathomable.

As a consequence, with Kristeva, I delineate as twofold what Rizzuto joins as one. Rizzuto writes that the mirroring provided by the mother's face in the oral stage of development is the first experience the child uses in the formation of a God representation.[43] However, with Kristeva, I suggest that the maternal matrix, the tain in that mirror, offers more original material: objectless and immediate, a not-yet-a-subject identifies with a not-yet-an-object.[44] From this material monsters emerge for the mythic imagination.

This process is visible when we note how Kristeva's theory develops from her observations of infants and toddlers, for whom separation from the maternal matrix is "a violent, clumsy breaking away, with the constant risk of falling back under the sway of a power as securing as it is stifling."[45] Embattled and beset, nascent subjects practice boundary making.[46] Not yet subjects of language or engaged in early object relations, they are abject: they demarcate space and place with their mouths. They bite, chew, and swallow sameness and difference. Bodily fluids, expelled or retained, enable them to experience difference as pleasure and as discomfort or loss. Echolalias and rhythms, not yet words belonging to "mother" or "child," lend texture to sound and space, forming an "archaic topos."[47]

These somatic rites secure for the human subject its most basic boundaries. However, the subject never rests easily. Notwithstanding its desire to wrest from difference a full unity of being, it repetitively confronts a lack of being. Summoning the resources of language and an emerging culture to secure its standing in the world, the subject labors in order not to die. Although all humans engage in what Kristeva calls death-work,[48] their labor is not always undertaken in unhallowed spaces haunted by monsters. Rather, under conditions of acute distress (e.g., personal crises, plague, famine, war), when humans second-guess their achievements in the cultural order and words fade, those in the throes of crisis revisit processes of differentiation that first won them a place in the world. Here, they reenact the moments when they first summoned the most archaic markers of difference in their quest to separate themselves from their maternal origins and secure an independent existence. This effort, evocative of monsters, is tracked in the premodern world by religion and attested to in works of art and literature still today.[49]

In her essay on bulimarexia, Rizzuto has captured much of the maternal narrative recited by Kristeva. Like Kristeva, she identifies an infant's connection with the maternal body, what Rizzuto calls the primal cavity, as a process antecedent to the formation of the subject in which the infant secures in oral play the boundaries of being: inside/outside, self/objects, incorporation/rejection. For Kristeva as for Rizzuto, the work that a young child does with that which is monstrous, hinging on the child's fears about completeness and incompleteness, fusion and separation, aggression and defense, pre-date its acquisition of language and have their origin in the primal cavity and its desires. So too are Rizzuto's insights similar to Kristeva's when she suggests that the work that goes on within the infant's mouth, which is described by her as the coenesthetic gastrointestinal state of fullness or emptiness, leaves mnemic traces that, if not directly available in adult life, still have a capacity to haunt us. Eating disorders in young women are symptomatic of that haunting.

But Rizzuto has not yet brought monsters fully to life as do Beal and Kristeva when they locate evidence of monsters' powers in crises of humankind that are attested to by religion, art, and literature. Rizzuto issues monsters work permits only for the premodern world. For Rizzuto, monsters today have only a shadowy existence in the homes of individuals who have not successfully negotiated developmental milestones. I suggest that Beal and Kristeva offer Rizzuto reasons to look for monsters elsewhere:

in humankind's abject origins and in a cultural unconscious at work on the stages of humankind in any era.

REASSESSING MONSTERS: OPENINGS IN RIZZUTO'S WORK

Openings for a reassessment of monsters are present in Rizzuto's work. In *The Birth of the Living God*, she already has laid the groundwork for freeing monsters in any era to do the work that monsters do. Rizzuto notes that, for Freud, the Devil is based on the splitting not only of a good-bad self-representation but also of an ambivalent paternal representation which itself has a divided origin: inherited memory traces of a primal father are joined with a child's personal history of a father. With Kristeva, Rizzuto could argue that monsters also have a dual origin via a primal mother who always pre-dates the emergence of the subject and remains accessible only in the embodied memories of the maternal body/primal cavity. She could suggest that, after childhood, we continue to access these embodied memories in moments of crisis, notwithstanding the successful accomplishment of developmental milestones along the way to adulthood.

Rizzuto could find inspiration for such a project in her book, *Why Did Freud Reject God?* In this work, Rizzuto tracks the development and derailment of Freud's God representations. She notes that Freud is largely silent about his mother in his writings and, when he does speak of her, he associates her with death. Indeed, he suggests in his writings that his mother's death is the occasion for his own liberation.[50] According to Rizzuto, Freud's mother hardly offers viable materials for a God representation.[51] As for Freud's father, Jakob, Rizzuto claims that he also is an inadequate source for God representations. When the young Freud's father becomes mired in financial struggles Freud finds himself confronted simultaneously with a number of personal losses and separations. These troubles leave his father a depleted figure in Freud's eyes.[52] As a consequence, Freud is unable to draw from his father features of a God representation that would offer him support or consolation. These problematic interactions with his parents set Freud on a path to self-sufficiency in childhood, which make of the adult Freud "a godless Jew."[53]

Nevertheless, as Rizzuto compellingly argues in *Why Did Freud Reject God?*, the death of Freud's father occasions a transformation in his parental and God representations. Indeed, after the death of his father, Freud pulls down from the shelf of his life the box in which, at the close of his childhood, he packed away his God representations. Now, Freud quite literally fills the shelves and tables of his study with an antiquities collection that offers him new material for God representations.[54] Rizzuto writes that the antiquities, which Freud began collecting six weeks after his father's death, connect Freud in profound ways to his father.[55] Many of the images in his collection—Egyptian gods and artifacts from Roman ruins—match images from the Philippson Bible, a German/Hebrew bible from the mid-1800s that Freud and his father read together during Freud's childhood and which Freud's father presented to him on his thirty-fifth birthday.[56] After his father's death, Freud writes of setting the images he has collected before him on his desk like an audience, playing with them, even "sacrificing" an image now and then.[57] Rizzuto argues that the images function as God representations for Freud while simultaneously reconnecting him with his father, this time in ego-syntonic ways. Writes Rizzuto: "It can be said that Freud was never alone as long as he was with his gods and his antique objects. Jakob remained with him in this sublimated form until his son joined him in death."[58] Freud's wished-for father was unable to afford him the protection he sought as a growing child. But, as Rizzuto notes in comments in an essay, Freud's actual father, to whom Freud reconnected via mnemic traces when he looked at or touched artifacts in his antiquities collection, "offered him a loving and playful presence which he needed and cherished."[59] Concludes Rizzuto: "in an unconscious and roundabout way, Freud had created his ad hoc ancestor temple and cult."[60]

Rizzuto does not indicate that Freud's mother features in Freud's rehabilitation of his God representations. However, with their curious amalgamation of human and animal bodies, some of the Egyptian gods with which Freud surrounded himself do suggest monstrosity. Further, a maternal referent is visible in Rizzuto's account of Freud's relationship with his antiquities collection. Rizzuto observes that, in the wake of his father's death, Freud revisits twin terrors of early childhood: the emotional distance he felt from his mother and the traumatizing loss of the nanny who had met his psychic needs before her abrupt dismissal from service. Absent his father, whose affection, playfulness, and lightheartedness had helped the young Freud to "go on living" after the traumatizing departure of his nanny,[61] the adult Freud wonders anew how he can go on living. His dream of the Three Fates, written less than two years after his father's death, which includes Freud's famous misquoting of Shakespeare—"Thou owest Nature a death"—demonstrates that an unholy cluster of God-Nature-mother-death still besets Freud.[62]

With Diane Jonte-Pace, I associate this cluster with Freud's "counter thesis," in contrast to his "master thesis" (the Oedipal complex).[63] Freud offers a rough outline of the counter-thesis in his reporting on the dream of the Three Fates. He focuses on three images of the mother: dead mothers, mothers as instructors in death, and uncanny maternal bodies.[64] Together, these images take us to the edge of life and death, home to a monstrous uncanny, which is typified in Freud's counter-thesis as maternal in its origin.[65] Rizzuto writes, "Freud's inner experience demanded a protector who could ward off the dangers of the Fates." With the death of his father, no one stood between him and "the Fate-mother." Rizzuto believes that Freud's antiquities collection provides that missing buffer. Freud wrote to Fliess that "These things put me in a good mood and speak of distant times and countries."[66] Rizzuto says that these "distant times and places" refer to the playful times he had with his father as together they read and looked at the images in the Philippson Bible.

But does Freud's collection of antiquities serve as an occasion only for revisiting the lands and times of his Father? Rizzuto acknowledges that the death of Freud's father prompts Freud to revisit his relationships with both parents. That the antiquities collection serves as an occasion also for Freud to visit a strange and unsettling place associated with his mother is suggested by Freud's description of a childhood nightmare about his mother. Uncharacteristically referring to her in his recounting of this dreadful dream as his "beloved mother" and noting her "peculiarly calm sleeping countenance" (the sleep of death?), Freud recalls that he watched as his mother was carried into a room by two or three people with bird beaks and laid on a bed. Frightened by these monstrous presences, he awakened "crying and screaming and disturbed his parents."[67] In his analysis of this dream, Freud recognizes the imagery in his dream as coming from an Ancient Egyptian funerary relief that was one of the illustrations in the Philippson Bible.[68] This image is included in the Philippson Bible's commentary on 2 Samuel 34:31–35 and is replicated in Rizzuto's book.[69]

I suggest that when Freud takes up the figures of his antiquities collection, his play is not unlike that of his nephew Ernst, who in his famous fort/da game works through issues of maternal separation and connection.[70] The paternal nexus of loving care proffered to Freud by his father as they poured over the Philippson Bible, adhering as mnemic residue to images in his antiquities collection that Freud's fingers now touch,[71] may afford Freud the support he needs to reconnect not only with his father but also with the mother of earliest childhood: the mysterious and uncanny maternal matrix or primal cavity. Rizzuto acknowledges that some of the images in the Philippson Bible could have frightened the young Freud as a child.[72] And certainly, Freud's own words confirm that, as a child, he was especially frightened by Egyptian gods whose bodies were a monstrous mix of human and animal bodies. Under the mnemic protection of his father, perhaps the adult Freud works through those fears when, seated safely at the desk in his study, he plays with small figures that once appeared in a nightmare as grotesque, life-size monsters. Perhaps the joy he experiences creates a safe bridge of connection, enabling Freud to re-traverse the land of death-bearing and uncanny maternity and to emerge from that land with a renewed connection to his mother.

A narrative that would show the role that fathers may play in reconciling not only Freud but also all children to the monsters of their childhood, thereby renewing their God representations, paternal and maternal, is available to Rizzuto in the work of Kristeva. Kristeva is noted for retrieving from the Freudian corpus and bringing to others' attention a paternal presence that is not Oedipal. With Freud, she calls this presence the "father of individual prehistory." Not the father of the law, this father supports the nascent development of the human subject, establishing its capacity for forgiveness and intimacy.[73] Solicited through affective memory, he offers protection. The father of individual prehistory is not the model the child will know in the world of symbols and signs; rather he is a non-object, a pattern, with which the child will bind by way of semiotic play—sounds, touch, and laughter. In these ways, he facilitates metaphorical transference to a place of meaning. Taking in these sounds, the child becomes a "subject of enunciation" and love. Writes Kristeva of this moment:

> it is on the basis of that harmonious blending of the two facets of fatherhood that the abstract and arbitrary signs of communication may be fortunate enough to be tied to the affective meaning of pre-historical identifications, and the dead language of the potentially depressive person can arrive at a live meaning in the bond with others.[74]

In the absence of nonrepresentational and affective elements in language associated with this paternal function, the world is an alien, even monstrous, place. Facilitating a bridging to the social, the father of individual prehistory enables us to reach across a void. He does not do so by means representation—mimetic modeling in the Symbolic order is secondary—but by means of embodied patterning. Metaphors link sound, speech, and affect in an original triangle of empathic connection. Through him, our bodies connect with those of others.

With the support of the father of individual prehistory, the infant's orientation in the world moves from its mouth to its ears. Just as a present and absent breast within a buccal space demarcates boundaries for an infant *within* the primal cavity (maternal body), so also do sounds demarcate sameness and difference for an infant *on the edges* of the social matrix (a voice directed toward the infant now turns away from it toward another).[75] Because the vocal chamber that is the infant's world resonates for it as triangulated space, the difference mirrored by this space is not offered to the child as interdiction (the Oedipal Father/Law of the Father) but as gift. As one's sounds directed toward an Other immeasurably enlarge the infant's world, they promise an alternative to the potentially imploding or exploding space of the primal cavity/maternal body.

Kristeva writes that, early on, *before* our desires become acts in the world, we are *for-given*.[76] With the French word "pardon," Kristeva depicts a process of for-giving. When we are novices at the task of living, *we find ourselves already accepted and protected*. Kristeva writes, "It is possible to forgive ourselves by releasing, thanks to someone who hears us, our lack or our wound to an ideal order to which we are sure we belong."[77] Significantly, a loving father, not the father of the law, is "primitive guarantor of our safeties."[78]

I suggest that, when Freud plays with his antiquities collection, primary in his recollections of his father may not be his father's commentary on the words and images in the Philippson Bible, but the sounds of his father: the warmth and timbre of his voice and his laughter may create an affective bridge of protection for Freud across time, a bridge whose mnemic traces come surging forth when Freud touches and plays with his collection. These embodied memories may re-present Freud with a father before whom the young Sigmund is always already for-given.

I concur with Rizzuto that the statue of *The Dying Slave*, the first purchase by Freud for his antiquities collection, and the Philippson Bible image of the Egyptian jumper, whose facial features are so similar to the slave's, bookend the death and resurrection of Jakob Freud. Rizzuto believes that the statue of *The Dying Slave* proves oddly liberating for Freud because it recalls for him the text in Job in the Philippson Bible, for which the Egyptian jumper serves as an illustration. The text describes the untamable Leviathan, "primeval monster and mythical symbol of evil"; however, contravening the text, the woodcut shows the jumper lightheartedly subduing the crocodile that lies beneath it. When Freud brings the image of the statue in his study together with his memories of the woodcut of the Egyptian jumper and his father's sonorous voice reading the book of Job, Freud is transported to the lands and times of his childhood. Then as now, a laughing father subdues the monster, evoking the most archaic of primal scenes. If this laughter connects Freud to the reassuring father of individual prehistory, we may imagine that, for Freud, these joyful sounds reverberate within a previously uncanny maternal abyss, subduing the monster that lies within.

On such a reading of the meaning of Freud's antiquities collection for him, an opening appears for a new interpretation of Freud's relationship with his mother. Perhaps Freud found in the antiquities collection a way of reimagining his relationship not only with his father but also with his mother. If the dream of the Three Fates is Freud's last *word* on the mother, the image on Freud's desk of *Isis Suckling Horus* may be the definitive *image*. Already in his childhood, Freud became familiar with an image in the Philippson Bible of an Egyptian mother and her infant, which is very like that of Isis and Horus.[79] One imagines that Freud must have identified with Horus; for, Horus's father, Osiris, is not unlike Freud's father.[80] Freud has witnessed his father's emasculation: he has observed his financial failures and has listened to his father's report of a humiliating harassment by a Christian during a chance encounter on the street.[81] Perhaps memory traces of a father's voice play a role in the adult Freud's reaction to the image of *Isis Suckling Horus*. Freud's hunger for an intimate connection with his mother, first forged with the maternal matrix/primal cavity, may be met in this image. Undergirding Freud's connection to Isis and the suckling Horus may be the supportive father who laughs at the threatening crocodile and whose warm voice promises a bridge across archaic time to communion in difference.

DISCUSSION

Ana-María Rizzuto

Professor Reineke suggests that, contrary to my purported opinion, monsters do not disappear because parents do not affirm their existence. I want to clarify that I have not theorized about monsters as such. In *The Birth of the Living God,* I have described the developmental moment in which monsters appear as a psychic phenomenon during a limited time, in the so-called phallic phase in relation to narcissistic issues of smallness, self-definition, and psychic elaboration of internal conflicts. Many children during that period of their lives are convinced and truly frightened that there are *actual* monsters in the closet, under the bed, in the toilet, and in other places. They are not only frightened; but they may also find some gratification in the fact that the monster represents what they cannot bear. These monsters are *psychical creations of the child* that serve the purpose of helping the young person to modulate internal tensions and conflicts. The externalization of perceived feelings, intentions, wishes, and fears onto a monstrous creature attributes to its appearance, purported ugly intentions, or feared misdeeds what the child cannot tolerate in him/herself. These are the *private, idiosyncratic monsters* that *do* disappear after the child has managed to find some resolution of his/her conflicts and moved to the next stage of development when these conflicts can no longer serve a useful purpose. In the book I acknowledge the cultural existence of many creatures from popular mythology as well as the numerous personages offered by children's literature, television, cartoons, comic books, and Disney.[82] Of course, these imaginary beings, monstrous or not, are there to stay in the culture and do have a sort of life of their own.

In my paper, *Eating and Monsters: A Psychodynamic View of Bulimarexia,* I do not talk about monsters in general but about the *private* experiences of individuals with severe eating disorders in the context of a scientific medicine that "leaves the individual alone with his or her feelings of being evil, bad, dirty." Medicine does not have cleansing rituals for such feelings in an environment that has removed from its scientific understanding all "devils, spirits of the dead, monsters, and all sorts of unspeakable creatures . . . with their gracious availability to accept the badness we did not like as part of ourselves."[83] In saying this, I was not theorizing about monsters but about the type of culture in which eating disorders have become a frequent condition for young people.

Having clarified these points, Reineke's paper offers me the opportunity to talk *for the first time* about cultural mythologies and the ubiquitous presence of monsters everywhere. I believe together with Freud that "a large part of the mythological view of the world which extends a long way into modern religions *is nothing but psychology projected into the external world.* The obscure recognition of psychical factors and relations in the unconscious is mirrored . . . in the construction of supernatural reality."[84] We have only two choices in relation to myths and monsters—either we *believe* that they are *factually* true, that what they portray exists in reality, or we accept that our "mythic imagination" bestows their peculiar reality upon them. I favor the second option. I believe that we should speak not about the birth of *a* living monster, but the birth of *many* monsters and of the disappearance of some of them when no longer necessary, as well as the creation of new monsters when personal or cultural circumstances require them.

First, let's attend to the *birth* of monsters. Clinical psychoanalysis has demonstrated the psychic origin of the belief in some individuals that they harbor a monster that must be kept secret and the dynamic processes that contribute to the creation of monsters outside of ourselves. These are the monsters that Timothy Beal describes so well as part of cultures and religions. Reineke writes, "Beal demonstrates that monsters continue to shape our lives."[85] I question where these mythic creatures get their *agency* to act upon us. As a psychoanalyst I claim that we create them to make believe that *they*, not ourselves, regulate our lives. We gladly bestow such power upon them to free ourselves of our unacceptable responsibilities. The dynamic processes between individual psyches and the culture sustain the *belief* in the existence and power of monsters. They represent individual and collective processes to articulate, master, and give some tangible meaning to personal and social realities that cannot be confronted by other means. In brief, we will continue to create monsters to allocate into other beings what we do not want in ourselves. And if we cannot do it, then, we convert the other, the enemy into a monster as Hitler did when he decided that the Jews had to be eliminated for the salvation of Germany. Here are two sentences from *Mein Kampf:* "(The Jew is) a true blood sucker that attaches himself to the body of the unhappy peoples" and "the nation is no longer willing to be sucked dry by these parasites . . . [who] plundered the nation without pity."[86] Hitler was neither the first nor the last leader to convert his enemies into actual monsters.

WHERE DO MONSTERS COME FROM?

Citing Beal, Reineke proposes that monsters "personify otherness within sameness," "are in the world but not really of the world" and they represent the uncanny we encounter.[87] She continues: "The uncanny otherness of the other—an otherness with the same—shakes us to the core of our being." I do agree and affirm that such uncanny realities result from the projections, displacements, and mythic anthropomorphic narrative elaborations of what is internal to our minds and unacknowledged. We spook ourselves with what we cannot bear to feel and accept as ours. That said, I propose mitigating existential circumstances for our need for monsters. Our existential circumstances prevent us from fully possessing ourselves. We are too much for ourselves. Our body is as much internal as external to us. Its openings, its interior and exterior constitution escape our conscious control. Our mouths incorporate things, make them disappear, and become very early in life, together with the rest of the senses in particular the eyes, our means of taking the other in. In this manner, our psychic body is built in conjunction with the maternal other by keeping what is pleasurable and struggling to avoid unpleasure. The other will become internal to ourselves and at the same time remain a mystery, regardless of loving ties. The external world exceeds us at every level; we can only master limited domestic realities, but an earthquake or a severe toothache are enough to confront us with our impotence. Our reasonable scientific explanations and beliefs have a limited power to help us modulate the enormity of our limitations, lack of mastery, and inability to know that which is most vital for our well-being. The uncanny *is* within us. Perhaps this is our true abjection throughout life.

Clinically, the circumstances that contribute to the individual's conviction that she/he harbors a monster are related to the felt sense that the mother is unable to see the child as herself eliciting the fantasy of being a monster that must remain hidden. Severe early physical illness or surgeries may interfere with the formation of a pleasurable bodily self and lead to the feeling that one is monstrous. Profound and prolonged narcissistic humiliation, actual abandonment, and parental rejection convince the growing child that there is something monstrous about herself. The inability to rectify these predicaments leads the growing child to develop a profound sense of impotence, narcissistic depletion, and rage together with compensatory grandiosity and the need to hide. These predicaments involve the impossibility of obtaining indispensable maternal and other objects' love, thus eliciting a lasting hunger for maternal recognition and response, a hunger that nothing can assuage. In treatment, the emotional revival of these predicaments and the exposure of the monstrous aspects of the self to the therapist offer the only possibility to help the patient change her conviction.

This extremely brief description helps us understand why most monsters are devouring, destructive, powerful, uncontrollable, and always ready to act if properly provoked. They all reveal in their great and frightening powers our psychic impotence.

I deeply regret that time limits do not permit me to elaborate on the rich ideas presented in Professor Reineke's paper. I could talk for hours about this fascinating subject.

NOTES

1. The "imagination" is referenced by Rizzuto in the epigraph which prefaces chapter 10 in *The Birth of the Living God.* Louis Couperous reminds us that we "live in the imagination"; indeed, thanks to its powers, we both enjoy and suffer life (Peter Cowan and Louis Couperus, "The Imagined Life," in *Short Story International* vol. 2, no. 7 [Great Neck, New Jersey: International Cultural Exchange, 1978] as cited in Ibid., 176). Accordingly, as she begins chapter 10, Rizzuto affirms that "imaginative living," in the form of "intense experiences," consists of human cultural activity and creativity, including religion (Ibid., 177).
2. Ibid., 193.
3. Ibid., 194.
4. Timothy K Beal, *Religion and Its Monsters* (New York, NY: Routledge, 2002).
5. Rizzuto, *The Birth*, 193.
6. Ibid., 196.
7. Ibid., 197. Rizzuto typifies the difference between the two devils by spelling with lower-case letters the "devil" of early childhood. The post-Oedipal Devil is accorded the titular recognition he has earned in the cultural history of the West.
8. Ibid., 198.
9. Ibid., 19–36.
10. Ana-María Rizzuto, "Freud, God, the Devil and the Theory of Object Representation," *International Review of Psycho-Analysis* 3 (1976): 168; Rizzuto, *The Birth*, 21.
11. Ana-María Rizzuto, "Freud, God, the Devil and the Theory of Object Representation," *International Review of Psycho-Analysis* 3 (1976): 168; Rizzuto, *The Birth*, 21.
12. Rizzuto, "Freud, God, the Devil and the Theory of Object Representation," 169; Rizzuto, *The Birth*, 20–21.
13. Rizzuto also distinguishes between God concepts and God representations. The God concept emerges in "secondary-process thinking." It is "the God of the

theologians, the God whose existence or nonexistence is debated by metaphysical reasoning." See Rizzuto, *The Birth*, 47–48. Ibid.

14. Rizzuto, "Freud, God, the Devil and the Theory of Object Representation," 172. Rizzuto observes that Freud makes a "conceptual leap from image to idea of God." She makes note of this gap while discussing Freud's brief account of the late entrance and early exit from human history of a maternally marked sacred. Julia Kristeva addresses this gap also in *Powers of Horror*, when she observes that, of the two taboos of totemism—murder and incest—only one is elaborated on by Freud (Julia Kristeva, *Powers of Horror: An Essay on Abjection* [New York, NY: Columbia University Press, 1982], 57–59). I address this point later in the essay.

15. Ana-María Rizzuto, "One God, Two Genders: Psychoanalytic Reflections," in *Die Zwei Geschlechter Und Der Eine Gott*, ed. Elmar Klinger, Stephanie Böhm, and Thomas Franz (Würzburg, Germany: Echter Verlag, 2002), 37.

16. Ibid.

17. Ibid.

18. Ana-María Rizzuto, "Eating and Monsters: A Psychodynamic View of Bulimarexia," in *Theory and Treatment of Anorexia Nervosa and Bulimia: Biomedical, Sociocultural, and Psychological Perspectives*, ed. Steven Wiley Emmett (New York, NY: Brunner/Mazel, 1985), 196.

19. Ibid., 197.

20. Ibid., 200. The primal cavity may be likened to Merleau-Ponty's notion of "the buccal space": for the infant, the world consists of that which can be contained in and explored by its mouth (Maurice Merleau-Ponty, "The Child's Relations with Others," in *The Primacy of Perception*, trans. William Cobb [Evanston, IL: Northwestern University Press, 1964], 122). The primal cavity also appears similar to Julia Kristeva's notion of the "maternal matrix" or "maternal body." Not actually a "body," this matrix is a thoroughfare, a threshold, a filter for a nascent subject who, with its mouth, experiences an initial division within being that precedes its differentiation from that matrix (Julia Kristeva, "Motherhood According to Giovanni Bellini," in *Desire in Language*, ed. Leon Roudiez, trans. Thomas Gora and Alice Jardine [New York, NY: Columbia University Press, 1980], 238, 247). Like Rizzuto's primal cavity, the maternal matrix/body is never directly accessed because it is experienced prior to the child's inception of language. There is no subject present in this encounter to signify what is going on.

21. Rizzuto, "Eating and Monsters: A Psychodynamic View of Bulimarexia," 206.

22. Ibid., 200.

23. Ibid., 206.

24. Ibid., 207.

25. Ibid., 207.

26. Ibid.

27. Ibid., 204.

28. Ibid., 205.

29. Ibid., 204.

30. Ibid., 208.

31. Ibid., 209.

32. Literature enables persons to encounter monsters in ways comparable to direct encounters with terror. Neuroscientific and cognitive findings in recent research on literature suggest that embodied cognition is at work when we read literature. See Guillemette Bolens's *The Style of Gestures (*Guillemette Bolens, *The Style of Gestures: Embodiment and Cognition in Literary Narrative* [Baltimore, MD: The Johns Hopkins University Press, 2012]). Bolens draws on research on mirror neurons to offer a theory of corporeal narrativity whereby narratives are linked through kinesis to sensory experiences. She cites the work of Beilock and Lyons, for example, who define as "motor resonance" the process by which the same neural substrates are recruited whether one is reading about another's actions or modeling action on another's actual performance. Bolens's theory has strong similarities with Vittorio Gallese's notion of intercorporeity (Vittorio Gallese, "The Two Sides of Mimesis: Mimetic Theory, Embodied Simulation, and Social Identification," in *Mimesis and Science: Empirical Research on Imitation and the Mimetic Theory of Culture and Religion* [East Lansing, MI: Michigan State University Press, 2011], 87–108). Defining "intercorporeity" as "the mutual resonance of intentionally meaningful sensor-motor behaviors," Gallese grounds intercorporeity in mirroring neural mechanisms. Significantly, he claims, as does Bolens for kinesis, that intercorporeity is crucial for our knowledge of and capacity to interact with others. His research complements insights such as Julia Kristeva's about the analytic power of art and literature which aligns them with psychoanalysis as well as Rizzuto's own work in essays such as "Metaphors of a Bodily Mind" (Ana-María Rizzuto, "Metaphors of a Bodily Mind," *Journal of the American Psychoanalytical Association* 49 [2001]: 535–68). In fact, in this chapter, it is evident that their respective notions of metaphor place Rizzuto and Kristeva on common ground. Each dissents from a common understanding of metaphor as referring only to a figure of speech (Ibid., 549). For Rizzuto and for Kristeva, metaphor literally embodies a function of the mind. Rizzuto understands that "language is a fully embodied function" and that mediation by the body is essential for building connections between the world and the self (Ibid., 537). So also does Kristeva concur that an affective connection governs human experience. Kristeva cites metaphor as a vehicle of translation whereby sensations, perceptions, and trauma are joined with the language of cognition (Suzanne Clark and Kathleen Hulley, "Cultural Strangeness and the Subject in Crisis," in *Julia Kristeva Interviews* [New York, NY: Columbia University Press, 1996], 55). The metaphor, joining sensation and perception, creates a bridge between the body and the idea that results in the transubstantiation of words into flesh (Julia Kristeva, *Time and Sense*, trans. Ross Guberman [Columbia University Press, 1998], 195). Similarly, Rizzuto writes, citing Deacon, "The physical changes that make us human are the incarnations, so to speak, of the process of using words" (Rizzuto, "Metaphors of a Bodily Mind," 536). Both appeal to what I have defined as a process of kinesis, through which metaphors acquire lived meaning. When links are drawn between Rizzuto and Kristeva, a way appears for eliminating from contemporary psychoanalytic theories of mentalization problematic remnants of Cartesian thinking that portray children as connecting with others only after they have negotiated an internal/external divide through processes that suggest a kind of mind-reading exercise. But a theory of metaphor suggests that we are always,

already outside ourselves. With Merleau-Ponty, Kristeva observes that metaphor is an immediate mapping of existence via neural connections. Cognition is not separate from bodily existence in perception and movement. The embodied mind is always, already a mind in connection with the other. On this count, psychological dysfunction does not manifest itself as a failure to get outside oneself to the other (a failed negotiation of an internal/external divide); rather it presents as a distortion within a metaphorical process that forecloses on embodied connections with the other that were always, already the human subject's birthright. Rizzuto writes in "Metaphors of a Bodily Mind" that anorexics and bulimics "make minimal use of metaphor" (Ibid., 551). Their embodied suffering, we could say, attests to a restriction in their capacity for metamorphosis. I take this observation as a point of entry to further conversation with Kristeva which would enable Rizzuto to reconsider ways in which not only bulimics but also all of us live with monsters when crises in our lives lead us replay those somatic rites through which we first negotiated standing in the world.

33. Julia Kristeva, *Powers of Horror: An Essay on Abjection*, trans. Leon Roudiez (New York, NY: Columbia University Press, 1982), 6.

34. Julia Kristeva, *Hatred and Forgiveness*, trans. Jeanine Herman (New York, NY: Columbia University Press, 2010), 186.

35. Ibid., 184.

36. Julia Kristeva, *Black Sun*, trans. Leon Roudiez (New York, NY: Columbia University Press, 1992), 27.

37. Beal, *Religion and Its Monsters*, 1–3.

38. Ibid., 4–5.

39. Ibid., 6.

40. Ibid., 7.

41. Julia Kristeva, *Revolution in Poetic Language*, trans. Margaret Waller (New York, NY: Columbia University Press, 1984), 75–79.

42. Ewa Ziarek, "At the Limits of Discourse: Heterogeneity, Alterity, and the Maternal Body in Kristeva's Thought," *Hypatia* 7, no. 2 (1992): 100.

43. Rizzuto, *The Birth*, 185–86.

44. Julia Kristeva, *This Incredible Need to Believe*, trans. Beverley Bie Brahic (New York, NY: Columbia University Press, 2009), xi.

45. Kristeva, *Powers of Horror*, 1982, 13.

46. Julia Kristeva, *Tales of Love*, trans. Leon Roudiez (Columbia University Press, 1987), 23.

47. Julia Kristeva, "Place Names," in *Desire in Language: A Semiotic Approach to Literature and Art*, trans. Leon Roudiez (New York, NY: Columbia University Press, 1980), 284–285.

48. Julia Kristeva, "Within the Microcosm of the Talking Cure," in *Psychiatry and the Humanities*, ed. Joseph H. Smith and William Kerrigan, trans. Thomas Gora and Margaret Waller (New Haven, CT: Yale University Press, 1983).

49. Kristeva, *Revolution in Poetic Language*, 70.

50. Ana-María Rizzuto, *Why Did Freud Reject God?: A Psychodynamic Interpretation* (New Haven, CT: Yale University Press, 1998), 227.

51. Rizzuto writes that because Freud's mother represented death (in the Three Fates dream) and because she was emotionally unavailable to him, he wanted to distance himself from God representations that would be stem from that relationship (Ibid., 239–40). By contrast, the affective relationship he had with his nanny provided more material for God representations; however, her early departure from his life, when combined with his mother's disapproval of the nanny, led Freud to link the nanny with death: on the one hand, her departure constituted a kind of death; on the other hand, he feared that his Rizzuto writes that because Freud's mother represented death (in the Three Fates dream) and because she was emotionally unavailable to him, he wanted to distance himself from God representations that would be stem from that relationship (Ibid., 239–40). By contrast, the affective relationship he had with his nanny provided more material for God representations; however, her early departure from his life, when combined with his mother's disapproval of the nanny, led Freud to link the nanny with death: on the one hand, her departure constituted a kind of death; on the other hand, he feared that his mother's disapproval would register on him and he too would disappear/die (Ibid., 241).

52. Rizzuto, *Why Did Freud Reject God?*, 244, 246–247.

53. Rizzuto, *Why Did Freud Reject God?*, 253.

54. The image is suggested by Rizzuto, *The Birth*, 180. The affective connection Freud has with these images suggests that, in collecting them, he is not interacting with them solely on the level of a God concept (albeit concepts from archaic religion). As transitional objects (Rizzuto, *Why Did Freud Reject God?*, 18), the images connect Freud to the territory of God representations Freud thought he had left behind. As reported below, Rizzuto concurs with this assessment.

55. Ibid., 4–6.

56. Ibid., 105 ff.

57. Ibid., 18–19, 259.

58. Ibid., 259.

59. Ana-María Rizzuto, "God in the Mind: The Psychodynamics of an Unusual Relationship," *The Annual of Psychoanalysis* 34–35 (2007): 41.

60. Ibid.

61. Rizzuto, *Why Did Freud Reject God?*, 242.

62. Ibid., 257.

63. Diane Jonte-Pace, "At Home in the Uncanny: Freudian Representations of Death, Mothers, and the Afterlife," *Journal of the American Academy of Religion* 64, no. 1 (1996): 61.

64. Rizzuto, *Why Did Freud Reject God?*, 218–22.

65. Jonte-Pace, "At Home in the Uncanny: Freudian Representations of Death, Mothers, and the Afterlife," 82.

66. Rizzuto, *Why Did Freud Reject God?*, 258.

67. Sigmund Freud, "*The*" *Interpretation of Dreams* (Macmillan, 1913), 460. Rizzuto, *Why Did Freud Reject God?*, 216.

68. Rizzuto, *Why Did Freud Reject God?*, 94.

69. Ibid., 94, note 3; ibid., 97, figure 6.2.

70. Sigmund Freud and C. J. M. Hubback, *Beyond the Pleasure Principle* (London, England: The International Psycho-analytical Press, 1922), 12–13. Lacan, among other interpreters, argues that Ernst is negotiating his ascension to the Symbolic order, the world of language and meaning. Kristeva and Irigaray locate the affective power of the fort/da game earlier in the pre-Oedipal work of separation from the maternal body. Both emphasize that Ernst's gestures play a key role in the game. They also suggest that Ernst's limited vocabulary places this game within the buccal space: Ernst plays his game within his mouth, as his teeth, tongue, and larynx "bite" into the maternal body from whom he is separating in his play. For a full account of Kristeva and Irigaray's arguments, see *Sacrificed Lives (*Martha J. Reineke, *Sacrificed Lives: Kristeva on Women and Violence* [Bloomington: Indiana University Press, 1997], 56–59.

71. Freud's memory work is facilitated when he touches the objects, as is supported by Rizzuto and Kristeva's understandings of embodied meanings.

72. Rizzuto, "God in the Mind: The Psychodynamics of an Unusual Relationship," 41.

73. Because the "father" of individual prehistory references experiences prior to the child's acquisition of language, I emphasize again that, for Kristeva, paternity refers to a *function*, not to empirical fatherhood. In a recent and extended commentary on this paternal presence, Kristeva writes (quoting Freud), "This identification anterior to any objective relation of desire is not destined for the Oedipal father but for a . . . loving father, who would have . . . the 'attributes of both parents'" (Kristeva, *This Incredible Need to Believe*, 10).

74. Julia Kristeva, *Black Sun*, 23–24.

75. Of course, the Symbolic order or Father's law, with which we are familiar from Freud's description of the Oedipus complex, will read this perceived difference as an interdiction: the mother's desire is directed elsewhere and I am not the phallus she seeks. But the Father of individual prehistory suggests a metaphorical reading of the social space that balances the interdictory Law of desire with the gift of love (Julia Kristeva, "Julia Kristeva in Conversation with Rosalind Coward," in *ICA Documents*, vol. 1 [London, England: Institute of Contemporary Arts, 1984]), 22.

76. Ibid., 200.

77. Ibid., 216.

78. Kelly Oliver, *The Colonization of Psychic Space: A Psychoanalytic Social Theory of Oppression* (Minneapolis, MN: University of Minnesota Press, 2004), 139.

79. Ana-María Rizzuto, *Why Did Freud Reject God*, 121, figure 7.9.

80. Osiris is god of the afterlife who also is associated with the cycles of nature. In Egyptian mythology, Osiris is killed and torn part. Isis puts back together the fragments of his body, but his penis is missing. Isis replaces the missing member with a golden phallus. Subsequently, she becomes pregnant with Horus.

81. A Christian approached Jakob Freud and knocked his cap in the mud while shouting "Jew! Get off the pavement." See Rizzuto, *Why Did Freud Reject God?*, 10.

82. Ana-María Rizzuto, *The Birth of the Living God: A Psychoanalytic Study* (Chicago: University of Chicago Press, 1981), 193.

83. Ana-María Rizzutto, "Eating and Monsters: A Psychodynamic View of Bulimarexia," in *Theory and Treatment of Anorexia Nervosa and Bulimia - Biomedical, Sociocultural, and Psychological Perspectives*, ed. Steven Wiley Emmett (New York: Brunner/Mazel, Inc., 1985), 196.

84. Sigmund Freud, "Psychopathology of Everyday Life," *Monograph for Psychiatry and Neurology* (1901): 258-259.

85. Martha Reineke, "Birth of a Living Monster."

86. Richard A. Koenigsberg, *Hitler's Ideology: A Study in Psychoanalytic Sociology* (New York, The Library of Social Science, 1975), 20.

87. Martha Reineke, "Birth of a Living Monster."

BIBLIOGRAPHY

Beal, Timothy K. *Religion and Its Monsters*. New York, NY: Routledge, 2002.

Bolens, Guillemette. *The Style of Gestures: Embodiment and Cognition in Literary Narrative*. Baltimore, MD: The Johns Hopkins University Press, 2012.

Clark, Suzanne, and Kathleen Hulley. "Cultural Strangeness and the Subject in Crisis." In *Julia Kristeva Interviews*, 35–58. New York, NY: Columbia University Press, 1996.

Freud, Sigmund. *The Interpretation of Dreams*. London: Macmillan, 1913.

Freud, Sigmund, and C. J. M. Hubback. *Beyond the Pleasure Principle*. London, England: The International Psycho-analytical Press, 1922.

Gallese, Vittorio. "The Two Sides of Mimesis: Mimetic Theory, Embodied Simulation, and Social Identification." In *Mimesis and Science: Empirical Research on Imitation and the Mimetic Theory of Culture and Religion*, 87–108. East Lansing, MI: Michigan State University Press, 2011.

Jonte-Pace, Diane. "At Home in the Uncanny: Freudian Representations of Death, Mothers, and the Afterlife." *Journal of the American Academy of Religion* 64, no. 1 (1996): 61–88.

Julia Kristeva. "Julia Kristeva in Conversation with Rosalind Coward." In *ICA Documents*, 1:22–27. London, England: Institute of Contemporary Arts, 1984.

Kristeva, Julia. *Black Sun*. Translated by Leon Roudiez. New York, NY: Columbia University Press, 1992.

———. *Hatred and Forgiveness*. Translated by Jeanine Herman. New York, NY: Columbia University Press, 2010.

———. "Motherhood According to Giovanni Bellini." In *Desire in Language*, edited by Leon Roudiez, translated by Thomas Gora and Alice Jardine, 237–270. New York, NY: Columbia University Press, 1980.

———. "Place Names." In *Desire in Language: A Semiotic Approach to Literature and Art*, translated by Leon Roudiez, 271–94. New York, NY: Columbia University Press, 1980.

———. *Powers of Horror: An Essay on Abjection*. New York, NY: Columbia University Press, 1982.

———. *Powers of Horror: An Essay on Abjection*. Translated by Leon Roudiez. New York, NY: Columbia University Press, 1982.
———. *Revolution in Poetic Language*. Translated by Margaret Waller. New York, NY: Columbia University Press, 1984.
———. *Tales of Love*. Translated by Leon Roudiez. New York, NY: Columbia University Press, 1987.
———. *This Incredible Need to Believe*. Translated by Beverley Bie Brahic. New York, NY: Columbia University Press, 2009.
———. *Time and Sense*. Translated by Ross Guberman. New York, NY: Columbia University Press, 1998.
———. "Within the Microcosm of the Talking Cure." In *Psychiatry and the Humanities*, edited by Joseph H. Smith and William Kerrigan, translated by Thomas Gora and Margaret Waller. New Haven, CT: Yale University Press, 1983.
Merleau-Ponty, Maurice. "The Child's Relations with Others." In *The Primacy of Perception*, translated by William Cobb, 96–155. Evanston, IL: Northwestern University Press, 1964.
Oliver, Kelly. *The Colonization of Psychic Space: A Psychoanalytic Social Theory of Oppression*. Minneapolis, MN: University of Minnesota Press, 2004.
Reineke, Martha J. *Sacrificed Lives: Kristeva on Women and Violence*. Bloomington, IN: Indiana University Press, 1997.
Rizzuto, Ana-María. "Eating and Monsters: A Psychodynamic View of Bulimarexia." In *Theory and Treatment of Anorexia Nervosa and Bulimia: Biomedical, Sociocultural, and Psychological Perspectives*, edited by Steven Wiley Emmett, 194–210. New York, NY: Brunner/Mazel, 1985.
———. "Freud, God, the Devil and the Theory of Object Representation." *International Review of Psycho-Analysis* 3 (1976): 165–80.
———. "God in the Mind: The Psychodynamics of an Unusual Relationship." *The Annual of Psychoanalysis* 34–35 (2007): 24–46.
———. "Metaphors of a Bodily Mind." *Journal of the American Psychoanalytical Association* 49 (2001): 535–68.
———. "One God, Two Genders: Psychoanalytic Reflections." In *Die Zwei Geschlechter Und Der Eine Gott*, edited by Elmar Klinger, Stephanie Böhm, and Thomas Franz, 29–46. Würzburg, Germany: Echter Verlag, 2002.
———. *The Birth of the Living God: A Psychoanalytic Study*. Chicago, IL: University of Chicago Press, 1981.
———. *Why Did Freud Reject God?: A Psychodynamic Interpretation*. New Haven, CT: Yale University Press, 1998.
Ziarek, Ewa. "At the Limits of Discourse: Heterogeneity, Alterity, and the Maternal Body in Kristeva's Thought." *Hypatia* 7, no. 2 (1992): 91–108.

Chapter 6

Ana-María Rizzuto and the New Atheism

Science and Religion in Light of Psychoanalysis

Jacob Waldenmaier

A typical, though not universal, assumption in the psychology of religion is that theology declines in relevance and usefulness when natural accounts of mental phenomena expand. Psychology also debates whether the elimination of God from humanity's field of belief would improve the overall well-being of humankind, as William Meissner noted in "Toward a Psychology of Religious Experience."[1] Meissner not only drew attention to what lies beneath this debate—the status and value of illusion—but also suggested a way out; he recommended that the discipline of psychology confines itself to the study of the mind in relation to its environment, thereby recusing itself from judgment as to whether God is objectively real. Since God is not an observable artifact of sense-perception, psychology must, for the sake of methodological consistency, understand that religious experience in all its dimensions is human; psychology "puts aside the supernatural character of religious phenomena and restricts itself more or less to their natural manifestations."[2]

Ana-María Rizzuto expresses views similar to Meissner's in her groundbreaking book, *The Birth of the Living God.* Rizzuto accepts that religion is "an institution consisting of culturally patterned interactions with culturally postulated superhuman beings."[3] She does not discuss the actual existence of God because her method of inquiry enables her "to deal only with psychic experiences."[4] For Rizzuto, the manner in which God is perceived and the subject's relationship history with that ever-modifying perception contribute to a sound understanding of the value of God in a person's psychological well-being. Rizzuto develops these insights by linking psychoanalytic theory with clinical practice and reflection in *The Birth of the Living God.*

In this chapter I examine how *The Birth of the Living God* has enriched across disciplines our understanding of and engagement with the tensions between faith and reason and between reality and illusion. I review the way in which continental theology, social theory, and natural philosophy—all three often mingled with atheistic sentiments—contributed to the nascent science of psychology leading up to and during the era in which Freudian psychoanalysis and its materialist roots developed. I describe also how Rizzuto utilizes tools from the psychoanalytic tradition to develop a manner of interpreting theology that fully appreciates its importance and relevance throughout human life without making discrete ontological claims about theology's referent. Finally, I discuss ways in which Rizzuto's work continues to address the contemporary resurgence of atheistic sentiment, especially with reference to the psychology of religion. Rizzuto maintains the importance and vitality of the God-concept against two incompatible polarities claimed in new atheism: reason with faith and reality with illusion. Rizzuto addresses the century of atheism poignantly, yet obliquely with respect to her discipline, showing how theology and psychology might be understood together. Physicians and psychologists around the turn of the twentieth century opened new forays into the study of the mind by examining and systematically describing events, functions, and processes that often had been attributed to divine, soul-related, or otherwise preternatural mental agencies that supersede the brain. The enigmas of innate talent, epiphany, intuition, and clairvoyance, along with specifically supernatural events (such as spiritual guidance, prophecy, and glossolalia), acquired natural explanations by William James, Wilhelm Wundt, Sigmund Freud, and others, especially with the exploration of unconscious or subconscious mental phenomena.

As a result, "commonsense psychology" and philosophies of mind acceded to the absence of both full conceptual access and comprehensive understanding of our own mental processes[5]—a shift in attitude which promoted the convention that mysterious peculiarities, or anomalies of the mind, likely have strong natural explanations to be discovered as neurologists prod, stimulate, and scan brains. Psychology, as exemplified by Freud, began to understand mental events vis-à-vis regulatory constraints like laws of conservation, which contributed to explanations of suppressed memory and numerous pathologies, neuroses, conditions, and complexes. Human experience became a closed system. After all, the space into which one might insert a *deus ex machina* was closing. This movement prompted some to endorse and include in their treatment the elimination of the very conception of those spiritual influences from the human psyche. Mental health would improve, once individuals were rid of these illusions.

For Freud, religion originated in primitive society, which he compared to childhood. Just as adolescents can mature and discard their naïve superstitions, outgrowing their juvenile fantasies and transitional objects, civilization can also shake off its primal illusions. Atheism in the psychoanalytic community shares not only the materialism of Freud but also, and more broadly, the tradition of unbelief coincident with the intellectual roots of psychology as an academic and clinical discipline and profession. Thus our discussion of Rizzuto's address of atheism will benefit from a description and analysis of the nineteenth-century dialog between psychology, theology, and materialism, which exerted a formative influence on Freud and also shaped his legacy well into the final century of the second millennium.

FAITH, REASON, AND MATERIALISM WITHIN THE FOUNDATION OF PSYCHOANALYSIS

In their theoretical origins, the roots of many of Freud's contributions to psychology are connected with theological and atheistic sentiments. Philosophers, physicians, theologians, and sociologists whose thought occupied Freud's intellectual repertoire contributed also to the affirmation (though perhaps not the origin) of his atheism. Not only did the nineteenth century progressively introduce material explanations for religious phenomena, but it also had elements emerge of what would become Freudian thought.[6]

Following the eighteenth-century Enlightenment emphasis on rationality and humanism (with its characteristic skepticism toward religious metaphysical claims), theologians needed to cultivate an understanding of faith that was compatible with the new wave of criticism. Friedrich Schleiermacher (1799), pioneer of liberal theology, relegated religion to its affective, private, and experiential manifestations in an effort to rescue religion from its "cultured despisers." His faith is a matter of "feeling" and "intuition" rather than doctrine or ethics or ritual. He thereby stressed the centrality of religious experience, most essentially that of "absolute dependence" on the divine source of human existence.

The humanization of theology produced a number of implicitly and explicitly atheistic echoes. Ludwig Feuerbach's project near the middle of the nineteenth century turned the arc of theology back toward its origins in human thought, interpreting religious convictions, practices, and dogmas as anthropological statements reflective of human aspirations (a position reminiscent of the Narcissus legend, which Freud would later incorporate as a psychoanalytic motif representing self-adoration). Feuerbach developed especially the conceptualization of God as a fulfillment of desire, the brainchild of a wish to feel protected and loved by an ultimate personality. Karl Marx's social critique of theology exposed its motivations for the upper and labor classes in dialectic: the faith of the proletariat was a hopeless "sigh," a resignation to their lot. Life on earth was destitute and fixed but tethered to the assurance of posthumous redemption.

Inasmuch as theological and socioeconomic accounts of the human condition provided the backdrop for psychoanalysis, philosophies of the self placed the individual human being at the center of study. The ego as a subject of interest, revitalized by Descartes and criticized during the Enlightenment, was restored to prominence by nineteenth-century aesthetes, idealists, and transcendentalists and made its way to Freud through Theodor Meynert, director of the psychiatric clinic at the University of Vienna.[7] Freud's characterization of the ego would be squarely personal and psychological, avoiding metaphysical claims. Freud's ego paradigm included a dialectical model whereby the ego exists in tension between instinct (the id) and social expectations (the superego); in Hegelian fashion, the consciousness is joggled between the unconscious pleasure principle and the morally constraining reality principle. Capable of voyaging further than phenomenology (as Paul Ricoeur notes), psychoanalysis offers connections between conscious life, its substrate id, and its conscientious modular superego.[8]

A strong preference for physical or material solutions—together with the assumed obsolescence of supernatural explanations—characterized many of these psychological theories of the ego. This materialist disposition bourgeoned in the physical sciences, medicine, and philosophy as the disciplines now delineated as physics and chemistry saw advanced mechanization. The more readily measurable concept of "drive" became useful for describing electricity and even mystical natural phenomena such as magnetism were formulated and explained by Michael Faraday and James Clerk Maxwell. As a neurologist, Freud understood the psyche on similar terms: he presumed that every internal, mental phenomenon had a natural origin, that is, a closed relation to its material causes. "It is my assumption," Freud wrote in *Psychopathy of Everyday Life*, "that the displacement [of name recollection] is not left to psychic arbitrariness, but that it follows lawful and rational paths."[9]

Hermann von Helmholtz (1847) and others similarly argued for the "conservation of energy." A now-legendary pact among colleagues who exerted an influence on Freud reads, in part, that "no other forces than the common physical-chemical ones are active within the organism."[10] Biology also began to succumb to law and principle-based analysis, especially with the advent of Darwinian theory. With some regard for the evolutionary primacy of reproduction and survival, Freud articulated that the reasons for all of our actions are ultimately expressions of an instinct with the will to sensual gratification at its fundament (the pleasure principle ensconced in the id). And yet Freud was distinctly aware that psychoanalysis was developing a linguistic system of its own, independent, it seemed, of the quantitative terminology of physics and chemistry.[11] Nonetheless, Freud still followed principles of conservation. He maintained that "in mental life nothing which has once been formed can perish."[12] No trauma, for example, dissipates. Trauma is either expressed or repressed. Freud's psyche was, in Ronald Fairbairn's words, "a conglomeration of inert, immutable and indivisible particles to which motion was imparted by a fixed quantity of energy separate from the particles themselves."[13]

Among the most strident naturalizers of religion and, perhaps, the philosopher with the strongest influence on Freud was Friedrich Nietzsche, whose interest in the source of morality and religion led to unflinching dissections of what modernity had come to accept as normal, especially in *Beyond Good and Evil* (1886) and *Genealogy of Morality* (1887). Commensurate with his training in classics, Nietzsche accessed many features of ancient Greek theology for models of human behavior. His paradigmatic dichotomy between Apollo and Dionysius carried forward into twentieth-century psychoanalysis[14] as did his stress on the "will to power" which he saw as endemic to desire in its deepest rudiments (the satisfaction of which Freud would fashion as wish-fulfillment). In his diatribes on idolatry, Nietzsche referred to sublimation as the gratification of will to power through more socially acceptable—or indeed religious—means. Freud would inherit this psychological maneuver through Heinrich Heine's *The Harz Journey*[15] and would understand sublimation to desexualize the libido by converting "object-libido into narcissistic libido,"[16] in effect defusing instincts even at the risk of "maltreatment and death."[17] While Alfred Adler encouraged patients to surmount their wills-to-power,[18] Freud recognized their inherent and irreplaceable role in human nature which must be either expressed (often sublimated under pressure from the superego) or repressed into a self-defeating neurosis. "In the new Freudian perspective," writes Norman Brown, "the essence of society is repression of the individual and the essence of the individual is repression of himself."[19] Nietzsche philosophized with a hammer; Freud psychoanalyzed with one.

NARRATIVE, PSYCHOANALYSIS, AND THEOLOGY: TOWARD A MATERIALIST PSYCHOANALYSIS

Schleiermacher's reorientation toward humanistic interpretations of religion entailed that he give significant attention in his hermeneutics to the authors of sacred texts.[20] He promoted the notion that, inasmuch as one reads a piece of literature for its subject, the composition also contains a great deal of information about the mind behind it. The author's imagination "creates" its subject through the author's personal perspective. One of Nietzsche's distinctly methodical influences on Freud was the repudiation of Kantian categorical logic, which crumbled under perspectivism, narrative, drama, and power. Freud would refer to "thinking" as "the equivalent of the hallucinatory wish."[21] Nietzsche made extensive use of classical literature to revitalize the personal drama expressed by the characters of Hellenic tragedy and comedy. Similarly for Freud, personal narrative—complete with subplots, hidden forces, and symbolism—became the primary source for psychological information and the context for psychoanalysis, and he, too, drew from ancient Greece profound narrative illustrations for the secrets of the psyche.[22]

Through Sophocles, for example, Freud had read Jocasta's reassurance to Oedipus: "Don't be afraid that you may marry your mother. Many a man before you, in dreams, has shared his mother's bed. But to live at ease one must attach no importance to such things."[23]

Accordingly, with multiple references to Schleiermacher,[24] Freud argued that wishes provoke the dreams that fulfill them; thus, the proper excursus of a dream narrative locates its origin in the id and interprets the sequence through the pleasure principle.[25] The interpretation of dreams is the "*via regia*'" to the unconscious.[26] Schleiermacher also noted an important difference between dreaming and wakefulness, the former of which is governed by pictures and the latter by ideas. For him, sleep begins as "undesirable" or unchecked, and amoral hypnogogic imagery predominates over conscious thought. Accordingly, Freud's hermeneutic method for interpreting dreams exposits their narrative form as authored by the dreamer.[27] This method further illustrates that psychoanalysis "is a theory of reading first and foremost; moreover, it suggests that there are always more meanings to any statement than there appear to be at first glance."[28]

The formulation of Freud's complex views on theology now can be discerned. God for Freud was "the object of sublimated libido after the resolution of the oedipal crisis."[29] The Oedipus complex explained both the imagery used in religious narratives and the social customs associated with them: "the Father loomed as a gigantic figure in primeval times and, raised to the status of a deity in the racial unconscious, returned to the memory of mankind."[30] While some anthropologists (such as E.B. Tylor) and psychologists (such as Wundt) would attribute the origins of religion to dream interpretation and fear of the inimical and mysterious, Freud sought a filial account of religion that accessed the fullness of the psyche in all aspects of personal and social life. [31]

Freud further presented the proximity between "savage" superstition and doctrines subsumed under modern religions, to the same effect that the psychic dynamics expressed in ancient Greek tragedies are still lived out today. No longer could the civilized, cosmopolitan, modern monotheist claim a loftier, more developed, advanced, enlightened theology because all forms of the divine are but variations of a common ancestral "compulsion neurosis."[32]

The hollowing of religion's supernatural contents and the retainer of their real effects on the psyche were both theoretical and personal for Freud. Even from youth, he felt "no need" to believe in the reality of God,[33] in part, because of his 1880s education in Vienna where Darwin's theory of natural selection was embraced as a sound explanation of human origins, entailing that the verisimilitude of design can emerge absent of a designer. And yet, "the teenager who knew that God did not exist"[34] espoused some abstract notions of the transcendental that seemed to defy his naturalism,[35] and Freud remained markedly Jewish in his family decisions, residence, and social status.[36] Indeed, he wore his Jewish identity without demure and with ever greater resolution as German prejudice against Jews intensified.[37] However, maintaining intellectual consistency, Freud also considered Judaism the myth of his ancestry[38] and seems not to have believed in the objective factuality of its stories or theology.[39] Further, because Freud's thought was imbued with materialism, little held Freud back from eventually regarding theology as pathology. Freud considered the theological illusion "a universal mass neurosis" (with some resemblance to Marx's views on religion), a sort of global obsession which, though nearly universal, should be considered pathological.[40] In all these ways, Freud took a journey in his own thought that followed the same course theology took during the nineteenth century in Germany, moving from Schleiermacher to Nietzsche.

Was psychoanalysis the brainchild of Freud, a unique force emergent from his peculiar life? Or might psychoanalysis have developed without him? The vectors of influence I have just traced affirm the latter:[41] The intellectual, aesthetic, and romantic products of the nineteenth century demanded rigorous application to the nascent study of the mind.[42] Materialism accompanied and endorsed the many conceptual means by which the mind was naturalized and mechanized. Further, the atheism of the twentieth century owes much to a momentum generated from its nineteenth-century expression with psychology—and Freud—among its many conduits. Janice Halpern invites a twentieth-century study of how the psychoanalytic community carried forth Freud's rejection of God, welcoming by corollary the question of whether its reasons have been similar to Freud's. Though mechanistic and reductive studies of the mind would continue to endure skepticism,[43] Freudian psychoanalysis could be conducted as a fully materialistic enterprise, with much of Freud's influence tied either to the absence or to the outright rejection of the relevance of the divine.

At the advent of the twentieth century, William James observed in his inquiry into experiences of the invisible, "'Science' in many minds is genuinely taking the place of a religion. Where this is so, the scientist treats the 'Laws of Nature' as objective facts to be revered."[44] The new science of the mind accordingly fueled tendencies toward reductionism because the elimination of the perceived necessity of preternatural mental events was seen to permit the distillation of any phenomenon into an aggregate of natural, mechanical causal constituents. The fluorescence of this philosophical trajectory brought forth what some have labeled "science chauvinism," or the view that the scientific method holds the final keys to unlocking every secret not only of the cosmos, but also of the mind. In this way, it decodes the enigmas of both the outer and inner worlds. This view insists that science has a monopoly on truth and that the methodological exclusivity of deductive and reductive natural science should apply everywhere.

Rizzuto's method draws from the manifold elements of Freudian thought described above. Although these elements have been saturated and inspired by materialism since their inception, including their twentieth-century development and application, Rizzuto channels these elements toward a personified absolute that stands at the denotative antithesis of atheism. As will be further discussed in this chapter, Rizzuto invites her clients to sketch their impressions of God. The clients' experiences of the divine emerge from within them, revealing something about their history: a religious institution does not centrally impart their experiences. As a consequence, these personal impressions provide a context for Rizzuto to discuss her clients' neuroses. Her approach is, in some respects, a variation and development of Donald Winnicott's "squiggle-line" method; moreover, it theoretically affirms James's insight into religious experience as independent of institutional doctrines or rituals.

THEOLOGY AS THERAPEIA: REALITY AND ILLUSION

After Freud a strong warrant to divide, or even set at loggerheads, can be detected between psychotherapy and religion.[45] In an attempt to legitimize a practical science of the mind, clinical psychology has at times dismissed the therapeutic value of incorporating or accessing the spirituality of subjects.[46] Furthermore, exceedingly transcendent models of spirituality that distance psychology from theology arguably have led to a dichotomy that presses patients to choose between a spiritualist "disenchantment of nature" and a secular course of recovery,[47] although psychology regularly has employed metaphors redolent of imaginal and religious metaphysical concepts.[48] In the process, a visceral part of the human psyche—and of human experience—has been neglected at the expense of holistic treatment,[49] though even Freud had come to recognize that the "'compelling emotional power' behind religion was related to 'actual but forgotten events'".[50]

In view of these circumstances, a social need has arisen to relate theology to psychological health.[51] In a manner similar to the way the American Psychiatric Association has weighed the credibility and status of presumed diagnosable disorders to better recognize potential cultural biases (e.g., the process by which homosexuality was removed as a disorder), the theology resulting from personal experience also has demanded acceptance and recognition as a visceral component of the thought-worlds of many.[52] The need for therapeutic theology is further augmented because of the disconnections between the abundant resources available to interweave religious and other life experiences and the ethical guidelines that can direct how these experiences are assessed and incorporated into the therapeutic context.[53]

A number of theologians and psychologists have recognized the compatibility of Freudian psychoanalysis with Christian principles.[54] Rizzuto writes that "all religions have a debt of gratitude to Freud for having provided us with a therapeutic tool capable of helping us to expose our spurious moves and thus to have the opportunity to modify them."[55] Further, Freud's broad "analysis of numerous examples from my own psychic life"[56] resembles in some ways introspective theological texts such as Augustine's deeply self-scrutinizing *Confessions* or Paul's letter to the Romans, in which the apostle laments the tension between desires of the flesh and his spiritual calling.[57] The primary inspiration for Freud's personal reflection seems especially to originate in Nietzsche, whom Freud admired for his "penetrating knowledge of himself."[58] Altogether the autobiographical genre demonstrates some (perhaps latent or, indeed, unconscious) foresight, as some psychoanalysts recently have promoted the value of "self-analysis" as, among other remedial acts, a demulcent of compulsions.[59]

Theology, when understood as a private creation[60] (Rizzuto aptly uses the word "birth") and connected intimately with personal narrative, can be highly therapeutic regardless of whether its content is independently real.[61] God often is a profoundly affective object and, therefore, a hub for emotional direction.[62] Even if religious belief is ontologically or epistemologically mistaken, it normally can be conscripted to good avail in the restoration of emotional tranquility and freedom.[63] When a doctrine remains inherent and nonnegotiable in a client's worldview, it is not only more feasible,[64] but also more humane and pacific for the psychotherapist to utilize or redirect[65] the theological object rather than expunge it altogether.[66]

However, a conspicuous hazard exists which requires careful consideration. In the development of a theological therapy, doctrinal commitments, variables between therapist and client, can be strong and inflexible. While the capacity of religion to ameliorate mental health issues has been broadly confirmed in recent decades,[67] a dramatic tension remains between psychotherapists who pursue the goal of mental health absent all metaphysical claims and clients who share religious beliefs with these psychotherapists. These beliefs appear to play significant roles in clients' lives and worldviews. How can they not also feature in the psychological challenges these clients face, either explicitly or tacitly?[68]

Because this dilemma raises important questions about the philosophical ground on which psychotherapy can stand with respect to the mind and to spiritual or theological claims, it is important that resolution be achieved.[69]

More than once the role of the therapist has been compared to clerical duties,[70] and Nietzsche stridently denounced as casuistry the hazy motives for practicing psychology.[71] A therapist's views on any number of topics, theological or otherwise, can fall outside that therapist's licensed area of competence. Best practice suggests that such views remain suspended when the therapist is engaged in the conduct of his or her professional responsibilities.[72] The consistency, trustworthiness, perseverance, and fidelity of the therapist are paramount, as the relationship between therapist and client makes the former "*emotional object constancy*," and this set of traits "creates the *conditions* for the exploration of all levels of psychic organization."[73] The therapist exhibits some of the attributes of God in this sense, as a reliable and faithful partner and companion in the interest of nurturing wholeness, freedom, and health.

OBJECT RELATIONS AND THEOLOGY

Object relations theory has played a significant role in the rapprochement between theology and psychology. Freud had thought that the libido and its corresponding id have no direction, but only seek gratification,[74] and that the ego represents "a passive structure without energy except such as invades it from the id."[75] In object relations, instinctual motivations originate from a drive toward functional connections between psychic objects (whereas Freud seemed to take the libido and other elements of the *id* as aimless).[76] W. Ronald Fairbairn argued that visceral drives like the libido should be considered conscious (ego-level) activity and, more fundamentally, that the structures and directions of related objects are more complex than earlier conceptualizations of motivation, the ego, and the pleasure principle.[77] For Fairbairn, we do not, at our core, simply seek the satisfaction of pleasure; instead, the challenge among instinct, personality, and ethics[78] is seen as a contest for psychic resolution and equilibrium (and thus the appeasement of the neurotic imbalance between their motives).

If understood in terms of object relations, then, theological reflection promises a dynamic and useful kind of therapy that is not limited to instincts, unconscious or otherwise, as foundational motives.[79] Theological dilemmas may be understood as consequences of "disrupted object relations," and psychotherapy can interact with these theological objects to help restore balance.[80]

MENTAL OBJECTS: REAL, ILLUSORY, OR BOTH?

Milestones in object relations exemplified by Fairbairn are not without theoretical difficulties and snares;[81] after all, abstractions in the psyche can be difficult to examine. Erik Erikson (1975), for example, challenged the reification of Freudian concepts such as libido or ego, since they are immeasurable.[82] Theological objects, by extension and because of their often obscure nature, are still more difficult to define, standardized measure. The crux of the matter must be determined. Is that which is "real" the psychoanalytic method used to interpret and treat the subject or the contents of the therapy that pertain to the nature of the subject? In short, the reality of the "objects" of object-relations is at issue.

Irrespective of the conclusion on this matter, mental objects' agency is undeniable, though they are present and efficacious in a wholly different way from material things. Early in the twentieth century, Lev Vygotsky assessed that psychologically relevant environments and processes are not reducible to biological mechana, since the constraints of the environment around a person and his psychological interaction with it operate and "develop according to completely different laws than the elementary or lower functions."[83] Rollo May observes,

> Many of the arguments of existential and phenomenological writers against "the unconscious" are themselves too legalistic, dealing in verbal logic, and fail to take the term in its dynamic, existential meaning. Surely, it is always inaccurate to speak of *the* unconscious, *the* preconscious or subconscious: these are never *places*. But we must be able to include *unconscious experience*.[84]

Therapeutic techniques that utilize empathy, such as Carl Rogers's "unconditional positive regard," seem compelled to make some metaphysical claim or suggestion. Rogers felt that his person-centered approach elicited a feeling of deep connectedness between his own and his clients' "spirits."[85] Paul Ricoeur understood the Freudian hermeneutic to make it possible to consider myth as "the symbolic exploration of our relationship to beings and to Being." He rejected the dichotomy between illusion and reality in favor of "the power of language" to disclose the heart of human experience.[86] Taking reification a bit further, James Hillman argued that what analysis does so effectively (and what makes it so attractive to psychology) is really a mythic effort to benefit and cultivate the soul; in his view, greater attention to the use of imagination and its role in "soul-craft" may make analysis obsolete.[87]

All psychological contents have "objective value" for psychological interpretation and therapeutic strategy.[88] Whether or not there is any substance to a wish, the desired object itself remains, nonetheless, as real to the wisher as anything.[89] May's hortative summary articulates this position concisely: "We must get over our fear of intellectual ghosts if we are ever to get anywhere. We need to overcome our illusion that things must be concrete to be real, or that only the quantifiable is true, if we are to make progress in the understanding of man and his problems."[90] Constructions such as these suggest a need to recognize the causal reality both of psychic objects and the means by which we communicate them. Rizzuto's method, to which we now turn, combines therapeutic experience with theological richness and versatility by using depiction as a baseline for symbolic object exploration.

AN OBJECT RELATIONS THEORY OF SCIENCE AND THEOLOGY: MINGLING REASON WITH ILLUSION

Rizzuto's combination of object relations and theology opens a number of connection points between religion and science,[91] especially inasmuch as both utilize the theoretical imagination. Scientific theories can behave cognitively (and sometimes affectively) like theological object formations. A tendency to denigrate the interior world and its ability to produce valuable models and relations relevant to nature also can be observed in the scientific community. Jung lamented that "man's greatest instrument," his psyche, is little thought of, and it is often directly mistrusted and despised. "It's only psychological" too often means, "It is nothing." Where, exactly, does this immense prejudice come from?"[92] Scientific theories normally gain their legitimacy from mechanization and measurement. By contrast, theology shares features of psychoanalysis: it is specific to individuals and eludes statistical normalization and mathematical standardization.[93]

Philosophy of science has aimed to identify the best methods by which reality can be ascertained, effectively attempting to pry illusion out of the mind.[94] In Freud's view, illusion is associated with immaturity, so that adulthood is accompanied by the elimination of illusions just as it also entails the rejection of fairy tales; after all, maturity requires a realistic understanding of the world. The new waves of materialism share with the old this strident antagonism to illusion. Strong atheism assumes that those who reify supernatural beliefs or report religious experiences are hallucinating, deluded, or suffer from a neurosis. Strong atheism takes illusion to be inherently pernicious and anticipates that belief in God will gradually disappear with the expanse of humanity's comprehensive knowledge. Pargament's insights are helpful:

> The religion of any particular time and place is faced with a difficult dilemma. If made too concrete, it will lose much of its flexibility, mystery and vitality. Yet if left too abstract it will have little to say to the person confronted with very immediate and very real problems. Theologians are quite aware of this dilemma. The essential function of theology, Tillich (1951) says, is to create a balance between two poles, "the eternal truth of its foundation and the temporal

> situation in which the eternal truth must be received" (p. 3). A theology that confuses the truth of the moment with eternal truth is as untenable as a theology that is disconnected from present circumstances.[95]

Rizzuto challenges hostile dogmatism with respect to theology by recalling the implications of psychoanalytic theory for knowledge and method itself, scientific or otherwise. While Freud intended to apply a mechanistic ontology to the study of the mind, the means by which he did so had implications which, were psychoanalysis to be consistent, would also make psychoanalysis a useful illusion. A consistent psychology must then be able to acknowledge that the therapeutic value (and even the truth) of psychoanalysis rests on its usefulness.

Rizzuto's Theological Therapy: Illusion Vindicated

As Freud cultivated a link between phenomenology and psychology through the introduction of the analysis of the unconsciousness,[96] Rizzuto developed a robust pathway between psychoanalysis and theology in *The Birth of the Living God*, which has been "hailed as a classic in the field' of psychoanalysis"[97] and has inspired a number of useful studies on faith and mental health.[98] For Rizzuto, the representation of God is a special kind of transitional object because of its unique features and functions. It is an especially powerful, realistic, permanent presence sought "through the spaces of illusion between objective and subjective reality,"[99] which the mind continually creates and discovers throughout the life cycle. Furthermore, God "cannot be made to disappear; it can only be repressed, transformed, or used."[100] Carrying forward Freud's Oedipal construction, God is a person's "introjection" of relationships with parents and other significant individuals.[101]

Rizzuto also fosters lucid study of the broadly observed complementary acts of transference and projection by enabling the client to illustrate his/her permanent transitional object. Whereas typical childhood transitional objects are "gradually decathected, especially as cultural interests develop,"[102] for Rizzuto, the notion of God represents the illusion which remains as the ultimate repository of self-evaluation. Rizzuto argues that God "is increasingly cathected during the pregenital years and reaches his most appealing moment at the peak of oedipal excitement."[103]

Winnicott had argued that transitional objects "belong to the realm of illusion which is at the basis of initiation of experience"[104] and that this epistemological framework governs object relations from the very beginning of life. His exposition of a transitional phenomenon laid important groundwork for Rizzuto's synthesis:

> The child uses a position in between himself or herself and the mother or father, whoever it is, and there whatever happens is symbolic of the union or the non-separation of these two separate things. The concept is really quite a difficult one and I think it would make a difference to philosophy if this could be grasped. It would also perhaps put religion once more into the experience of those who in fact have grown up out of the concept of miracles.[105]

In contrast to attempts to pare theology from spirituality and secularism in psychotherapy,[106] Rizzuto's primary thesis in *The Birth of the Living God* is that one's private representation of God "is given all the psychic potentials of a living person,"[107] who follows principles such as "psychic defense, adaptation, and synthesis, as well as the need for meaningful relations with oneself, others, and the world at large."[108] Rizzuto proposes a necessary yet paradoxical model of God as "permanent transitional object." Whereas strong atheism has, on occasion, demonstrated a preference for an image of the ideal human as a fundamentally cognitive machine whose sense of reason is dulled by believed fantasy and mythology, Rizzuto shows how one can apply Freudian psychoanalytic techniques and reap its manifold benefits, without using the method to bludgeon religion or obviate theology. Rizzuto insists that "psychoanalysis does not deal with ontology."[109] Rizzuto provides means for psychotherapy to remain robustly theological without stepping outside its bounds by making claims about God independent of humanity.[110] Her theory preserves the integrity of psychoanalytical approaches to religious thought by carefully defining their methodological limits so that psychology does not overstep its epistemological boundaries.[111] Her definition of God as a permanent transitional object that organizes our perception of the world, our social context, and our personal history locates it within the very patterns of human thinking and experience, such that it extracts a clinically effective, ontologically neutral, and psychologically sound characterization of God (the scholastic utility of which can scarcely be overstated).[112]

In the second featured case study from *The Birth of the Living God* titled "A God in the Mirror," Rizzuto describes a police officer at age 39 struggling with the aftermath of vehicular trauma. Using his graphic and verbal depictions, Rizzuto identifies his understanding of God as maternal and interprets his ambivalence about God's existence as a means of diminishing his need for affection and affirmation from his mother, which helps him defend against the frustration and anger concomitant with her death. Instead of distancing himself from his mother in response to and as preparation for loss, his God-image carries those needs and, by proxy, fades into existential uncertainty. During this man's adolescence, God became the repressed object, so that the son can "have a less painful experience with his mother and keep his relation with her on relatively good terms until she died." This also contributes to an understanding of the son's preference for self-sufficiency and aggressive independence (followed by a reversal after a traumatic event involving great weakness and vulnerability).[113] That maternal God is found "in the mirror" because the officer coped by narcissistically enlarging himself to compensate for missing support from his mother.[114]

Both artistic images and God representations play a visceral role in the human psyche. As a consequence, one's understanding of God is as important, relevant, and meaningful to one as is artistic expression (following Winnicott). Hence, we can readily ascertain the salience of Rizzuto's psychoanalytic technique, wherein she asks participants to illustrate God and prompts them to use the visual representation to elicit their private theologies:[115] "God, our own creation, like a piece of art, a painting, a melody . . . will, in reflecting what we have done, affect our sense of ourselves."[116]

Noting the significance of a work of art for the artist as well as for those who admired it, Freud not only poured significant interpretive effort into analyzing works of art but also regarded art as psychoanalytically revealing. He observed: "until I have accomplished that interpretation I cannot come to know why I have been so powerfully affected."[117] Carl Jung, whose thought has in psychoanalytic circles seen some rapprochement with Freud's,[118] also affirmed the value of pictures and other artwork. Writing about artistic images he observed, "When [patients] look at them they feel that their unconscious is expressed. . . . [The sacred images] cast their magic into our system and put us right, provided we put ourselves into them."[119]

Inasmuch as art can be understood as therapeutic, creative "play,"[120] and because the creative child at play also abjures—or at least flouts—the reality-principle which is imposed on it by the external world,[121] Rizzuto's method of eliciting theological art from her patients opens up manifold avenues for analysis that lead to a deep understanding of a client's conscious and subconscious worldview. Her method also serves to reunite "a continuous linguistic community divided by a political borderline, one between psychology and theology,"[122] and invites theological vicissitudes that challenge one's traditional habits and customs. Such change functions as a kind of internalization of historical and social revolutions against the status quo, which, as Rollo May notes, emulate Paul Tillich's "god beyond god."[123]

Reductionist accounts of human beings have remained problematic,[124] failing to definitively separate illusion from reality. In the most advanced cases in which scientists face deeply counterintuitive experimental results, they must employ illustrations, metaphors, and models in order to provide their minds with some semblance, rubric, or primer as to how these fundamental features of nature operate. William James articulates a similar point when describing science:

> If we take the whole history of philosophy, the systems reduce themselves to a few main types which, under all the technical verbiage in which the ingenious intellect of man envelops them, are just so many visions, modes of feeling the whole push, and seeing the whole drift of life, forced on one by one's total character and experience, and on the whole *preferred*—there is no other truthful word—as one's best working attitude. Cynical characters take one general attitude, sympathetic characters another. But no general attitude is possible towards the world as a whole, until the intellect has developed considerable generalizing power and learned to take pleasure in synthetic formulas.[125]

Winnicott had located mental representations "outside, inside, and at the border" of the mind,[126] and Rizzuto similarly avers the mutuality of (rather than the disjunction between) reality and illusion.[127] Illusion can refer to theories and models by which we interpret information.[128] Even in cases where one metaphor is evidently more scientifically reliable or useful than another, the intrinsic nature of the subject remains open to interpretation. In short, the scientific method continually deals with illusions.[129] "The essence of the paradox of being human," Rizzuto writes, is that "the objects we so indispensably need are never themselves alone, they combine the mystery of their reality and our fantasy."[130] She concludes audaciously that "men cannot be men without illusions."[131] Because our illusory interpretations of the world form part of the bedrock of human experience, purging illusion is an impossible, unnecessary, and perhaps even (ironically) quixotic, venture.

Insofar as illusion is value-laden, Rizzuto wishes to examine even scientific illusions psychodynamically (rather than as neutral mechanical theories). For Rizzuto, "psychic reality cannot occur without that specifically human transitional space for play and illusion."[132] Accordingly, in one of the many poignant insights expounded in *The Birth of the Living God*, Rizzuto turns Freud's psychoanalytic method toward himself in order to account for his atheism: "Asking a mature, functioning individual to renounce his God would be like asking Freud to renounce his own creation, psychoanalysis, and the 'illusory' promise of what scientific knowledge can do."[133]

Psychoanalysis impressed "enormous charm" on Freud and his readers.[134] It became Freud's beloved in a similar way that personal theologies generate the living God. Rizzuto observes that "the type of illusion we select—science, religion, or something else—reveals our personal history and the transitional space each of us has created between his objects and himself to find a 'resting place' to live in."[135] Science, a psychological object, is transitional, yet permanent. It is permanent inasmuch as theories persevere in their contextual usefulness and relevance; indeed, paradigms such as Freud's psychoanalysis act as enduring objects in scientific thought because they aspire to be publicly accessible and eternally relevant.[136]

Yet evidence that science is transitional is visible in humble affirmations emerging from science which suggest that current theories may one day be overshadowed by grander, more reliable, more accurate theories. Not even the categories of psychology and psychoanalysis are necessarily fixed. For example, depth psychologist Hillman (1972) suggests that, as psychology studies itself, "the more mythical it becomes, the more it relies upon mythical substructures to give account—all of which Freud indicated very early on and then elaborated throughout his life."[137] Hillman accuses the analytic community of verbicide: the prevailing taxonomies of the analytic community are "fantasies that could be replaced with better ones."[138] For example, the category "unconscious" could subside and be replaced by the more robust and present "*memoria*."[139]

What makes an illusion useful is its capacity to facilitate whatever goal has driven us to develop it. Scientific principles (not too distant from Rizzuto's view of theology) are tools more than truth. In this manner, antirealist, instrumentalist, and pragmatist philosophies of science corroborate Rizzuto's account of the usefulness of illusions for human interpretation of the world. Further, as elaborated in her psychoanalysis of Freud, Rizzuto elucidates the experiential, human face of those illusions. Her work reveals, uniquely, the affective drive to create, harbor, and use scientific illusions as it also looks behind philosophical and scientific methods to expose the psychic means by which theories are developed.

THEOLOGY AND SCIENCE AS USEFUL ILLUSIONS

Popular conceptions of the relationship between religion and science have been shaped by a relatively small elite community of scientists and public intellectuals. Karl Giberson and Mariano Artigas have tracked and described the "ascendency" of six such figures to "oracular status,"[140] showing several ways in which charisma fused with intellect generates national renown and celebrity that beatifies these figures such that their understanding of the science-religion dialog is adopted prima facie. Especially insofar as their presentations are polemical and socially charged, these individuals' narratives also have permeated much of Western popular culture.

In the 1960s, notable sociologists such as Peter Berger anticipated that secularization would continue its advance against religious life. Freud's prediction of the fate of infantile illusion, it seemed, might be unfolding. However, a number of broad-scale religious revivals in the late twentieth century forced scholars of religion to reconsider that hypothesis. Moreover, this newly invigorated religiosity was matched by a revitalized atheism, as a stronger, more vociferous "new atheism" emerged early in the twentieth-first century, stoked by the perfect storm of flagrant mass-violence and religious fundamentalism (with concomitant anti-modern radicalism and anti-colonial bitterness) witnessed on September 11, 2001. A complacent old atheism subsided, replaced by a more aggressive movement led by Richard Dawkins, Christopher Hitchens, and others that insists not only that God is nonexistent but also that belief in God is morally reprehensible. This "strong" or "positive" atheism[141] considers belief in God to be a great blight upon humanity. Furthermore, the growing body of literature in evolutionary psychology and the cognitive science of religion have provided new atheists with choice reductionist and rhetorical weapons to wield against belief in God. Their rhetoric regularly refers to "delusion,"[142] a modification of illusion that assigns pejorative connotations to language about God.

Scientists avail themselves of models and metaphors which provide them with mental imagery by which they may "understand" deeply abstract and counterintuitive products of high-level experimentation and observation. Philosophers of science make note of this as do contemporary new atheists. Sam Harris, for example, relays the separation of Einstein and Bohr on the proper interpretation or mental model of quantum mechanics as a matter not merely of scientific, but also of philosophical, discourse.[143] Richard Dawkins insists that his seminal works *The Selfish Gene* (1976) and *The Extended Phenotype* (1983) do not propose new scientific theories, but rather provide explanation and perspective to our understanding of biological evolution—a "gene's eye view."[144] Those who might wish to discount the combination of God and rationality should, then, with as much resolve, discourage the association between affect and reason. Strong atheists freely use models, metaphors, and even rhetorical devices like "satire and ridicule."[145] Clearly, these models and devices can play important explanatory and persuasive roles in the dissemination of ideas.

As a result of new atheists' tenacity in polarizing faith and reason, science-versus-religion discussions seem to have eroded into an irresolvable stalemate between reductionism and idealism that offers little novel or updated criticism to levy against perceptions of God. The new atheism recapitulates earlier complaints with an additional century of ammunition plus some modified ethical qualms.

By contrast, by the mid-twentieth century a number of anthropologists (notable among them E.E. Evans-Pritchard) had come to recognize that members of indigenous societies, replete with the religio-cultural elements Freud considered puerile, exhibit as much intellect, maturity, and sophistication as humanity's technologically developed counterparts. Additionally, devout practitioners of religion within advanced civilizations regularly demonstrate all the marks of maturity shared with the secular and unaffiliated. Two members of a religion whose commitment to religious doctrine conform to one another may diverge dramatically in their behavior (one may be a paragon of virtue, the other a psychopath). An analytic explanation for these differences that examines the personal histories and developments of their theologies is required. Far more important than the presence of orthodox faith in God is the perception of that God, which transcends dogma and confessional theology.[146] The enterprise of psychoanalysis liberates individuals through "a complex, lifelong awareness of interiority, not 'empowerment' or utilitarian problem-solving."[147]

Recognizing this, new atheists have needed to select the worst specimens of religion to magnify their case against "faith-heads."[148] For example, Sam Harris's *The End of Faith* and Richard Dawkins's *Enemies of Reason* position faith in blunt opposition to rational thought. Little is new in their attempt to depict religion as irrational, God as anthropogenic, or values as utilitarian. However, the new atheism carries a new emphasis on ethics, giving particular attention to the welfare of children. Dawkins dedicates a chapter of *The God Delusion* to the matter of raising children as members of a faith. Harris uses corporal punishment of children, which some persons justify by appeal to passages of scripture, as a springboard for discussions about the measurable effectiveness (or ineffectiveness) of corporeal discipline.[149]

The new atheism demonstrates awareness of the role desires and emotions play in the formation of our beliefs and attachments. In some cases, its proponents invoke this connection between faith and feelings in support of their argument that religion is inherently harmful. As philosopher A.C. Graying writes, "Because religious belief does not rest on rationality but on emotions, it is unsurprising that faith visits violence on what it regards as heretics and other enemies."[150] The new atheism maintains that reason has surpassing value, to the extent that it, in effect, dethrones God. But the new atheism's emphasis on logic and neutral observation risks dismissing prematurely important questions about the source of ethics and values. Can science support even the value of our attempt to conform our subjectivities to each other over natural theory in the way that such a method requires?[151] Harris's *The Moral Landscape* addresses this question, highlighting discrepancies in the thinking of new atheists.

Harris argues that values are reducible to neurological facts and thereby may be dictated by the results of scientific experimentation. He addresses the reducibility of value to neurological facts, such that a precise look at brain states (correspondent to values) can determine which values promote the most optimal conditions of well-being. Society and its ethical principles, both governmental and legal, should be made subject to the findings of neurology toward the optimization of well-being. Harris's incipient method may encounter challenges similar to those psychoanalysis has encountered; as it currently presents, it ranks with psychoanalysis among the "less systematized sciences," which are productive as cultivators of new knowledge only inasmuch as they adopt "allow maximal productivity on a given level of insight into the relations between fact and hypothesis and according to the degrees of formal organization."[152]

One corollary of this argument requires that science dictate government, at the risk of freedom or perhaps flexibility for the individual. Here materialist programs bear resemblance to hollowed-out religious movements. Some theists suggest that the new atheists harbor a wish that society to succumb to "a new and militant atheistic priesthood."[153] Alister McGrath has presented multiple arguments that atheism "proved just as fallible, just as corrupt and just as oppressive as anything that had gone before it."[154]

Most significant, the new atheism often neglects the psychodynamic complexity of motives for moral malfeasance. It also appears oblivious to the possibility that the best remedy for malicious theology may very well be the transformation of that theology rather than its eradication. The illusion remains susceptible to malformation and misuse, but this is not an observation unique to the new atheism, and the new atheism is not the solution to these challenges. Rizzuto demonstrates how theology can act as a barometer of one's internal condition; indeed, she credits Freud with the discovery "that, wittingly or not, we create our own gods from the apparently simple warp and woof of our everyday life."[155]

Theology itself is not neurosis. Rizzuto and other psychoanalysts who utilize her theory show that "bad" theology is a symptom rather than a disorder or a neurosis. Such a perspective opposes Hitchens's overstatements that religion "kills" and "poisons everything."[156] Further, traumatic events actually can exhume "bad objects" that have been repressed and made dormant. Once they resurface, they can compete with the established benign superego.[157] Rizzuto recognizes that, even when a patient's God representations appear harmful to her patient's mental health, the patient's theology can still function positively as a vehicle for diagnosis since it locates and orients guilt. We may refer to Sophocles's Oedipus wallowing in ignominy, redolent of Freud's explanation of melancholia by the ego feeling "hated and persecuted by the super-ego":[158]

> Is there a more unhappy man alive than I? Who could be more hateful to the gods than I am? No foreigner or citizen may take me into his house, no one can talk to me—everyone must expel me from his home. And the man who called down these curses on me was I myself, no one else. . . . It was Apollo, friends, Apollo, who brought to fulfillment all my sufferings. But the hand that struck my eyes was mine and mine alone.[159]

As though he were treating Oedipus himself, Fairbairn examined self-blame as a process by which a client makes himself the scapegoat in the hope that

God will remain benevolent and the world generally good. Both neuroses can have theological resolutions.[160]

The case study in *The Birth of the Living God* entitled "God My Enemy" details the struggle of a woman with a negative self-image who drew a picture of God as a warm sun. For her, God was an unreachable source of love whom she did not deserve and who withheld affection indefinitely. She experienced "the eternal absence of love in the presence of a God who knows how to love."[161] Her image of God reflected a deficit in theological "elaboration" beyond the impersonal (in this case, the sun),[162] which psychotherapy is capable of encouraging. Whereas Fairbairn may have seen in personal theology a clue for diagnosis, Rizzuto sees in it both the vehicle for diagnosis and the therapy for its associated neuroses. She writes:

> Taking a history, during the evaluation, of the patient and his dealings with God at moments of crisis can be a precious tool for uncovering private events that have contributed to the patient's decompensation. This is particularly true . . . when the relations to primary objects need some transformation.[163]

Mental health entails that, in the words of May, "the patient moves *toward* freedom and responsibility in his living as he becomes more conscious of the *deterministic* experiences in his life."[164] Similarly Karen Horney argues,

> The patient is not responsible for [traits such as insincerity, haughtiness, and refined cruelty]; he could not help their developing. But in analysis he has to face them, not because it is the analyst's business to improve his morals, but because he suffers from them: they interfere with a good relationship with others and with himself and they prevent his best possible development.[165]

The ethical objective of psychotherapy should be to form our behavioral, emotional, and cognitive patterns so that they do not traumatize other subjectivities. In that case, Harris's utilitarian argument receives partial confirmation insofar as it connects goodness with well-being measurable as brain states. But Harris's reduction of values in this manner might backfire—suppose optimal well-being is shown to be best achieved through various types of illusion. Would Harris be pleased with the results, should experimentation reveal a great degree of net well-being associated with this permanent transitional object?

In Stephen Frosh's words, psychoanalysis "is a major tool for ideological struggle" which "supplies a set of criticisms of the distortions and despair that are suffered under conditions of domination."[166] Eli Zaretsky cautions that "we risk congratulating ourselves on knowing our own minds at the very moment when we are being most effectively manipulated into compliance and assent."[167] The fiats of neurology according to Harris, then, need not become another source of domination. Rizzuto's therapeutic goal is eminently useful here:

> Psychic freedom is the aim of analytic treatment. It is not the absolute removal of pain, it is not the absolute of all minimal symptoms, it is only the achievement of enough psychic freedom for the person to be able to use himself or herself in the service of his or her aims—in psychic relatedness with others to be able to love and to work.[168]

With these words, Rizzuto demonstrates that a psychoanalysis open to the religious experience of those it seeks to help can play a positive role in human life, notwithstanding the criticisms of the new atheism.

CONCLUSION

Our ability to embark on the perpetual trek toward self-knowledge, likened to one's perception of God, is tantamount to "the 'normal' as a range of functioning which is 'mental health'."[169] The illusions of theology and of science thrive in creative, imaginal open-endedness. The opposite extreme—the routine, mundane, '"normal," and "average"'—may even catalyze illness.[170] The superimposition of a social stigma onto one's permanent transitional object can unnecessarily induce anxiety and other neuroses.[171] The elimination of theology from the psyche, then, is unnecessary and inimical to the objectives of psychoanalysis.

Ana-María Rizzuto's work elucidates contemporary grievances against religion, especially those emerging from the atheist community. She maintains the importance and vitality of the God-concept against two incompatible polarities claimed in new atheism: reason with faith and reality with illusion. In making this case, I have highlighted how the historical-intellectual roots of psychoanalysis are imbued with materialism, but have proceeded to describe how Rizzuto compellingly develops the *permanent* transitional object ("God") as a central concept of psychotherapy, even in the setting of secular counseling outside of faith-based communities. I have demonstrated how Rizzuto shows how "God" is inherently relevant to the human psyche. As Rizzuto describes it, the centralization of the illusory, permanent transitional object in the human psyche has been shown in this chapter to carry strong implications for scientific theory, method, and knowledge in favor of pragmatism and antirealism; indeed, the illusory nature of theology transposes to the illusory nature of science. Indebted as we are to Rizzuto for illuminating how the transitional object is joined for the individual with perceptions of God, I have argued that contemporary atheist movements should recognize the deep imaginal and cathectic similarities between theology and science, such that neither science nor theology has the capacity to universally ascertain reality. They can only present what is personally and/or socially and/or technologically useful toward desired goals. Finally, I have offered words of caution concerning the new atheism lest it fashion a dictator out of science, undermining the psychic freedom that is valuable for the optimization of human experience, happiness, and self-actualization.

Far from usurping God, science shares theology's psychodynamic features, as both science and theology participate in the formation of pragmatic illusions.[172] Insofar as humanity is capable of advancing through science, it remains generative of theology, which cannot depart from humanity. Permanent, transitional illusions are inherent in human experience; as a consequence, any attempt to expunge theology from human experience is tantamount to an attempt to discard that which is fundamental to humanity itself. Because psychoanalysis seeks to work with illusion in order to attain freedom to "love and to work," therapeutic intervention in, rather than elimination of, personal theological illusions will advance the overall quality of human life.

DISCUSSION

Ana-María Rizzuto

Professor Waldenmaier's chapter focuses on the contribution that my elaboration of Winnicott's conception of illusion in psychic life could make to facilitate the conversation with present-day atheists, in particular well-recognized scientists.

Waldenmaier's chapter deals implicitly with ontology and epistemology. Ontologically the atheists affirm that God does not exist. Epistemologically, they propose the scientific method to gain access to knowledge of reality. Supposedly, belief and illusion cannot match what science is able to offer for us to know the world in which we live.

I propose that in scientific discovery the mind acts precisely as Winnicott suggests: *It creates what it finds.* Scientist Michael Polanyi in his book *Personal Knowledge*[173] demonstrated that science requires belief and that its principles are based on belief. I hope to demonstrate that scientists find precisely what they create.

Perception is our only tool to document that something exists. Perception is an extremely complex psychical process that cannot complete its task without belief and the structure of illusion. Harvard scientists Kosslyn and Sussman[174] affirm that there is no immaculate perception. Perception is not a replica of reality. It is an active process of organizing perceived reality that involves the subjective participation of the perceiver in the act of perception itself. Talking about the function of imagery, they propose that "images are formed by priming the representation of what one anticipates seeing": In other words, the mind uses the structures it has already formed to shape actively what it perceives. To me, this reads as the scientific version of the illusion that creates what it finds. This process encompasses all our perceptions in our construction of physical, interpersonal, intrapsychic, scientific, and cultural realities.

How does it apply to scientific knowledge? The French scientist Pierre Lecompte du Noüy[175] established that "the scale of observation creates the phenomenon." Science is incapable of studying "reality" in its entirety. Science has to *fragment* reality in order to observe limited phenomena. Each level of observation creates its own phenomenon: we go from the visible skin to the cell, to the cell's membrane, to the cell's structure, to the molecules that compose it, to the atoms that form the molecule, etc. Each has its own phenomenology and is not accessible without a defined methodology and apt instruments from microscopes to advanced chemical and physical analyzing equipment. Scientists do not observe reality directly. They form a question based on the scientific conceptions of the time that they *believe* to be objectively true, they create experiments that focus on limited phenomena, and then they have to *interpret* the facts they uncover in the light of the conditions they have placed for the experiment. In one word, the best of science consists in the *interpretation* of experimental data provided by tool-mediated experiments that focus on a very limited aspect of an existing reality. The interpretation of the real *facts* found in the experiment is a response to the *question* posed by the believing and searching scientist whose scale of observation has *created* the phenomenon. In conclusion, the scientist based on sound enough scientific beliefs creates what he finds based, as Polanyi says, on fiduciary acts.

It is clear that the scientific method does not have what it takes to assert or deny God's existence for the simple reason that God cannot be subjected to any type of experiment. Extrapolations from scientific knowledge about the origins of the universe or morality are no more than the *personal* interpretation of the scientist.

The same notion applies to any believer in God's existence. Attempting to offer *proof* of God's reality is no more than a matter of logical *interpretation*, not an *ontological* demonstration, regardless of the arguments we use.

Waldenmaier credits me for challenging the hostility between science and religious believers. When I propose that illusion relates to a lens by which reality is understood, my claim is not about reality *and* illusion. We cannot approach anything that exists from any point of view other than our *interpretation* of what we actually find based on our need to create meaningful percepts to sustain us, not a nonexisting immaculate scientific perception. That is what reality *is* for each of us.

NOTES

1. William W. Meissner, "Toward a Psychology of Religious Experience," in *Psychoanalysis and Religious Experience*, by W. W. Meissner (New Haven: Yale University Press, 1984), 3–19.

2. Meissner, "Toward a Psychology of Religious Experience," 6.

3. Rizzuto, *The Birth*, 3.

4. Ibid, 4.

5. This point is well explored in George Lakoff and Mark Johnson, *Philosophy in the Flesh: The Embodied Mind and Its Challenge to Western Thought* (New York, NY: Basic Books, 1999).

6. Luis A. Cordón, *Freud's World: An Encyclopedia of His Life and Times* (Santa Barbara, CA: Greenwood, 2012).

7. Heinz Hartmann, "The Ego Concept in Freud's Work," in *Essays on Ego Psychology: Selected Problems in Psychoanalytic Theory* (New York, NY: International Universities Press, 1964), 274–75.

8. Paul Ricoeur, *Freud and Philosophy: An Essay on Interpretation* (New Haven: Yale University Press, 1970), 416–18. Freud's use of the legend of Narcissus echoes Feuerbach's (1841) insights on self-projection and reflexivity.

9. Sigmund Freud, *The Psychopathology of Everyday Life* (New York, NY: The Modern Library, 1938), 35.

10. As reads an 1842 letter by Émil du Buis-Reymond, as quoted in Frank Sulloway, *Freud, Biologist of the Mind: Beyond the Psychoanalytic Legend* (New York, NY: Basic Books, 1979).

11. Frank Sulloway, *Freud: Biologist of the Mind: Beyond the Psychoanalytic Legend* (New York, NY: Basic Books, 1979), 19.

12. Sigmund Freud and James Strachey, *Civilization and Its Discontents* (W.W. Norton & Company, 2005), 256.

13. W. Ronald Fairbairn, "Endopsychic Structure Considered in Terms of Object-Relationships," *Psychoanalytic Studies of the Personality* (Boston: Routledge & Kegan Paul, 1952), 127.

14. Hillman, for example, refers to "the Western, Protestant, scientific, Apollonic ego" in contrast to the "mythical perspective, the erotic, the imaginal, and the Dionysian." See James Hillman, *The Myth of Analysis: Three Essays in Archetypal Psychology* (New York: Harper & Row, 1972), 8.

15. For more discussion, see Ken Gemes, "Freud and Nietzsche on Sublimation," *Journal of Nietzsche Studies* 38 (2009): 38–59.

16. Sigmund Freud, *The Ego and the Id* (New York: W.W. Norton and Company, 1960), 24.

17. Freud, *The Ego and the Id*, 59.

18. Alfred Adler, *The Practice and Theory of Individual Psychology* (Totowa, NJ: Littlefield, Adams & Co., 1969), 15.

19. Norman Brown, *Life against Death* (Middletown, CT: Wesleyan University Press, 1959), 3; quoted in Stephen Frosh, *The Politics of Psychoanalysis: An Introduction to Freudian and Post-Freudian Theory* (New Haven: Yale University Press, 1987). 21. This is one of Freud's primary arguments in *The Future of an Illusion.*

20. Schleiermacher, Friedrich. *On: Speeches to its Cultured Despisers.* (Louisville, KY: Westminster John Knox Press.)

21. Sigmund Freud, *The Interpretation of Dreams* (New York: Barnes and Noble Classics, 2005), 445.

22. Ricoeur, Paul. *Freud and Philosophy.*

23. Sophocles, *Oedipus the King* (New York: Simon & Schuster, 1994), 67.

24. Freud, *The Interpretation of Dreams*, 50, 68, 94.

25. Ibid, 111.

26. Ibid, 479. Jung further included dreaming as the key to grasping the Self (Marie-Louise von Franz, "The Process of Individuation," in *Man and His Symbols*, ed. Carl Jung. (New York, NY: Dell Publishing Co., 1964), 1. The importance and centrality of dreams did not evade later skepticism, of course; see, for example, Erik Erikson, *Life History and the Historical Moment* (W.W. Norton & Company, 1975), 39–40.

27. Freud, *The Interpretation of Dreams*, 98–111.

28. Pamela Thurschwell, *Sigmund Freud* (New York, NY: Routledge, 2000), 3. This chapter later examines Rizzuto's use of pictures as interpretive devices as expounded in *The Birth of the Living God.*

29. Rizzuto, *The Birth*, 178.

30. Howard Philp, *Freud and Religious Belief* (Westport, CT: Greenwood Publishing Group, 1974), 120.

31. Sigmund Freud, *Totem and Taboo* (Routledge, 2003), 34–35.

32. Freud, *Totem and Taboo*, 39–42; "It is a law of neurotic diseases that these obsessive acts serve the impulse more and more and come nearer and nearer to the original and forbidden act."

33. David Cohen, *The Escape of Sigmund Freud* (New York: The Overlook Press, 2012), 34.

34. Cohen, *The Escape of Sigmund Freud*, 51.

35. Gregory Zilboorg, *Freud and Religion: A Restatement of an Old Controversy* (Westminster, MD: The Newman Press, 1964), 17–18, with some reference to Jones's extensive biography written in the 1950s.

36. Cohen, *The Escape of Sigmund Freud*, 41. See also Sulloway, *Freud: Biologist of the Mind*, 423.

37. Eli Zaretsky, *Secrets of the Soul: A Social and Cultural History of Psychoanalysis* (New York, NY: Alfred A. Knopf, 2004), 243.

38. For example, in "The Moses of Michelangelo," Freud expresses complete openness to redaction criticism of the Hebrew Scriptures (*The Standard Edition of the Complete Psychological Works of Sigmund Freud,* Volume XIII [1913–1914]); *Totem and Taboo and Other Works* [1955], 537–39).

39. In part, by tracing how Freud's habitual collecting of religious bibelots rests like a layer over Freud's perception of his own parents and the absence of a secure attachment in his youth, Rizzuto (1998) recognizes the trend in Freud's God-image during his career from excitement to disappointment, from respect to contempt, from interest to disillusionment. See Rizzuto, *Why Did Freud Reject God? A Psychodynamic Interpretation* (New Haven: Yale University Press, 1998). See also Paul Vitz, *Faith of the Fatherless: The Psychology of Atheism* (San Francisco, CA: Ignatius Press, 2013). Vitz identifies neuroses of atheists derived from the Oedipus complex not only in Freud but also in other prominent early modern atheists like Diderot and Voltaire. For contemporary psychoanalytic analyses with reference to *The Birth of the Living God*, see Deborah van Deusen Hunsinger, *Theology and Pastoral Counseling: A New Interdisciplinary Approach* (Grand Rapids, MI: William B. Erdmans, 1995), 127–30; and John Surr, "Links Between Early Attachment Experiences and Manifestations of Spirituality," *International Journal of Children's Spirituality* 16, 2 (2011): 129–41.

40. Philp, *Freud and Religious Belief*, 36.

41. Rollo May reminds us that "our psychology, and indeed modern science itself, are historical products like any other aspect of culture"; see Rollo May, "Social Responsibilities of Psychologists," *Psychology and the Human Dilemma* (New York, NY: W.W. Norton & Company, 1967), 207. However, as Hartmann assesses Freud, "Among great scientists there are those who confront the world with strikingly new facts; but there are also those who not only demonstrate new facts but also teach the world to look at them in an entirely new way, thereby also changing the forms or modes of our thinking. There are only a few in our time whom we would put into this second category. But there is no doubt that Freud is among them" ("The Ego Concept in Freud's Work," 296).

42. Janice Halpern, Review of "Why Did Freud Reject God? A Psychodynamic Interpretation by Ana-María Rizzuto," *Journal of the American Psychoanalytic Association* 48 (2000), 1013. See further discussion of this matter in James Grotstein, "Reflections on a Century of Freud: Some Paths Not Chosen," *British Journal of Psychotherapy* 9.2 (1992), 181–87.

43. See, for example, Gilbert Highet's account of the mind's elusive "wonders" ("Man's Unconquerable Mind," New York, NY: Columbia University Press [1954], 114–15); knowledge is Promethian, and mystery, for Highet, is the endpoint of all knowledge and all pathways to it.

44. William James, *The Varieties of Religious Experience*, *William James: Writings 1902–1910* (New York, NY: The Library of America, 1987), 58. James also enumerated several others within "the eighteenth century anti-Christian movement" (such as Diderot and Rousseau) who replaced monotheism with their adoration of nature (78–79).

45. For example, Albert Ellis's *The Case Against Religion: A Psychotherapist's View* (New York, NY: Institute for Rational Living, 1971).

46. See Michael Miovic's "Introduction to Spiritual Psychology: Overview of the Literature, East and West," *Harvard Review of Psychiatry* 12, 2 (2004) as well

as Thomas Plante's "Integrating Spirituality and Psychotherapy: Ethical Issues and Principles to Consider," *Journal of Clinical Psychology* 63, 9 (2007): 892.

47. G. Michael Leffel, "Prevenient Grace and the Re-Enchantment of Nature: Toward a Wesleyan Theology of Psychotherapy and Spiritual Formation," *Journal of Psychology and Christianity* 23, 2 (2004): 130–39.

48. As argued and discussed in Robert Fuller, "American Psychology and the Religious Imagination," *Journal of the History of the Behavioral Sciences* 42, 3 (2006): 221–35.

49. See, for example, Ruth Layzell, "A Case of the Baby and the Bath Water?" *Practical Theology* 4, 1 (2011): 97–116 and Meissner, *Psychoanalysis and Religious Experience*.

50. Zaretsky, *Secrets of the Soul*, 242. Jung had argued that "we are so captivated by and entangled in our subjective consciousness that we have forgotten the age-old fact that God speaks chiefly through dreams and visions"; see Carl Jung, "Approaching the Unconscious," *Man and His Symbols* (New York, NY: Dell Publishing Co., 1964), 92.

51. Jonathan Wyatt's (2004) work bridging theory and praxis vis-à-vis psychotherapy and faith avails this point, as does William Meissner's (2008) study of the overlap between psychoanalysis and Roman Catholic theology. See Jonathan Wyatt, "Counselling and Religious Faith," *Psychodynamic Practice* 10, 1 (2004) and William Meissner, "Psychoanalysis and Catholicism—Dialogues in Transformation," *Psychoanalytic Inquiry* 28 (2008).

52. Harold Koenig et al., "Understanding Religion's Effects on Mental Health," *Handbook of Religion and Health* (New York, NY: Oxford University Press, 2001).

53. David G. Myers, *The American Paradox: Spiritual Hunger in a Land of Plenty* (New Haven, CT: Yale University Press, 2001).

54. See J.A.C. Murray, *An Introduction to Christian Psycho-Therapy* (Edinburgh: T&T Clark, 1938) as well as Gregory Zilboorg, *Freud and Religion*, (1964): 4–5 in reference to Peter Dempsey (1956) and R.S. Lee (1948), Vicar of The Church of St. Mary the Virgin at Oxford, each of whom authored blends of psychoanalysis and pastoral ministry.

55. See J.A.C. Murray, *An Introduction to Christian Psycho-Therapy* (Edinburgh: T&T Clark, 1938) as well as Gregory Zilboorg, *Freud and Religion*, (1964): 4–5 in reference to Peter Dempsey (1956) and R.S. Lee (1948), Vicar of The Church of St. Mary the Virgin at Oxford, each of whom authored blends of psychoanalysis and pastoral ministry.

56. Freud, *The Psychopathology of Everyday Life*, 176.

57. See Romans 7 and 2nd Corinthians 10–12.

58. Jones, *The Life and Works of Sigmund Freud*, 2; quoted in Hartmann, "The Ego Concept in Freud's Work," (New York: International Universities Press, 1964) 274, 344.

59. See especially Karen Horney, *Self-Analysis* (New York, NY: W.W. Norton & Company, 1942), 40–46 (perhaps with some allusion to Wundt's "introspection" methodology). Chris Schlauch (2009) develops an understanding of psychoanalysis whereby the clinician's role is to listen, reflect, and play in such a way that the client

cultivates the ability to seek what is yet internally unknown; see Chris Schlauch, "Do I Hear What You Hear? Thinking about Psychotherapy and Spirituality from a Self Psychological Approach," *Journal of Spirituality in Mental Health* 11, 1–2 (2009): 26–50.

60. Rizzuto parses representation of God as a coupling of "God-image," the personal and private construction of God—what Jordan (2013) names "operational theology"—and "God-concept," the technical, doctrinal, or confessional understanding of God as often inherited from institutional theology; see Merle Jordan, "Psychotherapy as an Operational Theology Process," *The Spiritual Horizon of Psychotherapy* (Routledge, 2013), 4. Pargament (1997) makes a similar distinction between religion as "a search for significance in ways related to the sacred" versus theological ideations with little relation to human concerns (though, in comparison to Rizzuto, Pargament places theology too comprehensively in this latter category). See Kenneth Pargament, *The Psychology of Religious Coping: Theory, Research, Practice.* (New York, NY: Guilford Press, 1997), 32. Worth mentioning also is Gordon Kaufman's 1992 work on "Nature, History, and God" wherein he argues for an understanding of God as "creativity" that generates and sustains both nature and the human imagination. See Gordon Kaufman, "Nature, History, and God: Toward an Integrated Conceptualization," *Zygon* 27, 4 (1992): 379–401. Elsewhere Kauffman explores the way God-images predominate in the imagination and become the acceptable subject of worship, even though it is known that God transcends them in reality: Gordon Kaufman, *The Theological Imagination: Constructing the Concept of God* (Philadelphia: Westminster Press, 1981).

61. For an inconclusive but helpful discussion on the nebulous distinction between illusion and delusion see Carr's "reflections on spirituality, religion and mental health," which he addresses in light of personal well-being, social function, and validation: Wesley Carr, "Some Reflections on Spirituality, Religion and Mental Health," *Mental Health, Religion & Culture* 3, 1 (2000).

62. See, for example, Glendon Moriarty, Louis Hoffman, and Christopher Grimes, "Understanding the God Image through Attachment Theory: Theory, Research, and Practice," *Journal of Spirituality in Mental Health* 9, 2 (2006).

63. Wikström (1998) argues that psychoanalysis can expose currents beneath theological and psychological difficulties so that, more so than theology or psychology can achieve on their own, "psychoanalytically-oriented therapy" enables awareness of (and autonomy over) more visceral, unconscious motives and neuroses. See Owe Wikström, "Depression and the Absence of God: Religious Studies and/or Theology in Clinical Research," *Studia Theologica—Nordic Journal of Theology* 52, 2.

64. Siang-Yang Tan and Natalie Dong, for example, argue that "patients should be encouraged to utilize spiritual resources that are consistent with their values and traditions. . ."; Siang-Yang Tan and Natalie J. Dong, "Spiritual Interventions in Healing and Wholeness," *Faith and Health* (2001): 295–6.

65. As Steinfeld's "cognitive constructivist" therapeutic model can support, in which growth is sought through a cognitive and affective philosophical "shift" with respect to oneself, others, and the world as a whole; see George Steinfeld, "Spiritual Psychology and Psychotherapy," *Journal of Contemporary Psychotherapy* 30,

4 (2000): 355. Further affirmation appears in Lance Dixon, "Reaching Out to the Divine: An Examination of God Images and Prayer Functions," (PhD diss., Texas Tech University, 2014), 112, in reference to *The Birth,* 52.

66. Len Sperry and Edward Shafranske, "Spiritually Oriented Psychodynamic Psychotherapy," *Spiritually Oriented Psychotherapy* (Washington, DC: American Psychological Association, 2005), 156. See also Gary Hartz, *Spirituality and Mental Health: Clinical Applications* (Binghamton, NY: Haworth Pastoral Press, 2005), 76–88, 98, as well as Gordon Lynch, "The Relationship between Pastoral Counseling and Pastoral Theology," *The Blackwell Reader in Pastoral and Practical Theology* (Oxford: Blackwell, 2000).

67. See, for example, Harold Koenig, *Is Religion Good for your Health? The Eeffects of Religion on Physical and Mental Health* (Binghamton, NY: Haworth Pastoral Press, 1997) and William Miller and Carl Thoresen, "Spirituality, Religion and Health: An Emerging Research Field," *American Psychologist*, 58, 1 (2003).

68. Rachel B. Blass, "Beyond Illusion: Psychoanalysis and the Question of Religious Truth," *International Journal of Psychoanalysis* 85, 3 (2004). Browning (2008), drawing some insight from *The Birth of the Living God*, similarly regrets psychiatry's "alienation" from a substantial portion of America's believing population, and calls for some degree of public conciliation. See Don Browning, "Internists of the Mind or Physicians of the Soul: Does Psychiatry Need a Public Philosophy?" *Zygon: Journal of Religion and Science* 43, 2 (2008): 375–77. Consider also the mild disappointment expressed in Glenn Hudak's 2003 review of Ulanov's *Finding Space* (2001) that metaphysical consequences of psychotherapy, specifically whether arrival at psychological health obviates belief in God, seemed inadequately considered: Glenn Hudak, Review of "Finding Space: Winnicott, God, and Psychic Reality," by Ann Belford Ulanov, *Journal of Religion and Health* 42, 1 (2003).

69. Brent Slife, Tiffani Stevenson, and Dennis Wendt, "Including God in Psychotherapy: Strong vs. Weak Theism," *Journal of Psychology and Theology* 38, 3 (2010); Daniel Helminiak, "Theistic Psychology and Psychotherapy: A Theological and Scientific Critique," *Zygon: Journal of Religion and Science* 45, 1 (2010).

70. Douglas Whitcher (1996), for example, examines how the therapist encourages a client to empathetically transcend him or herself, resulting in collusion that resembles pastoral counseling: Douglas Whitcher, *When Therapy Becomes Theology: A Critical View of Empathy*. (PhD diss., Syracuse University,1996). See also Marc Oraison, "The Psychoanalyst and the Confessor," *Problems in Psychoanalysis: A Symposium* (London: Burns & Oates, 1961), 171–93; and Igor Caruso, *Existential Psychology: From Analysis to Synthesis* (New York, NY: Herder and Herder, 1964), 216.

71. Consider Nietzsche's vigorous accusation that the psychologist "wants to gain little advantages over them, or big ones too—he is a politician! . . . You say he wants nothing for himself, that he is "impersonal." Take a closer look! Perhaps he wants an even *worse* advantage: to feel himself superior to men, to have the right to look down on them, no longer to confuse himself with them. This 'impersonal' man is a *despiser*"; Friedrich Nietzsche, *Twilight of the Idols* (New York, NY: Penguin Books, 2003), 87.

72. See Siang-Yang Tan, "Ethical Considerations in Religious Psychotherapy," *Journal of Psychology and Theology* (1994); Gary Moon, "Training Tomorrow's Integrators in Today's Busy Intersection: Better Look Four Ways Before Crossing," *Journal of Psychology and Theology* 25, 2 (1997); Wikström, "Depression and the Absence of God"; and Plante, "Integrating Spirituality and Psychotherapy," especially pp. 898–99. Adler similarly argued that his "individual" approach "must must leave Christian guidance to those qualified for it. But it cannot banish God from the world"; see Alfred Adler, "Religion and Individual Psychology," *Superiority and Social Interest* (New York, NY: W.W. Norton & Company, 1979), 306. Compare also May's phenomenological charge to refrain from transferring "*our* guild and *our* value judgments to the counselee and patient, but endeavor to help him bring out and confront *his* guilt and its implications and meaning for him," *Psychology and the Human Dilemma*, 180. Wyatt's (2002) relation of countertransference to Hans Georg Gadamer's (1980) "prejudice" or bias and Martin Heidegger's "horizon" provides additional substance to this discussion; see Jonathan Wyatt, "'Confronting the Almighty God'? A study of how Psychodynamic Counselors Respond to Clients' Expressions of Religious Faith," *Counselling and Psychotherapy Research: Linking Research with Practice* 2, 3 (2002).

73. Ana-María Rizzuto, "Reflections on Listening to and Speaking with the Patient During Analysis," in *Language, Symbolization, and Psychosis,* 2007. See also Claudio Neri's discussion of the psychic reification of faith both for the client and the analyst: "What is the Function of Faith and Trust in Psychoanalysis?" *The International Journal of Psychoanalysis*, 86, 1 (2005); and Duckham's helpful intersubjective account of psychotherapy in Bryan Duckham, "Bipolar Illness, God, and Object Relations: The Treatment of M," *Smith College Studies in Social Work* 81, 2–3 (2011): 271.

74. Fairbairn, "Endopsychic Structure," 126.

75. Ibid., 131.

76. As did Adler to some extent, while eliminating the *id* and anything outside the ego as a factor altogether. See Alfred Adler, "The Differences Between Individual Psychology and Psychoanalysis," *Superiority and Social Interest* (New York: W.W. Norton & Company, 1979), 216.

77. W. Ronald Fairbairn, "Object-Relations and Dynamic Structure," *Psychoanalytic Studies of the Personality* (Boston: Routledge & Kegan Paul, 1952), 149.

78. Fairbairn's three dynamic object-seeking egos (a variation of Freud's id, ego, and superego); see W. Ronald Fairbairn, "Steps in the Development of an Object-Relations Theory of the Personality," *Psychoanalytic Studies of the Personality* (Boston: Routledge & Kegan Paul, 1952), 160.

79. As compellingly argued in Moshe Halevi Spero, *Religious Objects as Psychological Structures* (University of Chicago Press, 1992) and Andrea G. Gurney and, Steven A. Rogers, "Object-Relations and Spirituality: Revisiting a Clinical Dialogue," *Journal of Clinical Psychology* 63,10 (2007). See also Peter Hill and Todd Hall, "Relational Schemas in Processing One's Image of God and Self," *Journal of Psychology & Christianity* 21, 4 (2002).

80. Duckham, "Bipolar Illness, God, and Object Relations," 289.

81. Vicky Genia, "Religious Issues in Secularly Based Psychotherapy," *Counseling and Values* 44, 3 (2000); Daniel Helminiak, "The Role of Spirituality in Formulating a Theory of the Psychology of Religion," *Zygon: Journal of Religion and Science* 41, 1 (2006) and "Psychology of Religion in Search of a Theory," *Child and Family Behavior Therapy*, 30, 2 (2008).

82. See, for example, Erikson, *Life History and the Historical Moment*, 36–37.

83. Lev Vygotsky, *The Collected Works of L.S. Vygotsky, Vol. 5: Child Psychology* (New York: Plenum Press, 1998), 83.

84. May, *Psychology and the Human Dilemma*, 136.

85. Carl Rogers, *A Way of Being* (Boston, MA: Houghton Mifflin, 1980).

86. Ricoeur, *Freud and Philosophy*, 551.

87. James Hillman, *The Myth of Analysis: Three Essays in Archetypal Psychology* (New York: Harper & Row, 1972), 6–7: "Analysis will be ended when we discover what myth it is enacting, a discovery which may not come all at once but which occurs as insights reveal the relation of analysis to soul-making." See also Carl Jung, *Modern Man in Search of a Soul* (New York: Harcourt Brace Jovanovich, 1970).

88. William F. Lynch (1965) is known for supporting this point using hopefulness as an imaginal-therapeutic focus; see William Lynch, *Images of Hope: Imagination as Healer of the Hopeless* (Baltimore: Helicon Press, 1965). See also Carl Jung, *Analytic Psychology: Its Theory and Practice* (New York: Pantheon Books, 1968), 173–79. The therapeutic value of all psychological contents holds even in cases of transference.

89. See, for example, an illustration in Rollo May, "The Man Who Was Put in a Cage," *Psychiatry* 15, 4 (1952): 469.

90. May, *Psychology and the Human Dilemma*, 192, adding that "one of the aspects of Freud's courage is that he frankly used the term 'psyche' and made no bones about it," in contrast to Erikson's *Life, History, and the Historical Moment* et al, as psychology saw advanced metrification in the late twentieth century.

91. Rizzuto is intent on remaining within the ambit of psychoanalysis, however: "as a researcher," she writes, "I will not make pronouncements appropriate for philosophers and theologians" (*The Birth*, 4). But the scope and implications of her research and developments within the study of the mind, in my view, cannot help but inform philosophy and theology; the mind is their sole habitat. Rizzuto in "Reflections on Listening to and Speaking with the Patient During Analysis" (2007) does later acknowledge that theology is enhanced by what psychoanalytic theory has to offer.

92. Jung, "Approaching the Unconscious," 93.

93. Winnicott concludes, "Statistics could not show these changes"; see Donald Winnicott, *Home is Where We Start From: Essays by a Psychoanalyst* (New York: W.W. Norton & Company, 1986), 18. James had also remarked "in the religious sphere, in particular, belief that formulas are true can never wholly take the place of personal experience" (*The Varieties of Religious Experience*, 409–10).

94. Rudolf Carnap propounded verificationism, insisting that no idea merits belief unless confirmed observationally through experimentation. In response to verificationism's challenges with respect to correspondence, presumption, and

confirmation bias, Karl Popper argued instead for a falsification method, whereby scientific proposals were expected to include conditions whereby they could be shown false. Both cases could make broad interpretive use of Russell's famous cosmic teapot illustration: the proposal that such a household object were in orbit around the sun (say, somewhere between the Earth and Mars), could hardly be regarded as a reasonable or relevant conjecture; it cannot be verified, nor does it provide criteria by which it could be disproven.

95. Kenneth Pargament, *The Psychology of Religious Coping: Theory, Research, Practice* (New York: Guilford Press, 1997), 165.

96. Antoine Vergote, "Psychoanalysis and Phenomenology," *Problems in Psychoanalysis: A Symposium* (London: Burns & Oates, 1961), 139–160.

97. Van Deusen Hunsinger, *Theology and Pastoral Counseling*, 106, with reference to reviews in 1981 by Merle Jordan and C.D. Hackett.

98. See especially Hanneke Schaap-Jonker et al., "Image of God and Personality Pathology," *Mental Health, Religion & Culture* 5, 1 (2002), but also Wikström, "Depression and the Absence of God"; Carr, "Some Reflections on Spirituality, Religion and Mental Health"; Wyatt, "Confronting the Almighty God?" and "Counselling and Religious Faith"; Miovic, "Introduction to Spiritual Psychology"; Moriarti, Hoffman, and Grimes, "Understanding the God Image through Attachment Theory"; Tacey, "The Gift of the Unknown"; Meissner 2008; Schlauch 2009; and Duckham, 2011. See also Pnevmatikos, "Conceptual Changes in Religious Concepts of Elementary Schoolchildren: The Case of the House where God Lives," (2002).

99. Ann Belford Ulanov, *Finding Space: Winnicott, God, andRpsychic reality* (Louisville, KY: Westminster John Knox Press, 2001), 106.

100. Rizutto, *The Birth*, 90.

101. Ibid, Ana-María. "Religious Development: A Psychoanalytic Point of View.'

102. Donald Winnicott, *Playing and Reality* (New York, NY: Tavistock, 1982), 14.

103. Rizutto, *The Birth*, 178.

104. Winnicott, *Playing and Reality*, 14.

105. Ibid, *Home is Where We Start From*, 134.

106. Brent D. Slife and P. Scott Richards, "How Separable are Spirituality and Theology in Psychotherapy?," *Counseling and Values* 45, 3 (2001), 190–206; Daniel A. Helminiak, "Treating Spiritual Issues in Secular Psychotherapy," *Counseling and Values* 45, 3 (2001).

107. Rizutto, *The Birth*, 87.

108. Ibid., 179.

109. Ana-María Rizzuto, "Paradoxical Words and Hope in Psychoanalysis," *Psychoanalytic Psychology* 21, 2 (2004): 97; see related discussion in Wikström, "Depression and the Absence of God," 136–39. This contrasts with Spero's argument that a sufficient level of disparity between the beliefs of analyst and patient risks reductionism on the part of the former and undermines the inevitable theological relevance of their relationship and of the therapeutic produce of their sessions; see Moshe Halevi Spero, "The Experience of Religious Transformation During Psychoanalysis as an Event Horizon," *Psychoanalytic Inquiry* 28 (2008).

110. Additionally, to improve the objectivity of theological therapy, there is a burgeoning number of methods for standardized measurement (and thus correlation) of spirituality and psychological conditions. See, for example, Peter Hill and Kenneth Pargament, "Advances in the Conceptualization and Measurement of Religion and Spirituality: Implications for Physical and Mental Health Research," *American Psychologist* 58 (2003).

111. *The Birth of the Living God* has inspired and contributed to work on religion and gender; see Diane Jonte-Pace, *Speaking the Unspeakable: Religion, Misogyny, and the Uncanny Mother in Freud's Cultural Texts* (University of California Press, 2001).

112. Rizutto, *The Birth*, 111.

113. Ibid., 112, 116.

114. Ibid., 120–21, 27.

115. These also promote the convergence of theory and practice; Winnicott's "clinical work is always integrated with his theorizing, so that each informs the other in a dialectical fashion" (Steven Tuber, *Attachment, Play, and Authenticity: A Winnicott Primer* (New York, NY: Jason Aronson, 2008), 202; see also Marcia Cavell, *The Psychoanalytic Mind: From Freud to Philosophy* (Cambridge, MA: Harvard University Press, 1996), 5–6.

116. Rizutto, *The Birth*, 179. See also Ulanov's discussion of Winnicott, art, God, and illusion in *Finding Space*, 93–100.

117. Freud, "The Moses of Michelangelo," 524.

118. David Tacey, "The Gift of the Unknown: Jung(ians) and Freud(ians) at the End of Modernity," *European Journal of Psychotherapy and Counselling* 9, 4 (2007): 423–34.

119. Jung, *Analytic Psychology*, 203–4. He proceeded, "Because these pictures of the unconscious express the actual psychological condition of the individual, you can use them for the purpose of diagnosis"; however, Jung insisted that analysis is not normative: "Each patient is a new problem for the doctor, and he will only be cured of his neurosis if you help him find his individual way to the solution of his conflicts."

120. Winnicott wrote, "The thing about playing is always the precariousness of the interplay of personal psychic reality and the experience of control of actual objects. This is the precariousness of magic itself, magic that arises in intimacy, in a relationship that is being found to be reliable" (*Playing and Reality*, 47).

121. Winnicott, *Home is Where We Start From*, 40.

122. Gavin Miller, "Crossing the Border: Pastoral Theology and Psychotherapy," *The Expository Times* 124, 4 (2013): 164.

123. May, "Social Responsibilities of Psychologists," 214. Caruso's observation resembles May's: "The object of the struggle is no longer God-Man, uniting in himself the fullness of human nature and of being itself, but relative autonomous man—and, all too often, only one aspect of man, is emphasized and turned into one absolute" (*Existential Psychology*, 214).

124. As Thomas Plante and Allen Sherman note in "Research on Faith and Health," *Faith and Health: Psychological Perspectives* (New York, NY: Guilford Press, 2001), 2–3. Caruso articulates, "To be human is a quality of being, and this

quality . . . can by its very nature never be expressed as the quantitative sum of biological characteristics" (*Existential Psychology*, 24).

125. William James, *A Pluralistic Universe* (New York, NY: The Library of America (1987), 639.

126. Donald Winnicott, "Transitional Objects and Transitional Phenomena," *The International Journal of Psycho-analysis* 34 (1953), 89.

127. Rizutto, *The Birth*, 177.

128. Ibid., 209.

129. Ernst Mach called the separation between the natural laws" utility and truthfulness "instrumentalism." See also George Lakoff and Mark Johnson, *Metaphors We Live By* (University of Chicago Press, 1980), and Bruno Latour and Steve Woolgar, *Laboratory Life: The Construction of Scientific Facts* (Princeton University Press, 1979).

130. Rizutto, *The Birth*, 53.

131. Ibid., 209.

132. Ibid., 209.

133. Ibid.

134. An observation from Wittgenstein quoted in Zaretsky, *Secrets of the Soul*, 3.

135. Rizutto, *The Birth*, 209. We hear here, perhaps, an echo of Augustine's well known introspection in his *Confessions* that our hearts are restless until they find their rest in God.

136. Consider Winnicott's formulation: "Relief from this strain [of relating inner and outer reality] is provided by an intermediate area of experience which is not challenged (arts, religion, etc.)" ("Transitional Objects and Transitional Phenomena," 13).

137. Hillman, *The Myth of Analysis*, 267.

138. Ibid., 4.

139. Ibid., 211. (After all, even scientific knowledge and memory are closely affiliated with the imagination.)

140. Karl Giberson and Mariano Artigas, *Oracles of Science: Celebrity Scientists versus God and Religion* (Oxford University Press, 2006), 16.

141. Jon Lanman, "On the Non-Evolution of Atheism and the Importance of Definitions and Data," *Religion, Brain & Behavior* 2, 1 (2012).

142. Richard Dawkins, *The God Delusion* (Houghton Mifflin Harcourt, 2008).

143. Sam Harris, *The Moral Landscape: How Science Determines Human Values* (New York, NY: Free Press, 2010), 179.

144. Richard Dawkins, *The Selfish Gene—with a new Introduction by the author* (Oxford University Press, 2006), xv.

145. Harris, *The Moral Landscape*, 175.

146. There is much to be developed about the benefits of dramatic contrasts between the goals and doctrines of some religious traditions and those of psychoanalysis, inasmuch as both parties exhibit a "sincere search for truth"; see Blass, "Psychoanalysis and the Question of Religious Truth," 630–31.

147. Zaretsky, *Secrets of the Soul*, 344.

148. Dawkins, *The God Delusion*, 5.

149. Sam Harris, The End of Faith (W.W. Norton & Co., 2004) and Richard Dawkins, *Enemies of Reason* (IWC Media, 2008).

150. Anthony C. Grayling, *The God Argument: The Case Against Religion and for Humanism* (New York, NY: Bloomsbury, 2013), 237.

151. Whereas many duly note, following Karl Jaspers and, ultimately, Hume, that "Strict separation of knowledge and value-judgments is essential in psychological analysis" (Caruso, *Existential Psychology*, 215).

152. Heinz Hartmann, "Psychoanalysis as a Scientific Theory," *New Ideas in Psychoanalysis: The Process of Change in Humanistic Science* (2013), 335.

153. Albert Mohler, "The "New Atheism" Movement Considers Religion Morally Wrong," Atheism: Opposing Viewpoints (Greenhaven Press, 2009), 45. He continues, "Science as defined by these new priests, would serve as the new sacrament and as the means of salvation." Mohler is president of Southern Baptist Theological Seminary.

154. Rizutto, *The Birth*, 5. Here, a discussion of Rizzuto's distinction between personal and official religion also is warranted.

155. Rizutto, *The Birth*, 5. Here, a discussion of Rizzuto's distinction between personal and official religion also is warranted.

156. Christopher Hitchens, *God Is Not Great: How Religion Poisons Everything* (New York, NY: Twelve, 2007), 13, 22, 25, 27.

157. W. Ronald Fairbairn, "The Repression and the Return of Bad Objects (with Special Reference to the "War Neuroses')," *Psychoanalytic Studies of the Personality*, (Boston: Routledge & Kegan Paul, 1952).

158. Freud, *The Ego and the Id*, 61.

159. Sophocles, *Oedipus the King*, 57, 87. (See also 53, 107).

160. Helminiak, Daniel A., 96.

161. Rizutto, *The Birth*, 171.

162. Ibid., 172.

163. Ibid., 210.

164. May, *Psychology and the Human Dilemma*, 175.

165. Karen Horney, *New Ways in Psychoanalysis* (New York, NY: W.W. Norton & Company, 1939), 231.

166. Frosh, *The Politics of Psychoanalysis*, 273. Frosh explores many ways in which psychoanalysis contests authority structures with proclivities toward domination and oppression (pp. 266–67). See also Erikson's emphasis through a comparative study of Freud and Mohandas Gandhi which demonstrates that they both move away from "the mentality of the pseudo-species" (Erikson, *Life History and the Historical Moment*, 187–89).

167. Zaretsky, *Secrets of the Soul*, 344.

168. Rizzuto, "Paradoxical Words and Hope in Psychoanalysis," 103. Compare also Caruso's summary that "as personalist depth psychology emerges from the crisis of our thinking, it will be seen to be devoted to freedom and life" (*Existential Psychology*, 216).

169. Cavell, *The Psychoanalytic Mind*, 234.

170. Edward C. Whitmont, *The Symbolic Quest: Basic Concepts of Analytic Psychology* (Princeton University Press, 1991), 310.

171. Horney takes the superimposition of such a social stigma as concomitant to neurosis when the stigma prompts "defensive tendencies which, although equally imperative, are nevertheless incompatible with one another"; see Karen Horney, *The Neurotic Personality of Our Time* (New York, NY: W.W. Norton & Company, 1937), 101.

172. Here one may recall Bernard Lonergan's description of faith as "knowledge born of religious love." He remarks also that "every inquiry aims at transforming some unknown into a known. Inquiry itself, then, is something between ignorance and knowledge"; see Bernard Lonergan, *Method in Theology* (University of Toronto Press, 1990), 22.

173. Michael Polanyi, *Personal Knowledge: Towards a Post-Critical Philosophy* (London: Routledge, 1962).

174. Stephen M. Kosslyn & Amy L. Sussman, "Roles of Imagery in Perception: Or, there is no such Thing as Immaculate Perception," in *The Cognitive Neurosciences*, ed. Michael S. Gazzaniga, (Cambridge, MA: MIT Press, 1995), 1040.

175. Pierre Lecompte du Noüy, *La dignité humaine*, (Paris: Champ-de-Mars, 1947), 30.

BIBLIOGRAPHY

Adler, Alfred. *The Practice and Theory of Individual Psychology*. Totowa, NJ: Littlefield, Adams & Co., 1969.

———. "The Differences Between Individual Psychology and Psychoanalysis." In *Superiority and Social Interest,* edited by Heinz L. Ansbacher and Rowena R. Ansbacher, 206–18.. New York, NY: W.W. Norton & Company, 1979.

———. "Religion and Individual Psychology." In *Superiority and Social Interest,* edited by Heinz L. Ansbacher and Rowena R. Ansbacher, 274–308. New York, NY: W.W. Norton & Company, 1979.

Beattie, Hilary J. "The Repression and the Return of Bad Objects"" W.R.D. Fairbairn and the Historical Roots of Theory." *International Journal of Psychoanalysis* 84, 5 (2003): 1171–87.

Blass, Rachel B. "Beyond Illusion: Psychoanalysis and the Question of Religious Truth." *International Journal of Psychoanalysis*, 85, 3 (2004): 615–34.

Brown, Norman. *Life Against Death*. Middletown, CT: Wesleyan University Press, 1959.

Browning, Don. "Internists of the Mind or Physicians of the Soul: Does Psychiatry Need a Public Philosophy?" *Zygon: Journal of Religion and Science* 43, 2 (2008): 371–83.

Carr, Wesley. "Some Reflections on Spirituality, Religion and Mental Health." *Mental Health, Religion & Culture* 3, 1 (2000): 1–12.

Caruso, Igor A. *Existential Psychology: From Analysis to Synthesis*. New York, NY: Herder and Herder, 1964.

Cavell, Marcia. *The Psychoanalytic Mind: From Freud to Philosophy*. Cambridge, MA: Harvard University Press, 1996.

Cohen, David. *The Escape of Sigmund Freud.* New York, NY: The Overlook Press, 2012.
Cordón, Luis A. *Freud's World: An Encyclopedia of His Life and Times.* Santa Barbara, CA: Greenwood, 2012.
Dawkins, Richard. *The Selfish Gene: – with a new Introduction by the author.* New York, NY: Oxford University Press, 2006.
———. *The God Delusion.* New York, NY: Houghton Mifflin Harcourt, 2008.
———. *Enemies of Reason.* IWC Media, 2008.
Dixon, Lance S. "Reaching Out to the Divine: An Examination of God Images and Prayer Functions." PhD diss., Lubbock, TX: Texas Tech University, 2014.
Duckham, Bryan. "Bipolar Illness, God, and Object Relations: The Treatment of M." *Smith College Studies in Social Work* 81, 2–3 (2011): 268–91.
Ellis, Albert. *The Case Against Religion: A Psychotherapist's View.* New York, NY: Institute for Rational Living, 1971.
Erikson, Erik H. *Life History and the Historical Moment.* New York, NY: W.W. Norton & Company, 1975.
Fairbairn, W. Ronald D. "The Repression and the Return of Bad Objects (with Special Reference to the 'War Neuroses')." In *Psychoanalytic Studies of the Personality*, 59–81. Boston, MA: Routledge & Kegan Paul, 1952.
———. "Endopsychic Structure Considered in Terms of Object-Relationships." In *Psychoanalytic Studies of the Personality*, 82–136. Boston, MA: Routledge & Kegan Paul, 1952. Originally published in 1944.
———. "Object-Relationships and Dynamic Structure." In *Psychoanalytic Studies of the Personality*, 137–51. Boston: Routledge & Kegan Paul, 1952.
———. "Steps in the Development of an Object-Relations Theory of the Personality." In *Psychoanalytic Studies of the Personality*, 152–161. Boston: Routledge & Kegan Paul, 1952.
Freud, Sigmund. "The Moses of Michelangelo." In *The Standard Edition of the Complete Psychological Works of Sigmund Freud, Volume XIII, (1913–1914): Totem and Taboo and Other Works* (1955): 209–238.
———. "The Psychopathology of Everyday Life." In *The Basic Writings of Sigmund Freud*, translated by A.A. Brill, 33–178. New York, NY: The Modern Library, 1938. Originally published in 1899.
———. *Totem and Taboo.* Oxford, Routledge, 2003.
———. *The Interpretation of Dreams.* Translated by A.A. Brill. New York, NY: Barnes and Noble Classics, 2005. Originally published in 1899.
———. *The Ego and the Id.* Translated by Joan Riviere; edited by James Strachey. New York, NY: W.W. Norton and Company, 1960. Originally published in 1923.
Freud, Sigmund, and James Strachey. *Civilization and Its Discontents.* New York, NY: W.W. Norton & Company, 2005.
Frosh, Stephen. *The Politics of Psychoanalysis: An Introduction to Freudian and Post-Freudian Theory.* New Haven, CT: Yale University Press, 1987.
Fuller, Robert C. "American Psychology and the Religious Imagination." *Journal of the History of the Behavioral Sciences* 42, 3 (2006): 221–35.

Gemes, Ken. "Freud and Nietzsche on Sublimation." *Journal of Nietzsche Studies*, 38 (2009): 38–59.

Genia, Vicky. "Religious Issues in Secularly Based Psychotherapy." *Counseling and Values* 44, 3 (2000): 213–21.

Giberson, Karl, and Mariano Artigas. *Oracles of Science: Celebrity Scientists versus God and religion*. New York, NY: Oxford University Press, 2006.

Grayling, A.C. *The God Argument: The Case Against Religion and for Humanism*. New York, NY: Bloomsbury, 2013.

Grotstein, James S. "Reflections on a Century of Freud: Some Paths Not Chosen." *British Journal of Psychotherapy* 9, 2 (1992): 181–87.

Gurney, Andrea G., and Rogers, Steven A. "Object-Relations and Spirituality: Revisiting a Clinical Dialogue." *Journal of Clinical Psychology*, 63, 10 (2007): 961–77.

Hall, W. Todd, and Hill, C. Peter. "Relational Schemas in Processing One's Image of God and Self." *Journal of Psychology and Christianity*, 21, 4 (2002).

Halpern, Janice. "Review of 'Why Did Freud Reject God? A Psychodynamic Interpretation by Ana-María Rizzuto.'" *Journal of the American Psychoanalytic Association* 48 (2000):1009–13.

Harris, Sam. *The Moral Landscape: How Science Determines Human Values*. New York, NY: Free Press, 2010.

———. *End of Faith*. New York, NY: W.W. Norton & Co., 2004.

Hartmann, Heinz. "The Development of the Ego Concept in Freud's Work." *Essays on Ego Psychology: Selected Problems in Psychoanalytic Theory*. 61:113–141. New York, NY: International Universities Press, 1964.

———. "Comments on the Scientific Aspects of Psychoanalysis." *Essays on Ego Psychology: Selected Problems in Psychoanalytic Theory*, 297–317. New York, NY: International Universities Press, 1964.

———. "Psychoanalysis as a Scientific Theory." In *New Ideas in Psychoanalysis: The Process of Change in Humanistic Science*, edited by Calvin F. Settlage and Reed Brockbank, 101–126. Hillsdale, NJ: The Analytic Press.

Hartz, Gary W. *Spirituality and Mental Health: Clinical Applications*. Binghamton, NY: Haworth Pastoral Press, 2005.

Helminiak, Daniel A. "Treating Spiritual Issues in Secular Psychotherapy," *Counseling and Values* 45, 3 (2001): 163–89.

———. "The Role of Spirituality in Formulating a Theory of the Psychology of Religion." *Zygon: Journal of Religion and Science* 41, 1 (2006): 197–224.

———. "Psychology of Religion in Search of a Theory." *Child and Family Behavior Therapy*, 30, 2 (2008): 187–93.

———. ""Theistic Psychology and Psychotherapy': A Theological and Scientific Critique." *Zygon: Journal of Religion and Science* 45, 1 (2010): 47–74.

Highet, Gilbert. *Man's Unconquerable Mind*. New York, NY: Columbia University Press, 1954.

Hill, Peter C., and Todd W. Hall. "Relational Schemas in Processing one's image of God and self." *Journal of Psychology & Christianity* 21, 4 (2002).

Hill, Peter C., and Kenneth I. Pargament. "Advances in the Conceptualization and Measurement of Religion and Spirituality: Implications for Physical and Mental Health Research." *American Psychologist* 58 (2003): 64–74.

Hillman, James. *The Myth of Analysis: Three Essays in Archetypal Psychology*. New York, NY: Harper & Row, 1972.

Hitchens, Christopher. *God Is Not Great: How Religion Poisons Everything*. New York, NY: Twelve, 2007.

Horney, Karen. *The Neurotic Personality of Our Time*. New York, NY: W.W. Norton & Company, 1937.

———. *New Ways in Psychoanalysis*. New York, NY: W.W. Norton & Company, 1939.

———. *Self-Analysis*. New York, NY: W.W. Norton & Company, 1942.

Hudak, Glenn. Review of "Finding Space: Winnicott, God, and Psychic Reality," by Ann Belford Ulanov. *Journal of Religion and Health* 42, 1 (2003): 77–83.

James, William. *A Pluralistic Universe*. In *William James: Writings 1902–1910,* edited by Bruce Kuklick, 625–819. New York, NY: The Library of America, 1987.

———. *The Varieties of Religious Experience*. Bruce Kuklick, ed. In *William James: Writings 1902–1910*, edited by Bruce Kuklick, 1–477 New York, NY: The Library of America, 1987.

Jonte-Pace, Diane. *Speaking theUunspeakable: Religion, Misogyny, and the Uncanny Mother in Freud's Cultural Texts*. Berkeley, CA: University of California Press, 2001.

Jordan, Merle. "Psychotherapy as an Operational Theology Process." In *The Spiritual Horizon of Psychotherapy,* edited by William S. Schmidt and Merle Jordan, 4–11. London: Routledge, 2013. Jung, Carl G. "Approaching the Unconscious." In *Man and His Symbols*, edited by Carl Jung, 1–94. New York, NY: Dell Publishing Co., 1964.

———. *Analytical Psychology: Its Theory and Practice (The Tavistock Lectures)*. New York, NY: Pantheon Books, 1968.

———. *Modern Man in Search of a Soul*. Translated by W.S. Dell and Cary F. Baynes. New York, NY: Arcourt Brace Jovanovich, 1970.

Kaufman, Gordon D. *The Theological Imagination: Constructing the Concept of God*, Philadelphia, PA: Westminster Press, 1981.

———. "Nature, History, and God: Toward an Integrated Conceptualization." *Zygon* 27,4 (1992): 379–401.

Koenig, Harold G. *Is Religion Good for Your Health? The Effects of Religion on Physical and Mental Health*. Binghamton, NY: Haworth Pastoral Press, 1997.

Koenig, Harold G., M.E. McCullough, and D.B. Larson. "Understanding Religion's Effects on Mental Health." In *Handbook of Religion and Health*, 214–28. New York, NY: Oxford University Press, 2001.

Lakoff, George, and Mark Johnson. *Metaphors We Live By*. Chicago, IL: University of Chicago Press, 1980.

———. *Philosophy in the Flesh: The Embodied Mind and its Challenge to Western Thought*. New York, NY: Basic Books, 1999.

Lanman, Jon. "On the Non-evolution of Atheism and the Importance of Definitions and Data." *Religion, Brain & Behavior* 2, 1 (2012): 76–78.

Latour, Bruno, and Steve Woolgar. *Laboratory Life: The Construction of Scientific Facts*. Princeton, NJ: Princeton University Press, 2013.
Layzell, Ruth. "A Case of the Baby and the Bath Water?" *Practical Theology* 4, 1 (2011): 97–116.
Leffel, G. Michael. "Prevenient Grace and the Re-Enchantment of Nature: Toward a Wesleyan Theology of Psychotherapy and Spiritual Formation," *Journal of Psychology and Christianity*, 23, 2 (2004): 130–39.
Lonergan, Bernard. *Method in Theology*. Toronto: University of Toronto Press, 1990.
Lynch, Gordon. "The Relationship between Pastoral Counseling and Pastoral Theology." In *The Blackwell Reader in Pastoral and Practical Theology*, edited by James Woodward and Stephen Pattison, 223–32. Oxford: Blackwell, 2000.
Lynch, William F. *Images of Hope: Imagination as Healer of the Hopeless*, Baltimore, MD: Helicon Press, 1965.
May, Rollo. "The Man Who Was Put in a Cage." *Psychiatry* 15, 4 (1952): 469.
———. *Psychology and the Human Dilemma*. New York, NY: W.W. Norton & Company, 1967.
McGrath, Alister. "The Incoming Sea of Faith," *The Spectator*, Sept. 18, 2004. Reproduced as "Atheism Does Not Have a Future." In *Atheism: Opposing Viewpoints.*, edited by Beth Rosenthal, 167–74. Farmington Hills, MI: Greenhaven Press, 2009.
Meissner, William W. *Psychoanalysis and Religious Experience*. New Haven: Yale University Press, 1984.
———. "Psychoanalysis and Catholicism—Dialogues in Transformation." *Psychoanalytic Inquiry* 28 (2008): 580–89.
Miller, Gavin. "R.D. Laing and Theology: The Influence of Christian Existentialism on The Divided Self." *History of the Human Sciences* 22, 2 (2009): 1–21.
———. "Crossing the Border: Pastoral theology and psychotherapy," *The Expository Times* 124, 4 (2013): 157–65.
Miller, William R., and Carl E. Thoresen. "Spirituality, Religion and Health: An Emerging Research Field." *American Psychologist*, 58, 1 (2003): 24–35.
Miovic, Michael. "Introduction to Spiritual Psychology: Overview of the Literature, East and West." *Harvard Review of Psychiatry* 12, 2 (2004): 105–115.
Mohler, Albert. "The "New Atheism" Movement Considers Religion Morally Wrong." In *Atheism: Opposing Viewpoints*, edited by Beth Rosenthal, 37–45. Michigan: Greenhaven Press, 2009.
Moon, Gary W. "Training Tomorrow's Integrators in Today's Busy Intersection: Better Look Four Ways before Crossing." *Journal of Psychology and Theology* 25, 2 (1997): 284–293.
Moriarty, Glendon L., Louis Hoffman, and Christopher Grimes. "Understanding the God Image through Attachment Theory: Theory, Research, and Practice." *Journal of Spirituality in Mental Health* 9, no. 2 (2006): 43–56.
Murray, J.A.C. *An Introduction to Christian Psycho-Therapy*. Edinburgh: T&T Clark, 1938.
Myers, D. *The American Paradox: Spiritual Hunger in a Land of Plenty*. New Haven, CT: Yale University Press, 2000.
Neri, Claudio. "What is the Function of Faith and Trust in Psychoanalysis?" *The International Journal of Psychoanalysis*, 86, 1 (2005): 79–97.

Nietzsche, Friedrich. *Twilight of the Idols*. Trans. R.J. Hollingdale. New York, NY: Penguin Books, 2003.

Oraison, Marc. "The Psychoanalyst and the Confessor." In *Problems in Psychoanalysis: A Symposium*, translated by Cecily Batten, 171–93. London: Burns & Oates, 1961.

Pargament, Kenneth I. *The Psychology of Religious Coping: Theory, Research, Practice*. New York, NY: Guilford Press, 1997.

Philp, Howard Littleton. *Freud and Religious Belief*. Santa Barbara, CA: Greenwood Publishing Group, 1974.

Plante, Thomas G. "Integrating Spirituality and Psychotherapy: Ethical Issues and Principles to Consider," *Journal of Clinical Psychology*, 63, 9 (2007): 891–902.

Plante, Thomas G., and Allen S. Sherman, eds. *Faith and Health: Psychological Perspectives*. New York, NY: Guilford Press, 2001.

Pnevmatikos, Dimitris. "Conceptual Changes in Religious Concepts of Elementary Schoolchildren: The Case of the House where God Lives." *Educational Psychology: An International Journal of Experimental Educational Psychology*, 22, 1 (2002): 93–112.

Ricoeur, Paul. *Freud and Philosophy: An Essay on Interpretation*.Translated by Denis Savage. New Haven, CT: Yale University Press, 1970.

Rizzuto, Ana-María. *The Birth of the Living God: A Psychoanalytic Study*. Chicago, IL: University of Chicago Press, 1979.

———. "Religious Development: A Psychoanalytic Point of View." *New Directions for Child and Adolescent Development* 52 (1991): 47–60.

———. "Christian Worshipping and Psychoanalysis in Spiritual Truth." In *Personhood: Orthodox Christianity and the Connection between Mind, Body, and Soul*, edited by John T. Chirban, 51–59. Westport, CT: Bergin & Garvey, 1996.

———. *Why Did Freud Reject God? A Psychodynamic Interpretation*. New Haven: Yale University Press, 1998.

———. "Paradoxical Words and Hope in Psychoanalysis." *Psychoanalytic Psychology* 21, 2 (2004): 203.

———. "Reflections on Listening to and Speaking with the Patient During Analysis." *Language, Symbolization, and Psychosis* (2007): 143.

Rogers, Carl. *A Way of Being*. Boston, MA: Houghton Mifflin, 1980.

Schaap-Jonker, Hanneke, et al. "Image of God and personality pathology: an exploratory study among psychiatric patients." *Mental Health, Religion & Culture* 5, 1 (2002): 55–71.

Schlauch, Chris R. "Do I Hear What You Hear? Thinking about Psychotherapy and Spirituality from a Self Psychological Approach." *Journal of Spirituality in Mental Health* 11, no. 1–2 (2009): 26–50.

Schleiermacher, Friedrich. *On Religion: Speeches to its Cultured Despisers*. Louisville, KY: Westminster John Knox Press, 1994.

Slife, Brent D., and Richards, P. Scott. "How Separable are Spirituality and Theology in Psychotherapy?" *Counseling and Values* 45, 3 (2001), 190–206.

Slife, Brent D., Tiffani D. Stevenson, and Dennis C. Wendt. "Including God in Psychotherapy: Strong vs. Weak Theism." *Journal of Psychology and Theology* 38, 3 (2010): 163.

Sophocles. *Oedipus the King*. Bernard Knox, trans. New York, NY: Simon & Schuster, 1994.
Spero, Moshe Halevi. *Religious Objects as Psychological Structures*. Chicago, IL: University of Chicago Press, 1992.
———. "The Experience of Religious Transformation During Psychoanalysis as an Event Horizon." *Psychoanalytic Inquiry* 28 (2008): 622–37.
Sperry, Len, and Shafranske, E.P., eds. *Spiritually Oriented Psychotherapy*. Washington, DC: American Psychological Association, 2005.
Steinfeld, George J. "Spiritual Psychology and Psychotherapy: Is There Theoretical and Empirical Support?" *Journal of Contemporary Psychotherapy* 30, 4 (2000): 353–80.
Sulloway, Frank. *Freud, Biologist of the Mind: Beyond the Psychoanalytic Legend*. New York, NY: Basic Books, 1979 (1983).
Surr, John. "Links Between Early Attachment Experiences and Manifestations of Spirituality." *International Journal of Children's Spirituality* 16, 2 (2011): 129–41.
Tacey, David. "The Gift of the Unknown: Jung(ians) and Freud(ians) at the End of Modernity." *European Journal of Psychotherapy and Counselling* 9, 4 (2007): 423–34.
Tan, Siang-Yang. "Ethical Considerations in Religious Psychotherapy: Potential Pitfalls and Unique Resources." *Journal of Psychology and Theology* (1994).
Tan, Siang-Yang, and Natalie J. Dong. "Spiritual Interventions in Healing and Wholeness." *Faith and health* (2001): 291–310.
Thurschwell, Pamela. *Sigmund Freud*. New York, NY: Routledge, 2000.
Tuber, Steven. *Attachment, Play, and Authenticity: A Winnicott Primer*. New York, NY: Jason Aronson, 2008.
Ulanov, Ann Belford. *Finding Space: Winnicott, God, andPpsychic Reality*. Louisville, KY: Westminster John Knox Press, 2001.
van Deusen Hunsinger, Deborah. *Theology and Pastoral Counseling: A New Interdisciplinary Approach*. Grand Rapids, MI: William B. Erdmans, 1995.
Vergote, Antoine. "Psychoanalysis and Phenomenology." Trans. Cecily Batten. In *Problems in Psychoanalysis: A Symposium*, translated by Cecily Batten, 139–160. London: Burns & Oates, 1961.
Vitz, Paul C. *Faith of the Fatherless: The Psychology of Atheism*. San Francisco, CA: Ignatius Press, 2013.
von Franz, Marie-Louise. "The Process of Individuation." Carl Jung, ed. In *Man and His Symbols*, edited by Carl Jung, 157–254. New York, NY: Dell Publishing Co., 1964.
Vygotsky, Lev S. *The Collected Works of L.S. Vygotsky, Vol. 5: Child Psychology*, translated by Marie J. Hall. New York, NY: Plenum Press, 1998.
Whitcher, Douglas Eames. *When Therapy Becomes Theology: A Critical View of Empathy*. PhD diss., Syracuse, NY: Syracuse University, 1996.
Whitmont, Edward C. *The Symbolic Quest: Basic Concepts of Analytic Psychology*. Princeton, NJ: Princeton University Press, 1991.
Wikström, Owe. "Depression and the Absence of God: Religious Studies and/or Theology in Clinical Research." *Studia Theologica—Nordic Journal of Theology* 52, 2 (1998): 130–146.

Winnicott, Donald W. "Transitional Objects and Transitional Phenomena." *The International Journal of Psycho-analysis* 34 (1953): 89.

———. *Playing and Reality*. New York, NY: Tavistock, 1982.

———. *Home is Where We Start From: Essays by a Psychoanalyst*. New York, NY: W.W. Norton & Company, 1986.

Wyatt, Jonathan. "'Confronting the Almighty God'? A Study of how Psychodynamic Counselors Respond to Clients' Expressions of Religious Faith." *Counselling and Psychotherapy Research: Linking Research with Practice* 2, 3 (2002): 177–183.

———. "Counselling and Religious Faith." *Psychodynamic Practice* 10, 1 (2004): 27–43.

Zaretsky, Eli. *Secrets of the Soul: A Social and Cultural History of Psychoanalysis*. New York, NY: Alfred A. Knopf, 2004.

Zilboorg, Gregory. *Freud and Religion: A Restatement of an Old Controversy*. Westminster, MD: The Newman Press, 1964.

Conclusion

Martha Reineke and David Goodman

Ana-María Rizzuto's groundbreaking explorations of the formation of God representations in early childhood and their elaboration throughout the life cycle have made their mark, enriching the practice of psychoanalysis and psychotherapy as well as scholarship within the psychoanalytic study of religion. Assessing Rizzuto's legacy on the thirty-fifth anniversary of the publication of *The Birth of the Living God,* contributors to this book have confirmed the significance of Rizzuto's contributions to psychoanalytic theories of religious experience. They also have underscored Rizzuto's most important contribution to clinical practice: rather than assert that psychoanalysis is incompatible with religious beliefs and practices or with spiritual concerns that patients may bring to a therapeutic context, Rizzuto makes room for the coexistence of psychoanalysis and religion in the therapeutic setting. And, perhaps even more audaciously, she carves out a creative and playful space where religious belief brings a richness into psychotherapeutic discourse. For Rizzuto, religious belief is not greeted immediately with the suspicion of the modern mind but with the illuminative potential of a more poetic spirit—a spirit in keeping with Freud's fundamental requirement regarding the analyst's attunement to patients' experiences. Rizzuto provides the reminder that, rather than being reduced and pathologized, God representations and religious beliefs must remain sites for curiosity.

Accompanied by illuminating commentaries by Rizzuto, the contributors to this book have addressed a range of topics: developmental processes associated with God representations, psychotherapeutic treatment models informed by Rizzuto's theory, psychotherapy in contexts shaped by Eastern religious traditions, monstrous referents in God representations, and the psychoanalysis of religion in light of the new atheism. In the years to come, how will scholars and clinicians engage Rizzuto? The contributors to this book point out three pathways for future influence: enhanced connections within and among psychoanalytic theories of religion, newly established pathways for developing psychotherapeutic approaches, and the possibility of a new mode of interdisciplinary conversations.

PSYCHOANALYSIS AND RELIGION: NEW CONNECTIONS

In their contributions, John McDargh and Mario Aletti highlighted the suggestive potential of Rizzuto's work for future developments in psychoanalytic theories of religion. When Rizzuto generated discrete definitions for "God representations" and "God concepts," she opened up for new consideration fundamental constructs of religious behavior. God concepts, linked with secondary process, feature regularized attributes (e.g., "loving" or "wrathful") and find their home in formal religious discourse among adults; by contrast, God representations are associated with primary process and are drawn from preconscious and even unconscious experiences of very young children, particularly from their parental figures. McDargh observed that, as a consequence of these distinctions, in recent years, psychologists have expanded and deepened research on God through such devices as the "God Image Inventory." Further advances in this area promise to inform clinical practice in helpful ways as well as to bolster Rizzuto's major insight: the God of primary process can be acknowledged in the therapeutic setting, to the benefit of patients and their psychotherapists. Patients need not park their God representations at their therapists' doors. Rather, thanks to Rizzuto's guiding analyses, it is incumbent upon therapists to put God representations in play in transference and countertransference, with salient implications for therapeutic outcomes.

Observing that the propensity for "personal religion"—the religion of God representations—is not innate but results from interactions of the human subject with organized religion and culture, Aletti identified another way that Rizzuto's work may influence future directions in the psychology of religion. As scholarship increasingly addresses the embedding of religion in culture, future research can further assess and more precisely engage how, in response to specific cultural stimuli, the God of primary process emerges from and within a psychocultural matrix of meaning. This promises to be a new frontier for psychoanalysis, one that will expand contemporary models of subjectivity and more capaciously attend to the complex intersections of human experience.

Aletti called our attention also to the ongoing significance of the feature of Rizzuto's work that was considered most noteworthy at the time of the initial publication of *The Birth of the Living God*. Rizzuto upheld and implemented an epistemologically conservative approach to the psychological experience of religion. Making no pronouncements concerning the truth of religion or the ontological existence of God, Rizzuto focused more narrowly on the psychic dynamics of belief. Aletti also reminded us of the most essential outcome of Rizzuto's neutrality: consistent demonstration of a profound respect for patients' values, beliefs, and spiritual practices. Including the future in his gaze, Aletti suggested that analysts in any era—past, present, and future—will find their interactions with patients challenged and enhanced when they model Rizzuto's stance. Remaining forever open to patients' religious experiences, nevertheless, they will not serve as apologists for or critics of religious beliefs and practices. In many ways, this is an extension of Freud's very own methodological wishes, despite the fact that this very sensibility was not available to him. Here, Rizzuto calls the psychoanalyst to a higher elevation—assisting the clinician and scholar in bracketing the prejudice of the discipline's father, all the while embracing his adventurous spirit of radical curiosity.

PSYCHOTHERAPY UNDER RIZZUTO'S INFLUENCE

Describing how Rizzuto's work informed work with patients at the Modem Bad Clinic, McDargh rightly cited one outcome with particularly strong potential for future influence: the application of Rizzuto's work in clinical practice. Through the case of Olav and description of the development of the VITA model at Modem Bad, contributors Gry Stålsett, Arne Austad, and Leif Gunnar Engedal drew on Rizzuto's theory to better understand the function of metaphors in psychotherapy. As reported in their case analysis, they found that Rizzuto's theory illuminated the sources of metaphors that were so demonstrably meaningful to Olav. They explained also how Rizzuto's theoretical reflections were instrumental to the VITA team's efforts to comprehend the interpersonal and communicative significance of these metaphors.

Notably, Rizzuto's theory facilitated the VITA team's capacity to access rich interpretive material beyond the confines of classical psychiatric language. As profoundly illustrated by their discussion of Olav's primary metaphors—*The Committee*, The *Persecuting God*, a *Crucified Self*, an *Occupied Land*—these authors describe experiencing enhanced sensitivity to the dimensionality of descriptive meaning involved in Olav's experience and more supportive ability in relieving Olav's suffering. Stålsett, Austad, and Engedal consider metaphor analysis to be an emerging area in psychotherapy and invite other clinicians to consider patient metaphors as "agents of change."

The Modem Bad experience suggests that, in the future, if psychotherapists attend more closely to layers of affect attached to these metaphors and to affective valuation in all representations, their clinical practice will be enhanced. The VITA team argued that this allows for a type of attending to patient experience and to the complexity of communication inherent to psychotherapy that contributes significantly to positive change. As a new generation of clinicians emerge who have the benefit of Rizzuto's scholarship and influence, case studies will be forthcoming that will further confirm the findings from Modem Bad. In short, Rizzuto's impact on psychotherapy is not yet fully appreciated, and this exciting new space is currently under construction.

INTERDISCIPLINARY KEYS TO A NEW CONVERSATIONAL MODE

One of the most potent opportunities for future engagement with Rizzuto involves the growing application of her insights to areas outside the original purview of her work. Religious and cultural landscapes have changed significantly since Rizzuto published *The Birth of the Living God*. Globalization, secularization, and new models and modes of subjectivity have introduced new configurations and considerations for understanding Rizzuto's insights. Contributors McDargh and Anthony Stern highlighted one extant example of this possibility: the augmentation of Rizzuto's insights to embrace Eastern meditative traditions. In extending Rizzuto's theory to cultural studies—a relatively new interdisciplinary field of study—I (Reineke) signaled the potential for Rizzuto's work to inform future scholarship in that field. Jacob Waldenmaier highlighted the potential implications of Rizzuto's work for contemporary philosophy, particularly for a more robust engagement by philosophers of religion with the new atheism.

Thirty-five years after the publication of *The Birth of the Living God*, globalization and increased immigration have made it increasingly likely that individuals who enter psychotherapy will present with familial contexts informed by Eastern spiritual and cultural traditions. This development may have the productive consequence of inspiring future engagement with Rizzuto's work that brings her insights to bear in completely new ways on the psychoanalytic theory and practice of religion. In his contribution to this book, Stern outlined two suggestive avenues for just such developments. First, he reassessed the work of metaphor in psychoanalysis in the context of Eastern traditions in which culture and spirituality appear as strands in a closely woven fabric and in which the central metaphor of existence is "no self." Second, he pondered the implications of Rizzuto's ontological neutrality, which she articulated with exclusive reference to Western theism, for individuals whose primary metaphors include a flow of energy evocative of the Tao and Buddhist enlightenment. Describing himself as an "amalgam of a spiritually oriented thinker and a clinical psychiatrist," Stern suggested that individuals who are immersed in Eastern meditative traditions may be precluded from adopting the stance toward the spiritual workings of the universe that Rizzuto advanced when she ceded to theologians all discussion of a manifest sacred. In creating openings for a new relationship between psychoanalysis and spirituality, Stern's essay exemplifies rich possibilities for future engagement with Rizzuto's work from locations that de-center the largely Christian and Jewish milieu in which her psychoanalytic theory of religion was developed.

My (Reineke's) contribution to this book demonstrated the potential for Rizzuto's theory to inform scholarship in the humanities where, in recent decades, innovative applications of psychoanalytic theory in fields such as literature, film studies, and cultural studies have generated strong interest. Extending Rizzuto's reflections on God representations to the mythic cultural imagination, I showed how one topic of substantial interest in the field of cultural studies—monsters such as vampires and zombies—can be illuminated by a psychoanalytic perspective even as new interpretative possibilities emerging from engagement with cultural studies can enhance the psychoanalysis of religion. Suggesting that monsters may play more meaningful roles in children's and adult's lives than Rizzuto recognized, I looked closely at monsters, drawing on Timothy Beal's scholarship that explores how the spiritual and psychological work that monsters do has been transposed from their earlier home in the world religions to fiction and film in modern and contemporary culture. Demonstrating that monsters remain existentially powerful, I sought to build a bridge from Rizzuto to scholarship in cultural studies as well as to scholars who have embraced the psychoanalysis of culture. Drawing on the work of Julia Kristeva, who has authored a number of psychoanalytic studies of culture and has contributed significantly to the psychoanalysis of religion, I also argued for the productive utility of bringing Rizzuto into conversation with theorists working in the tradition of Lacanian psychoanalysis. In both respects, I attempted to lay groundwork for dialogue between psychoanalysis and cultural studies upon which others may build in the future.

In chapter 6, Waldenmaier pointed to other ways Rizzuto may continue to be an influential voice in humanities scholarship. Waldenmaier explored the utility of her work for philosophical conversations undertaken at the intersection of religion and science, with particular concern for how philosophers might understand religion. Citing proponents of the new atheism, Waldenmaier brought a philosopher's eye to Rizzuto's work, showing its special relevance for two features of our contemporary scene: scholarship that draws on science to advance the new atheism and a religious landscape of belief and unbelief undergoing dramatic change. Bringing Rizzuto's work on transitional objects and the work of the human imagination to bear on scientific models that are undergirding the new atheism, Waldenmaier observed that the language of faith and the language of the new atheism share deeply imaginal and cathectic similarities: both are expressions of psychic desire. As a consequence, Waldenmaier championed the productive utility of placing faith and the new atheism under the same umbrella of psychic experience. Admittedly, psychic experience sometimes attests to neuroses; however, the open possibilities of meaning that attend its work also secure psychic freedom. Moreover, for Waldenmaier, God representations, which persist even in the professed absence of belief in God, can be the occasion for reinvigorating the philosophy of religion, especially in a time of growing unbelief and generalized "spirituality" among persons who increasingly have no affiliation with organized communities of faith.

LOOKING FORWARD WITH RIZZUTO

Under the guiding light of Rizzuto's own vision, the three pathways of influence explored here are proceeding with newly emerging qualities and considerations. Rizzuto's generous and insightful responses to each essay in this book confirm her openness to novel receptions of her work and provide a model for others. As Rizzuto observed in her discussion of McDargh's contribution to this book, central to all her work has been a commitment to encouraging persons to "tell their own life stories and to talk about the God of their understanding." Setting the parameters for future work in the psychoanalysis of religion, Rizzuto recommended that we respectfully explore "all types of religious experiences, regardless of how sublime or bizarre they may appear to the external observer." Acknowledging Freud as her own model for such inquiry, Rizzuto turns to the past to offer guidance for the future: Freud "insisted that to know the private life of a person we must invite him/her to speak without censoring what comes to mind." Rizzuto summons us to take up this task with utmost seriousness and with the expectation that, if we move forward with an open regard for the hearts and minds of believers and of unbelievers, we will continue to gain access to fundamental features of religious experience that she identifies and so eloquently describes in *The Birth of the Living God.*

Highlighting Ana-María Rizzuto's achievements, chapters of this book suggest that Rizzuto's groundbreaking scholarship will continue to raise questions and inspire new directions in scholarship and clinical practice. In bringing to the fore her work's significance, we have been honored to celebrate Rizzuto's field-defining contributions to the psychoanalytic theory of religious experience and its clinical application. Having sketched pathways in this conclusion for Rizzuto's continuing influence on this field, we anticipate that ours is not the last word on Rizzuto's legacy. We foresee that, building on her work, theorists and clinicians will have occasion in the future to discuss Rizzuto's legacy anew and to affirm yet again the significance of her work for scholarship and clinical practice.

Index

About the Contributors

Mario Aletti is a clinical psychoanalyst and professor of the psychology of religion in the Department of Psychology at the Catholic University of Milan. He founded (1995) and has served as the president of the Italian Society of the Psychology of Religion. He has published over 100 articles, book chapters, and several books. Among his most recent publications are *Percorsi di psicologia della religione alla luce della psicoanalisi* [*Pathways to the Psychology of Religion in the Light of Psychoanalysis*] (Roma: Aracne, 2010); *Preti pedofili? La questione degli abusi sessuali nella Chiesa* [*Pedophile Priests? The Matter of Sexual Abuse in the Catholic Church]* with P. Galea; *Assisi: Cittadella Editrice*, 2011; and "My Concern with Psychology of Religion: Defending Psychology, Respecting Religion." In *Psychology of Religion: Autobiographical Accounts,* edited by J.A. Belzen., New York: Springer, 2012.

Arne Austad is affiliated with the Modum Bad Clinic in Norway. Austad is a senior psychiatrist and approved supervisor in psychodynamic psychotherapy, with a specialization in existential psychotherapy.

David M. Goodman is the associate dean of academic affairs and advising at the Woods College of Advancing Studies at Boston College, an associate professor of practice in the Department of Philosophy at Boston College, the director of the Psychology and the Other Institute, a member of the teaching faculty at the Massachusetts Institute for Psychoanalysis, and a teaching associate in the Department of Psychiatry at Harvard Medical School/Cambridge Hospital. Dr. Goodman has written over a dozen articles and books on continental philosophy, Jewish thought, social justice, and psychotherapy, and edited several books including *The Demanded Self: Levinasian Ethics* *and Identity in Psychology* (with Duquesne University Press, 2012), *Psychology and the Other (*with Mark Freeman and Oxford University Press, 2015), and *The Ethical Turn: Otherness and Subjectivity in Contemporary Psychoanalysis* (with Eric Severson and Routledge, 2016). Dr. Goodman also is a licensed clinical psychologist and has a private practice in Cambridge, MA.

Leif Gunnar Engedal is affiliated with the Modum Bad Clinic in Norway. Engedal is a professor of practical theology at the Norwegian School of Theology, Oslo, Norway, with a specialization in the psychology of religion and pastoral care.

John McDargh is an associate professor in the Boston College Department of Theology. His book *Psychoanalytic Object Relations Theory and the Study of Religion: On Faith and the Imaging of God* explores the implications of Dr. Rizzuto's work for a clinical and theological understanding of religious development. He also serves as an adjunct professor of psychotherapy and spirituality at William James College, a school of professional psychology.

Martha J. Reineke is a professor of religion in the Department of Philosophy and World Religions at the University of Northern Iowa. A specialist in the thought of René Girard and Julia Kristeva, she is the author of *Sacrificed Lives: Kristeva on Women and Violence* (Indiana University Press, 1997). Her most recent book, which draws on Kristeva, trauma studies, and Girard's early work on sensory experience, is *Intimate Domain: Desire, Trauma, and Mimetic Theory* (Michigan State University Press, 2014). She is a member of the Editorial Board for *The Handbook on Mimetic Theory and Religion* (Palgrave MacMillan, 2017).

Ana-María Rizzuto, MD, an Argentina-born psychoanalyst, is a training and supervising analyst at the PINE Psychoanalytic Center. She was a clinical professor in psychiatry at Tufts University School of Medicine until 1991. In 1987, she was an invited lecturer in Religion and Psychology at the Harvard Divinity School. In 1960–1965 she was a professor of child and adolescent development at the Catholic University of Córdoba, Argentina. In 1964, she was a professor of pastoral anthropology at the Catholic Seminary in Córdoba, Argentina.

Rizzuto is the author of *The Birth of the Living God. A Psychoanalytic Study* (University of Chicago Press, 1979). She also is the author of *Why did Freud Reject God? A Psychodynamic Interpretation* (Yale University Press, 1998). In 2001, this book received the Gradiva Award for Best Book (Religion Subject), given by the National Association for the Advance of Psychoanalysis. She is the co-author, with W.W. Meissner and Dan H. Buie, of

The Dynamics of Human Aggression: Theoretical Foundations and Clinical Applications (Brunner-Routledge, 2004). Her most recent book is *Freud and the Spoken Word: Speech as a Key to the Unconscious* (Routledge, 2015).

In 1996, Rizzuto received the William C. Bier Award, given by Division 36, American Psychological Association, for outstanding contributions to the Psychology of Religion. In 1997, she received the Oskar Pfister Prize, given by the American Psychiatric Association, for outstanding contributions to the Psychology of Religion. She is a member of the American Psychoanalytic Association and the International Psychoanalytic Association. In 2000, she became an honorary member of the Italian Society for the Psychology of Religion. She is a regular participant in national and international psychoanalytic congresses and a frequent psychoanalytic lecturer in the United States, Latin America, Europe, and Japan.

Gry Stålsett is affiliated with the Modum Bad Clinic in Norway. Stålsett is a psychologist and psychotherapy researcher with specialization in the clinical psychology of religion. Her doctoral dissertation at the University of Oslo (Ph.D., 2012) is on *Existential and Religious Issues in Psychotherapy: Development and Evaluation of a New Integrative Treatment Model (VITA) for Comorbid Depressive Disorders.*

Anthony Stern is the editor of *Everything Starts from Prayer: Mother Teresa's Meditations on Spiritual Life for People of All Faiths* (White Cloud Press). After Harvard College and Mount Sinai medical school, Dr. Stern did psychiatry training at Cornell and a neuropathology research fellowship at the University of Vermont. In addition to his work with patients in crisis intervention and homeless outreach, he has been involved with the dialogue between religion and psychology for many years.

Jacob Waldenmaier has taught philosophy and religious studies at the University of Akron, Baldwin Wallace University, and High Point University. He holds a D.Phil and MSt from the University of Oxford and an MDiv from Ashland Theological Seminary. His research explores the phenomenological, epistemological, and psychological relationships between religious experience and natural science.

Lightning Source UK Ltd.
Milton Keynes UK
UKOW04n0044110917
308865UK00004B/106/P

9 781498 564243